Laughing at the Sky

Wild Adventure, Bold Dreams, and a Daring Search for a Stolen Childhood

A Memoir by
Heidi Love

Praise

"Heidi Love's story is compelling, exotic, and full of tension. She has lived a rare and very interesting life. But most importantly, she is an exciting writer. This is a powerful, tender, and smart book."

Meredith Hall, *New York Times* bestselling author of *Without a Map* and *Beneficence*

"What an incredibly powerful book. I was moved and deeply affected by it. It's clear she has an important story to tell. Brilliant!"

Alex Marzano-Lesnevich, Lambda Literary Award–winning author of *The Fact of a Body*

"Heidi Love's memoir Laughing at the Sky *is a gorgeous adventure through courage, trauma, and the quests we take to make ourselves whole. Beautifully written, heartbreaking and heart-mending, this book will remind you what it is to be alive."*

Tessa Fontaine, *New York Times* Editor's Choice author of *The Electric Woman* and *The Red Grove*

"In Laughing at the Sky, *a strong and brave Heidi Love overcomes fear, adversity, and trauma on multiple levels to fulfill a lifelong dream. Her raw, emotional, and gripping story is masterfully written and will touch readers in a profound way. It's a powerful page turner and the best adventure memoir I've read in years."*

Liesbet Collaert, bestselling author of *Plunge: One Woman's Pursuit of a Life Less Ordinary*

"Heidi Love distills her life in episodes shrouded in undertones that enhance their potency. Her writing is beautiful, powerful, and compelling."

Anna Moï, World Literature Prize–winning author of *The Butterfly's Venom* and *Riz noir*

"Heidi Love's memoir is an intense, intimate look at trauma, healing, and the powerful journey between the two. As it weaves together a seafaring adventure along with a haunting past, it shimmers with courage, resilience, and inspiration."

Ashley Davis Bush, psychotherapist and author of *The Little Book of Inner Peace* and *Light After Loss*

"Few books have affected me as profoundly as Heidi Love's memoir, Laughing at the Sky. Her true story of transcendence over childhood trauma via a daring five-year, 12,000-nautical-mile sailing journey to French Polynesia is both white-knuckle gripping and achingly beautiful. It's a journey no reader should miss."

Nancy Crochiere, author of *Graceland*

"Heidi Love's engrossing and beautiful memoir parallels two treacherous journeys: the ocean-sailing voyage she's dreamed of making since childhood and recovering from childhood trauma that seems impossible to heal. With exacting prose and profound insights, she shines light on the difficult passage women take as they transmute a history of terror into a present filled with joy."

Mary Carroll Moore, bestselling author of *Last Bets* and *A Woman's Guide to Search & Rescue*

"Heidi's courage is a gift to all of us. Facing her past, following the sea's call, and sharing her healing journey will undoubtedly inspire others to find their way to peace too."

Captain Liz Clark, author of *Swell: A Sailing Surfer's Voyage of Awakening*

"Author Heidi Love tells a story that too many of us relate to and too few of us have the courage to claim, taking readers along on her journey to face her past and create a fearless, love-filled future."

Lizbeth Meredith, award-winning author of *Pieces of Me: Rescuing My Kidnapped Daughters*, and *Grounded in Grit: Turn Your Challenges Into Superpowers*

"In this beautifully written memoir Heidi Love navigates us along her journey of recovery and healing from childhood trauma, showing what it looks like to thrive. It is raw, difficult, and powerful, but uplifting."

Madeleine Black, author of *Unbroken*

Laughing at the Sky

Wild Adventure, Bold Dreams, and a Daring Search for a Stolen Childhood

A Memoir by
Heidi Love

Author's Note

Laughing at the Sky is a work of nonfiction. I have reconstructed events from my personal journals, researched facts when I could, consulted with people who appear in this book, and relied on my own memory. I have changed the names of three individuals. I occasionally omitted people and events when that omission had no impact on the truth or substance of the story.

Also by Heidi Love:

Knowing Acts—Engage in Healing
A Calming Practice Workbook for Emotional Balance

Cover and Book Design: Judy Trepal

Cover Photos: Dennis Jud

Editor: Lynda Dietz, Easy Reader Editing

Laughing at the Sky Copyright © 2024 Heidi Love. All rights reserved. Printed in the United States of America. No part of this book may be used or reproduced in any manner whatsoever without the permission of Heidi Love except in the case of brief quotations embodied in critical articles and book reviews. Request permission at HeidiLoveAuthor@gmail.com.

Library of Congress Number TXu 2-253-512
ISBN 978-1-7375528-2-6

Dedication

For three generations of brave and honorable men.

Charles

my protector through storms
you worked tirelessly to make the world a better place

Dennis

my courageous captain, partner, and truest friend
you are the witness to my life, the champion of dreams

Nico

my love and inspiration
you fill my life with joy and beauty
You once told me,
"In this world anything is possible,"
and now—I believe you.
I love you "forever and for all the evers."

Contents

Author's Note vi
Dedication vii
Map: Maine to the Panama Canal x

Part One—The Boldness of Dreams 1

Prologue—Night Watch 3

1. The Journey Unfolds 7
2. There Was a Little Girl 15
3. The Graveyard of the Atlantic 27
4. Torment 37
5. Defeat 41
6. Sisterhood 49
7. Shadows 63
8. It's Not Your Fault 77
9. Alone 85
10. Providence Means Heaven 89
11. Seeking Courage 97
12. Dos Se Vie De Ti 111
13. A Whiter Shade of Pale 119
14. Guna Wisdom 127
15. A Woman's Place 137

Photos One 144
Maps: Panama Canal to the Marquesas Islands 148

Part Two—Crossing the Divide 149

16. If Life Is a Dream 151
17. A Patch of Clarity 161
18. A Journey of a Thousand Miles 169
19. The Galapagos 177
20. Rites of Passage 191
21. The Farthest Point 197
22. Conviction 203
23. Mayday 209
24. The Butcher's Knife 213
25. An Ant on a Toothpick 223
26. The Absence of Image 229
27. Pouring Light 237
28. Land Ho 241
29. Laughing at the Sky 247

Epilogue—Transcendence 261

Photos Two 270
Another Book by Heidi Love 275
Acknowledgments 277
How Readers Can Help 279
A Note to Survivors and Their Champions 279

MAINE TO THE PANAMA CANAL

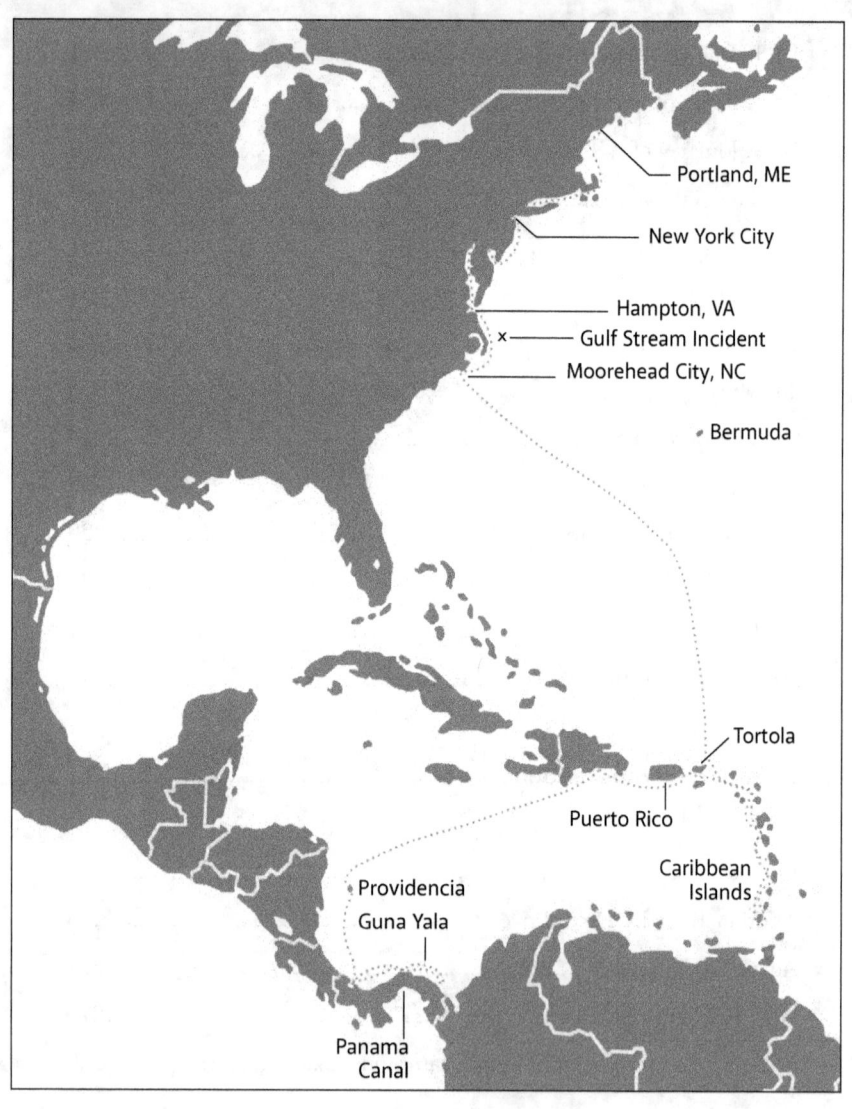

PART ONE

The Boldness of Dreams

*When you realize how perfect
everything is, you will tilt your head back
and laugh at the sky.*

Buddhist Saying

PROLOGUE

Night Watch

Remember that life is not measured by the number of breaths we take, but by the moments that take our breath away.

Vicki Corona, *Tahitian Choreographies*

The South Pacific Ocean, April 2015

The waves are tall, the ocean black and borderless. My thirty-nine-foot sailboat, *Centime*, glides and dips, rising through crests and troughs on waves higher than her stern. All is well for now, yet at sea, everything can change in a moment, life cleaved forever into before and after.

It happens on land, too. It's something I've known since my youth. It's why I'm here, on this sailing odyssey to reach the French Polynesian Bay of Virgins. I have embarked on a quest to sail nearly halfway around the world to search for an elusive Polynesian waterfall, carried in memory from my childhood, that may not exist.

The wind fills the mainsail and genoa, a large forward sail. *Centime* slices through the sea, creating patterns of glittering white foam. A river of glowing phosphorescence flows behind her.

My husband, Dennis, sleeps below, but I don't feel alone on deck. Someone is with me: the spirit of the eleven-year-old girl I once was—a skinny, high-energy tomboy who dreamed of this voyage. I have held her close, this fragile child, for a long time. Her dream is my dream: to sail away from our troubling past into a future where perhaps we can feel whole again. Will we succeed? It's impossible to know. But we're sure as hell going to try.

The wind propels us forward. Grabbing a handrail, I feel vibrations of energy flow through my sailboat as though her ecstatic soul trembles. The sky overflows with stars. Tears run down my cheeks as I sense a connection to something more powerful than myself. What am I feeling? Are molecules in my body expanding, blending into the sky and sea? Or am I losing my mind, 1,000 miles from land?

Long voyages at sea mess with your head. They also reveal who you are and what to set aside. Parts go overboard, the parts that hinder or make you cower, parts you didn't realize you carried. In their wake can come an overflowing peace that happens when you strip away everything nonessential, and discover your purest self, unburdened by weighty secrets held much too long. I'm nearing the edge of an epiphany, an essential truth. It's not me against the elements, against the pain and trauma that have shaped me. Instead, together we form a single, powerful, almost mystical whole.

But I am getting ahead of myself. What I didn't yet know is that in order to heal—to feel whole again—I must first break apart. And that is where my story begins.

Philadelphia, Pennsylvania, May 1967

It starts as a perfect day. I wake up with a smile, bound out of bed and run to the window. Sunlight streams through the panes, past white curtains with pink and red rosebuds. I can almost touch the brick house next door where my best friend, ten-year-old Terry, lives. She is one year younger than I. I look across to find her shade down, her room dark.

My room is cheery with soft blue wallpaper filled with complementary rosebud bouquets. A small wooden bookshelf holds my favorite, well-read classics: *Nancy Drew*, *Winnie-the-Pooh*, *Adventures of Huckleberry Finn*, and a stack of newer magazines: *Tiger Beat* and *Seventeen*, offering the promise of first love. A large book of poetry sits on top. Sometimes I imagine being the youngest poet ever published, but I would rather climb trees, scale walls, ride bikes, and be what Mother calls a tomboy.

Changing into blue shorts and a sleeveless shirt, my favorite with fish on the front, I slide my laced blue sneakers onto my bare feet. I grab a wooden brush and try to neaten my long, unruly, white-blonde hair. I toss the butterfly quilt that Grandma Katie made over my bed to hide the unmade sheets, stuff my pajamas under the pillow, and place my teddy bear and doll Patty on top.

It is Saturday morning and like most mornings, I have boundless energy. I think of Winnie-the-Pooh's friend, Tigger, and bounce from my bed back to the window. I wonder what Terry and I will do today. Shorter than I, she is wiry and strong—pure spunk. She leads me into adventure. In winter, we sled with wild abandon on the steepest section of "Deadman's Hill" at the city park, build snow forts, and lob snowballs at boys and trolleys. In summer, we climb the high limbs of the only neighborhood tree and pedal our bikes at top speeds before she crashes hers into the street trolleys.

Terry takes chances. I want to be wild like her. I wish I had her courage.

This Saturday I am excited for another day of freedom, after homework and chores are done and before Sunday obligations begin. I rush through my chores, spring out of the house, and skip next door.

The sun is out and people bustle about in the street. There is no activity at Terry's. Her house is dark, the windows are closed, the curtains drawn. At the front corner of her yard, I call out her name. No response.

I run along the narrow alley toward her backyard and call again. Trash and rusted junk are scattered across the dirt where there once was grass. The wire cage usually housing her pet ocelot is empty. Her broken bike leans against the wire fence, the tires flat.

I've lived next door to the Harts for seven years but have never been inside their yard or house. I play in all my other friends' homes. I know that Emily's bedroom has neat stacks of books and a microscope; Debbie's room has drab green peeling paint, few toys, and a well-worn Bible on a wooden night stand; and the twins have canopy beds with pink frills and a closet full of party dresses. Terry is my best friend, yet Mother says her house is off-limits. I don't know why.

This morning I run, once again, to the front of her house. I cross an invisible boundary—a boundary of no return.

Looking back at that eleven-year-old me, I want to grab her and violently shake away her naivety, to scream at this young child, STOP! Yet all I can do is envision her standing before the tall door, alone, wearing a smile of anticipation across her young face.

Would I change this scene, rewrite the start, if I could? The answer gushes out of me with a loud, resounding yes. Yet if I had, I would not have taken the transcending journey that was to come. I would not have embarked on this epic quest.

Now it's too late.

Bounding up the stairs to Terry's porch, I knock on the front door.

No one answers.

I turn to go. The door behind me creaks. A small opening reveals darkness, yet I can hear and sense a figure behind the door.

"Is Terry home?" I whisper.

Emerging from the crack in the door, several feet above me, the edge of a pair of eyeglasses appears, an oval shape with a remarkable orange-brown frame.

CHAPTER 1

The Journey Unfolds

For in my heart I needed to go, the pull of Everest was stronger for me than any force on Earth.

Tenzing Norgay, *Tiger of the Snows*

Portland, Maine, September 2011

Gazing at the horizon, I stand balanced at the edge of a floating dock. Waves lap and rock the float. Pulsing electric energy arrives with each swell. I breathe deep and feel the power of an unsettled sea.

Wisps of ocean kiss the air, filling it with brine. Bell-like chimes sound as a northeast breeze rattles stainless steel rigging. A disarray of sailboats lies in chaos in the boatyard in the aftermath of a recent hurricane. After a low-pressure system passes, the sky often clears, yet second and third storms can follow in its wake.

The bay outside Portland Harbor is large; the North Atlantic beyond is immense. The isolated island of Fatu Hiva, in French Polynesia, lies near the center of the South Pacific. You can't drive or fly there. My destination and destiny lie 12,000 nautical miles away, a bit more distance than half the world's circumference. I have waited long enough to sail away.

At age eleven, violence had carved my life into before and after.

My psyche too had split in half. At times, I was a risk-taking daredevil of a child; at other times, a terrified girl who ran from everything—police, memories, family, and myself. I ached for comfort, an end to my running, a secret place to heal and thrive.

Hiding in my neighborhood library one night as a teen, I had discovered a National Geographic image of a lush tropical oasis, filled with fruit trees, flowering bushes, and birds. At its heart was a shimmering waterfall, a dazzling sunlit cascade that surged over a cliff and vanished into mist. All of my senses were enlivened as I imagined wearing a sarong, bathing under the cascade, and disappearing in the spray. I could almost taste the juicy, ripe mangoes and feel the mist on my half-naked body. That image launched an obsession: escape my torment by sailing to French Polynesia and live near the alluring falls.

It has taken a far-reaching effort to develop courage and sailing skills, and to find a partner, my husband Dennis, as wild and crazy as I am: someone willing to brave turbulent seas and daring adventure to find the remote waterfall that lingers in the memories of my youth. Today, as we leave, I hope this sail will heal me. I want to overcome nagging self-doubt and hidden shame; I need to stop traumatic PTSD flashbacks.

Centime, a thirty-nine-foot, cutter-rigged sailboat, floats next to the wharf. She's a traditional beauty: bright white hull with a blue waterline stripe, long classic bowsprit, champagne-glass stern, sleek curves, and a graceful sheer. She's not shiny or new, but she's mine. The wind pushes her away from the dock, and she strains and pulls at her lines like she's anxious to flee to open water where she belongs.

On board, Dennis removes a canvas sail cover, stretching to roll it over the elevated boom. At six foot one, his lanky reach is beyond mine. My sailing-trimming abilities, oversized imagination, and ease at working in tight spaces complement his strengths. We work in tandem to begin our journey.

Kneeling on the floating dock, I prepare the lines for departure. A wave shakes the wharf. My heart flutters as I steady myself. Although we did extensive coastal sailing when we brought *Centime* from Virginia to Maine, and I had sailed thousands of nautical miles without Dennis, we have not yet ventured far offshore together. *Centime* is a strong, well-equipped, safe boat, yet she too remains untested by poor weather. At thirty-nine feet, a thirteen-foot wave breaking broadside could capsize her, destroying sails, rigging, engine, and possibly her crew.

Many of my friends believe I'm courageous. Others feel it's romantic to search for a Polynesian waterfall with my sweet husband, and are excited to visit us in tropical locales. Some worry I may never return.

Dennis is a hang-gliding, bungee-jumping risk taker and confident sailor. I'm filled with doubt. I have lived on land through the ravages of three hurricanes and have a clear understanding of the potential for danger, at least for the weather- and boat-related varieties. Looking back, I now realize I was unprepared for the emotional challenges I would face.

It is not unusual for me to teeter between bursts of courage, even recklessness, and then find myself debilitated by fear. I once hitchhiked next to burned-out cars on a run-down off-ramp in the Bronx of New York, only to later panic for no reason in the safe entry of a national park. I navigated and skippered a small boat for a month from Southern Spain to the Côte d'Azur, France, alone with a dying, medically-drugged, one-legged amputee, and later found myself in a cold sweat trying to row ashore. I have driven my car over one hundred miles per hour, skied out-of-bounds snowfields, and rock-climbed a steep face without a safety harness, only to become scared in my safe-neighborhood home, alone in my shower. I can trace these erratic behaviors back to my childhood, when my innate high spirits could get me into trouble or when trouble would come uninvited.

Friends arrive on the dock, wanting to be useful. They're not quite ready to let Dennis or me go. After long hugs, Dennis starts the motor and *Centime* springs to life. I push us off the dock, jump on board, and catch the free lines as they yell, "Fair winds," and "Be safe," and wave a bit harder than if we were just sailing around the bay.

Wearing his yellow rain slicker and Navy watch cap, Dennis grabs the helm and steers a course away from the dock, dodging a mooring buoy and a fishing skiff. My hand trembles as I continue to wave. I pull up the white plastic fenders that hang off *Centime*'s hull and coil her lines to clear the decks. We work together to raise the mainsail and unfurl the genoa. Working the lines is easy for him. At five foot three and 108 pounds, I have to work twice as hard in this boat designed and built by men. I adjust the sails and shut off the engine as *Centime* catches the wind.

The sun pokes through the clouds and streaks across our white sails, making them glisten. They are bright and full enough for a respectable exit. Our friend Paul from nearby Little Diamond Island hops in his small, red motorboat, *Lil' Hog*, and follows us out to the edge of the harbor, snapping photos and waving goodbye. The picturesque Maine harbor and Paul's waves are the last images I have of home.

With an abrupt change in the wind, *Centime* heels at an angle to the sea. She is alert, responsive to the wind that guides her. I grab the sheet to let out sail. Dennis grips the wheel and shouts, "We're doing it, honey." Flipping a switch, he turns on the autopilot and takes a step toward me. We fall together and steady each other on the angled cockpit deck.

I met Dennis five years earlier. It started as a blind date, on an ordinary Wednesday evening after meeting online. He had written that he liked to bike, hike, ski, and sail, and I teased that I enjoyed all of these sports and was looking for someone who could keep up. We made plans to share glasses of wine at a seafood restaurant on Portland's waterfront. For all my online bravado, I felt hesitant meeting him in person.

Golden light streamed through the restaurant's tall windows, creating a warm ambience on that cold November evening. As I opened the door, the welcoming heat of the room enveloped me, while mouth-watering aromas of garlic and seafood filled the air. Muted laughter flowed through the entryway. People dressed in professional garb, unwinding from the stresses of their day, were smiling and conversing.

Without warning, I felt a tingle through my body, like static shocks that come from shuffling across a carpet. I looked around the room but didn't notice anything unusual. Goosebumps covered my left arm as I removed my coat. I could not account for the burn on the left side of my face, yet I had an uncanny sense that something powerful was happening.

Similar sparks had occurred before, and I hadn't understood their portent. When I was forty, I had gone on a yoga retreat and was walking down a long, narrow, concrete corridor, chatting with a friend. All of a sudden, the hair on my left arm stood up; I felt vibrations in my neck, and the left side of my face burned. My whole being felt a sense of peace and joy that I had never experienced. I closed my eyes and turned to face the energy stream. Approaching me from the end of the corridor was Garchen Rinpoche, one of the Dalai Lama's highest monks, and the happiest man I've ever met.

I looked around the Portland restaurant but there were no Buddhist monks or exposed electrical wires. Instead, the hostess, a thirty-something woman in a black dress and high heels, arrived and asked how she could help. I was still uncertain of what was happening, my eyes darting in every direction.

"I'm … I'm meeting someone …."

A man exuding an air of confidence arrived behind her. He was tall, with a short-cropped, chestnut-hued beard. His button-down, collared shirt was well-pressed, his tie loosened at the neck. He smiled and reached out to shake my hand. It was warm and strong.

"Hi, I'm Dennis. I have a table for us over here," he said, cocking his head toward the bar. He extended his hand to direct me toward a high-topped table where a dark blue suit coat rested on the back of a chair.

We sat across from each other and ordered glasses of wine and appetizers of grilled shrimp and fried calamari. He began to ask questions. The buzzing on my face and arms continued, making normal conversation difficult. Every fiber of my being wanted to blurt out what was happening, yet I suspected if I told him he would think I was unstable. I sipped my wine, fidgeted in my chair, ignored the buzz, and tried to gain control. It was as though I was sitting in the center of an invisible vortex. I glanced around the restaurant. Nothing appeared unusual.

When our appetizers arrived, Dennis chatted about his life as a landscape architect, his two adult children, and his liberal political persuasions. At first, he sat up straight in his chair. After a few minutes his cheeks began to glow as he described his love of nature and adventure. Weeks later, he told me he had revealed secrets unknown to most of his friends, yet all I can remember is the unexplained whirlwind of energy flowing through me and a feeling of euphoria.

I excused myself to visit the bathroom, taking care not to trip with my higher-than-normal heels. A crowd of men I needed to walk past stood at the bar, and I could feel my cheeks getting hotter. Still, warm air, scented with pine cleaning fluid, greeted me in the claustrophobic powder room. Splashing cold water on my face was cooling, yet I felt drunk after consuming only a few sips of wine. In the mirror I saw a red-faced silly grin as I patted the excess water from my cheeks. It was not appealing.

Returning to my stool past the gauntlet of men, I brushed back my hair and took a sip of my zinfandel. "Do you really like adventure? Do you like to sail?" I asked, hoping to center the conversation on him.

"I would love to sail the world. How about you?" he replied.

I blushed. "When I was young, sailing was everything—nature, freedom, and escape. I came alive at sea. I sailed when I could in my teens and early twenties. When my son Nico was born it was extraordinary. Life with him, our adventures together, and my job to support our lives became all consuming. Now that he's a teen with his own friends, I go with my friends when I get the chance. Being at a tiller with a brisk wind, the boat heeling, the salt spraying on my face … it's exhilarating. I'd like to do more. Sail out of the harbor on a real adventure."

Dennis stared at me across the table, a smile on his face. "Where would you go?"

The answer shot out of me before I could stop it. "Fatu Hiva. I've tried not to think about it for years, but I was once obsessed with the Marquesan Islands in the South Pacific. As a child, I dreamed of sailing to French Polynesia."

He leaned closer, his eyes wide. "That's insane. You should go."

Walking with me to my car after our encounter, he said a polite goodbye. As I drove away, my phone rang. We talked through the evening.

I never did figure out what happened that night. Call it karma or serendipity: on the day I met Dennis, my thinking shifted in a profound way. My dream that I buried in my youth resurfaced with new possibilities, and old memories. After a month of dating, I sent him a card with a borrowed promise: "to live our dreams, to sit on the edge of the world, feet hanging over."

Three years after that first date, Dennis and I married and found *Centime*, a boat from South Africa capable of sailing the world. After picking her up in Norfolk, Virginia, we cruised to our home port in Maine. She sailed with perfection in fresh winds, with a turbulent sea under her keel.

"Feel that wind," Dennis said as we entered Portland Harbor. "Sixteen knots and building. We're doing seven. She's in her element."

"The breeze is fresh, but it's blowing in the wrong direction," I said, gripping the helm to hold her steady. "*Centime* wants to head out to sea."

"So do I." We looked at each other and smiled.

"Just say the word," I dared. "I can turn her around now and sail to Paris, or at least Brittany. At this rate we could drink champagne for breakfast."

"Don't tempt me," he said, jumping in front of me in a playful square off. He covered my hands with his, pretending to force a change of course.

As the wind blew from the west, away from the harbor, I knew *Centime* wanted to go with it and we wanted to go with her. She was like a sleek horse—beautiful, untamed, alive, and ready to gallop if we let go of her reins.

During that first, ten-day sail from Virginia to Maine we fell in love with *Centime* and the lifestyle she promised. Neither of us could wait to sail full time. Even though we liked our jobs, we dreaded returning to work that Monday morning. Sitting on our mooring in Portland Harbor at the end of our maiden voyage, my body was exhausted, my spirit energized.

Dennis and I worked hard through the fall: planning, figuring out what we could sell, how little we could live on, and how we might afford to sail away. We consulted with weather almanacs, reviewed storm patterns, and determined how to safely synchronize our sailing departure with Nico's start at college. While we both felt healthy, we visited a tropical medicine clinic near Portland for preventive vaccines, malaria pills, and remedies for dengue fever.

Chilled under hats, gloves, and multiple layers of dirt- and paint-streaked sweatshirts, we scraped, painted, rewired, and installed new safety equipment. Our life-saving gear and four-person life raft needed outfitting with dried food, water-collecting equipment, and locating devices. We read texts on emergency procedures: withstanding gale-force winds, and deploying a sea anchor. I listened to a Navy SEAL lecture on reducing tensions if boarded by a desperate trespasser.

Preparation continued through winter. We took classes at Massachusetts

Institute of Technology on storm tactics and survival at sea, launched a life raft in their swimming pool, and practiced person-overboard procedures. I shivered continuously while treading water in full foul-weather gear as we huddled together in the pool's deep end. The difficulty of launching and entering a lifeboat in a calm swimming pool, and then projecting this experience onto storm-ridden seas, made me acutely aware of the risks of our voyage.

By September, our journey unfolded. *Centime* was ready. Our wills were signed. The only item not addressed was my fear. I wore my courage as a façade, fooling friends and loved ones—and at times, myself. I didn't understand then how a momentary scare could bring to mind my uneasy youth, setting off a cascade of emotional triggers.

Leaving Portland Harbor for the open ocean that morning, in search of a resolution to my past, I recalled my seafaring grandfather. I had inherited his passions. I hoped that I hadn't inherited his misfortunes.

Grandfather Edgar left his pregnant wife, Katie, and their young son to work on a cargo ship when he was twenty-five. The vessel he boarded carried a deadly influenza virus. His unborn daughter, my mother, lost her father to the 1918 pandemic. Grandfather's headstone sits in a graveyard in Reading, Pennsylvania; his germ-infested body was buried at sea.

I picture a young Grandma Katie waiting for her husband to disembark after his ship pulls into Philadelphia Harbor. She stands with one hand holding tight to her two-year-old son dressed in his Sunday best, the other hand grasping her pregnant belly. Looking up at the large ship, she waits for what is never to be.

In Maine, late summer days on the bay are often cool. I shiver thinking of my two grandfathers: the one I never knew, and the one who replaced him.

CHAPTER 2

There Was a Little Girl

There is no greater agony than bearing an untold story inside you.

Maya Angelou, *I Know Why the Caged Bird Sings*

Seward, Alaska, July 1955

A volatile glacier surrounds my Alaskan motherland, still and peaceful one moment, unstable and terrifying the next. As the glacier calves, the frigid sea moves in powerful upheaval. The unsettled earth is at once awesome and frightening. All that appears as solid is not. It never was. This is the legacy I inherited.

My life began near the North Pacific Ocean. I was born in the small Alaskan town of Seward, at the head of Resurrection Bay. It's a stunning region on the southern coast of Alaska. Dramatic peaks rise 6,600 feet from the sea and rim both sides of the bay. Majestic eagles soar past mountains that pierce the sky. The steep, ragged peaks are covered with snow much of the year, more snow in one season than most areas receive in a lifetime. Here the vast sea calls to the spirit, as it has always called to mine.

In 1951, Dad became a missionary. Mother said she was horrified when she found out he was taking her away from Pennsylvania to go to Alaska, and told everyone she was afraid her baby, my two-year-old brother, Vern, would freeze. I was yet to be born. She later told me she only went because it was her "duty" as a wife. I suspect she was equally afraid of telling my dad her true feelings and of being left behind in her hometown with her stepfather.

My dad was ecstatic about the Alaskan wilderness. He loved to hunt, fish, kayak, and climb mountains. During the six years that my family lived in Alaska, he would use his free time to work as a cook on hunting and fishing excursions, heading off into the wilderness in helicopters.

His friends called him "Moose." During one of his wilderness trips, after he had finished his cooking duties and headed out of camp, he sat down on the snow with his back up against a tree, letting the sound of a nearby river lull him to sleep. He awoke abruptly with a large moose licking the salt off his face. Startled, he grabbed his hunting rifle to shoot the large animal, but he couldn't pull the trigger because the moose had kissed him.

"How could I kill an animal that was in love with me?" he said.

I was five when Dad brought our family to Wayne Avenue, North Philadelphia. His heart was filled with compassion for those he deemed "less lucky." Philadelphia was where I first found, and later lost, friendship and courage. It was the neighborhood that both ignited my spirit and then snuffed it out.

Terry Hart was my best buddy in my diverse neighborhood. We became instant friends the moment we met. At four she was a year younger, yet I thought of her as my twin. She had freckles and medium-length straight brown hair. Her body was thin and strong. Her grin hardly fit on her face.

She had more gumption than anyone I knew. There wasn't a risk she wouldn't take. What I liked most about Terry was her life-spark and contagious laughter. Terry and her family were as different from me and mine as jungle cats are from calico kittens.

One spring day when I was six, she led me to a forbidden wall that surrounded a small, abandoned church. The top of the wall was a foot and a half wide with flat rocks in the middle and knife-edged rocks and pointed shards of glass embedded in concrete along the top edges. It seemed curious that a church would have a wall with glass shards around it. Terry climbed easily to the top of the wall, navigating around the glass. I proceeded with caution.

Along the inside edge of the wall was a long, impenetrable row of bushes full of thorns. The bushes grew taller and the thorns larger as we moved to the far end of the wall.

Terry wanted to see how far we could get, jumping over each consecutive bush. She counted, "one, two, three," let out a big "whoop," and jumped with triumph onto the dirt below. I followed. She squeezed between two thorny bushes, clambered back up, around the glass shards, and jumped again over the next higher bush. We jumped, whooped, and laughed our way along the wall, over higher bushes, until we found ourselves in a mess of brambles, scratched, and bleeding from the one that we could not conquer.

Mother didn't approve of my tomboy activities. Many Saturday evenings I arrived home dirty, with dried blood on my arms, skinned knees, and torn pants. It made her furious. She didn't like to see me messy, and she hated the sight of blood.

That day I limped back with bloodstains on one knee. Our tiny backyard was quiet and sunny with clean laundry drying in the light wind. There were large white sheets and small white towels strung on a clothesline from the far side of the yard to the house. I ducked behind the sheets, breathing in their fresh scent, edged up the back steps toward the kitchen door, and peeked through the window. The path appeared clear. Mother was nowhere to be seen. I opened and shut the screen door, entering like a stealthy cat. I had ample experience avoiding Mother.

I could hear the tick of our wall clock in the kitchen. I crossed the room to the back stairway on tiptoe. Several items lined the narrow staircase: a stack of old magazines, a pile of folded, clean clothes, a new bottle of mouthwash, and an unopened box of toothpaste. As I crept up the wooden treads, my tender knee gave out and I slipped, banging the step and landing hard on my recent wound.

"Ouch," slipped out of my mouth before I could catch it.

"Heidi Lynn Malin, where are you?" Mother asked.

"I'm okay," I replied. "Just going to the bathroom."

"Come up here at once," she said.

"I just have to go to the bathroom first."

"Now!"

I continued climbing the stairs in slow motion, taking care of my sore knee and trying to hide the bloodstain with my hand. She stood at the top wearing a worn housedress with faded purple flowers and a matching apron. Hands on her hips, she blocked the way, her eyes scanning my body. Her face was red, her mouth open.

"You come with me, young lady!" She grabbed my shirt and arm at the shoulder, pulled me up the final steps, and shoved me down the hall to the bathroom. The door slammed closed behind us. "Take these off," she said, tugging at the waist of my pants as I unzipped them and pulled them over my hips.

"Sit," she said as she pushed me toward the toilet.

Falling backward, I turned to put the toilet lid down and sat without a word, my pants tangled around my ankles. She pulled off my bunched up clothes and sneakers in a quick, rough sweep to a dirty heap on the floor. As I swung my legs back and forth, drips of blood stained the floor. Mother turned on the water in the sink, grabbed an old, ragged, blue washcloth from the closet, and wiped it against the soap. She scrubbed hard at my raw knee. The blood seeped out, covering the blue cloth as I winced. I grasped the toilet and looked away.

"Heidi, why do you do this to me? What's wrong with you? Are you stupid? Every Saturday you make yourself ugly on purpose, just in time for Sunday church. I'm at my wits' end. Are you trying to drive me crazy? You are disgusting. Just wait 'til your father gets home." She pulled out the hydrogen peroxide in a large, brown glass bottle, and red Mercurochrome in a short bottle with a stopper. I watched the peroxide bubble at my cut and grimaced at the sting as she applied the red liquid and then a bandage. I kept quiet; I knew enough to not make her angrier.

"Now go to your room," she said, propelling me forward and slapping my exposed backside. "And think about what you did to me. I'm sick of you."

These frequent scrubbings and criticisms weren't so painful, yet when Mother lost control, she scared me. I learned early that I didn't want to make her mad. Yet, as a child, I didn't know how to avoid her screams.

Mother was an enigma to Vern and me. She was an average-sized woman, slim, with medium-brown hair. She dressed conservatively, often covering her neck with high-collared shirts or turtleneck sweaters and wearing cover-ups to the beach. Except for her eyes, her features were average, not striking. Her eyes sparkled a deep saturated blue. They were not Grandma Katie's muted blues; instead, they had a vibrant intensity that sharpened with her changing moods. I wondered if she inherited them from her biological father.

Although she never met the seafaring Edgar, the story of his death was forever imprinted on her heart. Six months after Mother was born, her mother, Grandma Katie, married Grandpa Lloyd. He had been married before. His wife had left him; I never knew why. He was a farmer and a hard worker on the Reading Railroad. More comfortable in sweat-stained work clothes than Sunday best, he shaved and bathed once a week for church.

As children, Vern and I weren't aware that Mother's life had begun surrounded by loss and Grandma's grief. I did notice that pictures of my brother and I perpetually appeared and disappeared on her bureau, while she always displayed a photo of the biological father she never knew.

Our family moved often throughout my youth. Mother's fine wooden chest of drawers and photo collection moved with her to the various homes where we lived. At times, a lace doily graced the top of her bureau with an assemblage of family photos. Other times the polished walnut top gleamed with a solitary photo of Grandfather Edgar.

I once asked Dad why Mother continued to display her father's photo when she had never met the man. Dad's face reddened and his gaze bounced across their bedroom.

"You better not mention him to your mother. She's very fond of him," he said.

"Why shouldn't I mention him if she likes him?" I asked.

"Don't even ask," he said and walked out.

Grandma Katie and her second husband, Grandpa Lloyd, lived in a brick row house in Reading, a blue-collar Pennsylvania town famous for railroads and coal. Grandma kept her two-story home immaculate except for the basement.

Grandpa's farmer hands were rough when he grabbed mine one Saturday morning and led me down the narrow, wooden stairs to his realm. I was about six and a half the first time.

Grandma and Mother were napping upstairs after Grandma's filling noontime supper. Grandma loved to cook and often made hearty soups with fresh ingredients from Grandpa's small farm or chicken and dumplings with birds that Grandpa slaughtered. I had avoided the chicken that afternoon and ate an extra dumpling or two, but I wasn't interested in a nap. I wanted to play with my dolls.

(Trigger Warning) As we headed down to the basement, underneath the bright kitchen, a cold, dampness seemed to envelop us. I began to shiver. A light dangled over Grandpa's workbench hanging from an orange extension cord. There was a brown bottle of Reading Premium beer on the worktable next to a high stool. He grabbed me under my armpits and lifted me onto his lap. My breath seemed to stop when I saw a calendar with topless women hanging on his wall and magazines with naked ladies on his workbench. I wriggled to get down. He held me tight, his hands pressing across my chest. He smiled as I squirmed and twisted around to look at him. I loved Grandpa and didn't understand why he was being strange.

"Shh," he said. "Don't wake Grandma from her nap. She won't like it if you do. Mommy will be mad too." His breath smelled of beer; his body smelled of sweat. He gazed at his magazine and drank his beer. I squeezed my eyes shut to block out the naked women and what Grandpa was doing. I stiffened my body and stayed quiet while he bounced me on his lap like I was his pet. I hoped it would be over soon, yet the time seemed to lengthen.

Eventually he lifted me off his lap. I bolted up the stairs to an empty kitchen, ran out the back door, and sat in the alley. I held my head in my hands and watched the neighbor children play. Later, Mother called me in to say goodbye. Giving Grandma a lasting hug, I buried my face in her oversized belly and breathed deep as her arms wrapped around me. Katie's hugs were pure love. I froze at Grandpa's hug. He bent down, smiled, and then patted me on the head.

"Be a good girl," he said.

Whenever we visited over the next several years, he brought me downstairs. When he grabbed my hand, I would feel numb, following him like a rag doll. Before we left his basement he always said, "Remember, this is our secret. You mustn't tell. Mommy will know you are a very, very bad girl."

Our secret haunted me. Later, I learned another family member, as a child, experienced sexual assault by Grandpa, too.

The years of silence deepened. Grandpa's basement excursions and other sordid incidents during my childhood brought on a simultaneous fear of men and a longing to flee. Throughout my youth I plotted elaborate schemes to escape.

At seven, I would tuck myself behind a bush in my front yard. By age eleven, I skipped school and crawled beneath low-hanging branches of a weeping willow. As I became braver that year, I would stay out alone through the night, sleeping under a New Jersey boardwalk or the nearby beach umbrella shack, only to be found and returned home by local police. No one seemed to question why the pastor's daughter felt the need to run away. By age thirteen, the daredevil in me would sail alone across Sunset Bay near my grandmother's New Jersey cottage, then I would hide, secluded in a maze of high grasses in a salt marsh, until dusk set in.

Early attempts to stay hidden eluded me. I longed for a safer place to live. My destination emerged on a Friday evening in November when I was fifteen. Earlier that afternoon, I had socialized with girlfriends who were getting ready for a high school dance. We tried on orange and purple miniskirts and varying shades of red lipstick and blue and gray eye shadow. My adolescent attempts at makeup looked garish and quite ridiculous, with my fair skin and blonde hair. I laughed with my friends, yet the idea of attracting a boy made me uneasy. As my friends headed toward our gymnasium in Radnor, Pennsylvania, I ducked into my neighborhood library. The shelves of books and magazines had a calming impact. I felt less anxious.

The light in the library was uneven, dampening my mood. Harsh fluorescent bulbs glared between aisles of books; table lamps exposed dark wooden paneling and dusty corners. My body became tired after sitting for an hour on a stiff wooden chair. I massaged my left shoulder.

The library was soon closing, the sunlight fading. I shivered thinking of the long, dark walk home. Will Mother be in the kitchen when I arrive?

Will she even notice that I've been gone? She spent much of her time those days alone in her room. Though she had been a watchful disciplinarian when I was in grade school, after her breakdown when I was nearly twelve, she barely acknowledged me.

Slumped over, head in hand, I perused a *National Geographic* journal. I turned a page and brightness appeared. I sat up and strained my eyes to discover a brilliant waterfall, glinting as it surged and plunged. Warmth radiated through my body.

Page after page revealed luminous black-and-white photos of French Polynesia and vibrant paintings by Paul Gauguin. His paintings, infused with feminine energy, awoke a passion that I had previously smothered. He painted abundant tropical jungles in bright uplifting colors, and sensual women with exposed breasts and voluptuous curves.

Throughout adolescence, I had envisioned feminine nature as weak and tainted. In contrast, Gauguin portrayed his figures with a light of enchantment and strength, or so I believed at the time. One painting, Mohana No Atua, depicted the powerful Goddess Hina who could use the moon to summon feminine forces and control the sea. Gauguin's work shaped a lifelong desire to flee to an equitable utopia, a place where society celebrated women and girls and imbued them with power.

I returned to the Journal's page with the waterfall and traced the sparkling light at the top of the rock face to a still reflecting pool below. Although I did not understand it at the time, I was surprised by a tingling on my left arm and face, and heat that spread through my body.

My eyes stopped and my breath caught as I read the caption—"The Bay of Virgins."

That evening a dream to find the Bay and Gauguin's hidden waterfall crystallized. I closed my eyes and could see my reflection in the clear azure pool at the base of the falls. The image returned my euphoric smile.

Calm seas bordering enchanting seascapes beckoned and brought to mind a possible means of escape. My most treasured possession was an eleven-foot sailboat. It was more of a surfboard with a mast and sail, yet when the wind filled her canvas, I felt free. My small surfboard of a boat rested in a bay near my Grandmother Elsie's New Jersey cottage, where she had lived alone before her brain ceased to function properly. I had heard about sixteen-year-old Robin Graham, with his boat *Dove*, who was circumnavigating the world's oceans; after seeing Gauguin's tropical seascapes, I wanted to join his ranks. In my longing to escape my unstable teens, my plan to find this bay and the entrancing waterfall became my touchstone when life became erratic.

Life with Grandpa Lloyd and Mother continued to present disturbing patterns. Both of them seemed to adore me at times and then mistreat me. Grandpa would appear loving, combing my hair, giving me treats, and letting me ride with him on his tractor, before taking me to the basement. Mother would buy me clothes she could barely afford and tell everyone of my achievements. Then, behind closed doors, she would berate me. Her behavior confused me. I tried, over time, to better understand her.

Years after I left home for college, married, and had a child of my own, she wrote me a curious note. My son Nico was four, an endearing, lively child. He resembled his father's Italian heritage with warm brown eyes, a curly mop of rich brown hair, and smooth olive skin. We had just moved, Nico and I, to a home in southern Maine, separating from his father.

Separation for me, like for many, was painful. I was concerned about how it would hurt Nico, afraid of living alone, and heartbroken over marital quarrels. At the time, I had more experience running away than addressing conflict. My guilt for leaving Nico's father was overwhelming, my sleeping fitful. Therapy sessions were often filled with tears.

One crisp winter morning, shafts of sunlight filtered through spruce and white pine. My mailbox stood at the end of a long drive that meandered through the woods. There was a small pile of letters, six or seven in long business envelopes and one in the shape of a greeting card. On the upper left corner of the card's envelope was a return-address sticker, the free kind from charities seeking donations. Mother loved anything free; she saved and rearranged boxes of these treasures every few weeks. Her name was on the sticker.

I brought one hand up to my throat, a habit since childhood. Mother had called a few days earlier. I had been afraid to tell her of my separation; she'd found out on her own.

As I stared at the envelope, a hardness formed in my gut, a heavy shifting weight, a burdensome obligation. Although I had left home twenty-one years earlier, I still obeyed her unspoken demands. I opened the envelope.

A pre-printed message on the card said, "Thinking of you," and below, in her formal script, she had written "Your Mother." A separate white note folded in quarters fell from the card. Time seemed to slow as the note fluttered to the ground. At first, I just stared at it, then I sat down on the frozen earth, picked it up and unfolded it. The paper had two types of writing: small letters, and all capitals. My eyes were drawn to the caps.

> Dear Heidi,
> YOU PUT A BUTCHER KNIFE THROUGH MY HEART!!! HOW DARE YOU DO THIS TO YOUR MOTHER!!!
> Aunt Betty came for dinner last night. She asked about you. I told her you were fine. I served baked chicken with cornflake crumbs, frozen peas, boiled new potatoes, and iced tea. For dessert, I bought a shoofly pie from the farmers' market.
> YOUR MOTHER

My heart raced. Reading the words formed in all caps was akin to hearing her scream. I quickly stuffed the card and letter back in the envelope and returned it to the mailbox.

It was the first of several jarring letters I would receive, which would one day shed light on an emotionally-charged time of our lives. While they were unsettling, her letters would later provide clearer glimpses into our tangled relationship. All I knew then was to run into the woods.

Two years later on Mother's Day, I invited her to dinner at a local restaurant. Nico was now six; my divorce from his father complete. Mother had arrived at my home in Maine in the late afternoon and went to work to make her classic sweet tea. She had learned to make southern-style iced tea as a newlywed, and served it to my family and me every day I lived at home.

Nico kneeled on a counter stool, leaning over our kitchen island while she encouraged him to stir the tea, squeeze a lemon, taste, and evaluate the evolving brew. He smiled, his dark curly hair framing eyes filled with mischief, and then threw in some extra sugar and laughed. Mother laughed too.

Early in the evening, the weather became cool as we departed for the restaurant. Mother dressed in a ruffled shirt, buttoned tight around her neck, and a gray turtleneck cardigan. She wore a white scarf over her short-cropped hair and carried a large brown leather purse which she had found at her church rummage sale.

The historic farmhouse restaurant was dark and cavernous, yet cozy. Candles on the table and a fire in the brick hearth provided a warm ambience. We savored a full Sunday dinner and then indulged in chocolate cake and steaming cups of coffee and hot chocolate. She grinned and leaned forward as she listened to Nico chat about his new bike and how fast he could ride. Nico was physically strong and fit, with endless energy.

In mid-discussion, she sat up straight, cleared her throat several times, and picked at her chapped dried fingers and broken nails. Nico stared in silence at his grandmother, waiting for her to speak.

"I already know what kind of mother I am. I don't need you to tell me." Her striking blue eyes flashed. "I'm only curious if your perceptions are accurate. Did you think I was too mean? Too strict?"

My legs swung under the table. Nico waited for my response, his elbows near his cake, chin in his hands, eyes darting from her to me and back.

"You weren't too strict, yet I wonder if you might have been … at times … unhappy."

Her body stiffened; her face fell. The intensity of her eyes receded as she stared across the room. Her voice seemed to come from far away.

"Of course I was happy. I had my husband. I had my family," she said in a staccato rush of syllables. It was almost as if she was reeling off a well-practiced line or that her voice and words were not fully connected to her body.

The gray rings of sleepless nights showed beneath her eyes. Her brow wrinkled in despair. Her chest rose and fell; her breathing became rapid as if she were running, escaping, as she sat beside me.

I touched her hand. She recoiled.

She placed her hand on her throat. Without looking at what she was doing, she pulled out an old white handkerchief, edged with lace, from her purse. Her hand shaking, she brought it to her eyes. I looked for tears that weren't there.

I wanted to know more and fought against the silence that surrounded us whenever her handkerchief appeared. "Did you like Grandpa Lloyd?" I asked.

"I had my husband. I had my family," she whispered to the room.

"Are you okay, Mother?"

She sank lower in her chair and nodded in a slow circular motion. I took her home. She was silent for the rest of the evening. The next morning, she put the kettle on to make a second pitcher of iced tea. She never said another word to me about Grandpa or her happiness.

For ten more years, I too kept silent.

CHAPTER 3

The Graveyard of the Atlantic

*You drown not by falling into a river,
but by staying submerged in it.*

Paulo Coelho, *The Alchemist*

Hampton, Virginia, November 2011

"It would be insane to leave tomorrow," warns Ken, our weather advisor from Maine. There's a tropical depression building off Cape Hatteras and a stationary, extratropical cyclone between Bermuda and the Bahamas. I'm monitoring a sailboat off Bermuda. She's a strong boat, got an experienced captain, and she's had three knockdowns. When do you need to leave?"

Dennis clears his throat and replies, "The fleet is scheduled to leave tomorrow."

After departing Portland Harbor in Maine two months ago, Dennis and I have sailed *Centime* to Hampton, Virginia. Other than dodging high-speed ferries in the fog at Cape Cod, and screaming through New York's Hell's Gate, we've been joyfully day-hopping along the Atlantic coast. Our first serious, multinight passage will soon extend from Virginia toward the Caribbean Island of Tortola. This first two-week offshore route is 1,500 nautical miles and crosses the Gulf Stream, notorious for unsettled weather.

To be safer, we've joined seventy boats for this two-week passage. The fleet shares a boat-to-boat radio network and weather information to reduce risks. The World Cruising Club organizers provide rigorous boat inspections, safety checks, and safety seminars.

The docks are crammed with yachts and nervous crew hoping for a weather window to depart between the end of hurricane season and before winter gales begin. The organizers haven't yet delayed tomorrow's start.

To ease our journey, we have found a third crewmember, Lauren, a fiftysomething engineer consultant for the nuclear power industry and avid sailor. Her short curly hair matches her calm Midwestern personality.

"I've pulled up a few weather maps," Lauren says. "The wind, waves, and currents are … interesting. Look, you can see what Ken's talking about."

Dennis and I hover over her shoulder at our small, wooden navigation table. The boat's computer flashes a vibrant firework display of colors and motion. Light streaks across a color-coded background depicting wind strength over the western Atlantic: blue and green for light winds; yellow for twenty and thirty knots; pink, red, and purple for gale force and higher. A fierce vortex of swirling pinks and purples are southeast of our marina, the direction we plan to travel.

Centime's cabin is cramped with food, gear, and charts. With closed hatches, the air is stale. Rushing away from the flashing screen, I slip on worn blue sneakers and tired black sweatpants, open the hatch, and duck under the Bimini cover. Rain falls steady on the docks and the wind whips through trees as I jog away from *Centime*. The streets are deserted except for occasional passing cars which splash my legs with watery mud.

Running calms my thoughts, creating a near-meditative state. Today, however, somber images intrude. The computer screen with neon colors, Lauren's and Dennis's bleak stares, and Ken's warnings crowd my mind. Premonitions of *Centime* deserted by the rally, alone in a vast ocean, are eerie. Visions of a knockdown, our boat overtaken by wind and waves, her mast underwater, frighten me more. I jog for miles in drenched clothes, shivering.

Returning to the dock forty minutes later, I pace back and forth through the drizzle waiting for the rally organizers to decide the larger group's fate. At 4:00 p.m. on Sunday, they delay the start for twenty-four hours. I return to *Centime*'s cabin to prepare dinner and pour three large glasses of red wine.

Dennis sets aside his wineglass and pours a glass of Pusser's rum.

The depression strengthens into Tropical Storm Sean, wreaking havoc at sea.

On Wednesday, the Coast Guard reports that a thirty-eight-foot boat sailing from Newport, Rhode Island, to Tortola, has been hit by a thirty-foot wave. The wife of the husband-and-wife team has been washed overboard and not found.

Throughout the week we're told to prepare to leave in twenty-four hours, then late in the afternoon the organizers delay the start another day. The Cruising Club rents facilities and staffs a full British crew, losing money every day that passes.

As Sean strengthens, I continue to run hard through wind and rain.

Mariners can be superstitious about leaving port on a Friday. After a five-day delay, the organizers tell us the rally will truly start tomorrow—Friday, 11/11/11. I take a deep breath and scramble through final preparations. The yellow emergency ditch bag bulges as I squeeze in extra containers of Ensure.

We wake at dawn. The tide is low, and I stretch to remove our lines from the tall wooden pilings. I use my whole body to push us away. Lauren coils the lines as Dennis backs *Centime* out of the slip. Our side channel is calm with moderate winds. A heron stands in the mudflats searching for small fish. Seagulls cry out as they swoop overhead.

As we reach the open sea, the wind builds to twenty-two knots. We fly toward the Gulf Stream. *Centime* moves with agitation, sails flapping, plastic windows rattling in her cockpit. Pounding waves are erratic and relentless. We start the engine and begin to motorsail to gain better control.

Heavy rain seeps through Gore-Tex seals on my jacket. Heeling over, waves break over our stern, the cockpit fills with several inches of water and drains as the boat springs back. Water rushes in and out, over Dennis's high navy boots, splashing his legs like river rapids.

In the cabin below, the galley stove rocks. The swiveling gimbals work to keep the stovetop level. A tall pot of premade chicken cacciatore, wedged onto the stove, sloshes around like a microcosm of the sea around us. The aromas, which envelop the small living area, aren't helping my stomach. I stumble around the galley trying to avoid falling against the hot stove. Lauren takes her food at the salon table below and I cover a portion for Dennis to eat after his watch. I have no appetite.

Darkness descends. I start my watch alone. Since I was eleven, I have been afraid of the dark. I've experienced flashbacks and night terrors. Despite years of therapy, my fear of darkness remains.

As waves build, *Centime* rolls up each short wave. Her aft, or back end, lifts to the right, forcing her bow left, then as the wave passes her bow surfs right, like a twisted ride. The autopilot steering groans, responding to wind gusts and forceful waves. By midnight the winds are thirty-four knots, and the waves eleven feet, over twice my height, throwing *Centime* around like a toy. The sails are reefed like small handkerchiefs. The wind and current drive the boat at nine knots, even with her tiny sails. I adjust them to keep us on course to race through unsettled weather.

Torrential rain pounds on our canvas bimini muffled by howling gusts. Black-on-black visibility is broken by white foam from breaking and splashing waves. No ship lights are visible on the seesawing horizon, yet I must remain vigilant.

Centime's steep angle to the seas, and wet deck, makes movement across the cockpit sluggish. My layers of foul-weather gear and a bulky life jacket increase the difficulty. At each step I check instruments, motor temperature, wind direction, and sails. Remembering the wife who washed overboard, I carefully unhook one of two ends of my safety tether, as the boat moves side to side through the waves, and quickly re-hook it, with cold wet hands, to reach the farthest corner of the opposite side.

The scene reminds me of the book, *Captains Courageous*, that I read in high school. The book's dramatic sailing scenes were the first hints I had of the challenges to my South Pacific sailing scheme. Today, my childhood dream seems far away. I long to be home in a warm, safe bed.

The sails flap with an abrupt change in the wind. Cool air turns warm, yet the sea remains confused. Just before midnight, my three-hour stint soon complete, I can't stop yawning. I move from side to side and splash my face with rainwater. I try to do a brief dance in place.

Lauren pokes her head up from below. "How are you doing?" she asks.

"Tired," I yell. The rain and sea are deafening. "We've made it to the

Gulf Stream. It's warmer but the seas are coming from every direction."

"I can tell. Hard to sleep. I'll be up soon."

After Lauren takes the watch, I remove my wet gear and squeeze into a tight double berth next to Dennis. His snoring competes with the engine's groan. With the boat heeled over, I struggle to find a position where I'm not rolling into him. I place blankets and pillows to buffer the hard edges of the hull, and one on top of my head to muffle the noise. Exhaustion takes over.

An alarm sounds with a jarring reverberation through our small cabin. I wake suddenly as Dennis rushes out of the berth. An unsettling green glow from the clock shows that it's near 2:00 a.m., not yet time for his watch. I vault out of my warm berth. My head pounds, cloudy from fatigue and too much seasick medicine.

Centime moves in sporadic fits, the floor trembles and shifts like slight earth tremors. Waves vibrate through the hull. Holding on with one hand, I sort out the tangled crotch straps on my life jacket and put it on. I climb the companionway stairs, hook my tether into place just outside the cockpit, climb into the night air, and steady myself on the bench to get my bearings.

A gust of wind slaps my face. I suck in damp air.

Centime is heeled far over. Lauren's body angles against the wheel, one foot braced on the cockpit seat, both hands gripping the wheel. The autopilot alarm continues to shriek. Dennis is nowhere to be seen.

Holding on with both hands, I nudge close to the corner of the cockpit to locate him. Without warning, cold water pours over my head. Plastic windows on the sides of the cockpit and a canvas top should enclose the space, keeping me dry. I'm sitting under a stream of water gushing through the enclosure like a garden hose.

I spring to the left to get out of the flow. It surges over me and splashes into my eyes. As I strain my neck and shield my eyes to find the source, I spy a thick piece of metal swinging in an arc, inches from my skull.

A fifty-pound solar panel, longer than my torso, jerks up and down, as if on a spring. The panel's sharp metal edges are adjacent to my right eye. My heart pounds as I duck and cover my head. The canvas Bimini is shredded. The solar panel, a swinging metal beast, has flipped 180 degrees, ripped from its stainless-steel frame.

"Where's Dennis?" I yell.

"Up on deck," Lauren says, her voice muffled by the wind and rain.

Dennis's yellow rain slicker moves in and out of focus in the dark of night. Waves jerk his body as he wrestles to hold onto the boom. His bright headlamp flashes strobe-lit panic, like a black-and-white film. Out-of-control lines fly and snap close to his face. Our lazy jacks, lines that maintain control when dousing, or lowering, the mainsail, are torn apart. One line is in the water. If it catches the propeller, our motor will surely shut down, leaving us to the mercy of the wind and sea. We work for several hours through the night to secure the lines and steer the boat through squalls.

Dawn breaks with lighter wind. Though the seas remain choppy, clear weather is ahead and the frenzy of the night before has diminished. A fleeting moment of calm blows through the boat and we try to secure the hazardous, sharp-edged solar panel that takes up a large portion of the cockpit. Sweat runs down my face and neck as Dennis and I strain to lift the dislocated panel while Lauren steers the boat.

The panel moves in convulsions, mimicking the sea. After several failed attempts to move it, we tie it angled across the cockpit. It hangs, hinged overhead, like a precarious steel girder ready to collide with an unlucky sailor. Apprehensive about the solar panel, we decide to turn *Centime* around.

Heading back across the Gulf Stream, *Centime* is a high-strung racehorse, reluctant as she bucks against strong currents and a west wind blowing on our bow.

The area around Cape Hatteras is known as the "Graveyard of the Atlantic." It's riddled with shoals where numerous ships have sunk. The land juts into the Gulf Stream, often bringing chaotic weather. Dennis downloads weather information using our single sideband radio and finds that a second front is approaching. Though the weather is unpleasant now, the forecasts appear worse. He sends a high-frequency radio email to Ken, our weather router. An hour later, we receive his written response:

Dennis and Heidi –

A front is heading your way, producing nasty thunderstorms over eastern South Carolina. Some storms have produced tornadoes. The squall line will reach Hatteras between 11:00 p.m. and midnight.

You should be ready for strong storms through the wee hours of the morning. You could see lightning, heavy downpours, possibly hail, and localized wind gusts of fifty knots or more. If you approach what looks like a strong storm, get all the sails down before you get into a gusty wind situation.

Maybe you'll get lucky.
Ken

I rub my growling stomach and notice my hands. Extra coffee on an empty stomach makes me jittery. I force down dry crackers and sweet tea. I don't feel lucky.

We head toward a marina 30 nautical miles away. If we continue at three to four knots sailing into strong winds it will take us the full day. We should arrive before the next front.

Dennis calls the marina by VHF radio. "Morehead Marina, Morehead Marina, this is *Centime*. Do you read?"

"This is Morehead Marina. I read you loud and clear. Go ahead, *Centime*."

"We're off the coast and plan to arrive late this afternoon or early evening, possibly after closing. Can you accommodate a thirty-nine-foot boat with a six-foot draft, and can we get help with our lines and directions to the slip if we arrive after dark?"

"You're coming in tonight? There's a big storm coming. Do you know there is a big storm?" I tremble at the sound of his voice. "I'll ask if one of the skippers here will help in case you arrive after closing. Call me back before 17:00 with your progress."

By early afternoon, I take the watch as the weather again deteriorates. Rain falls through the torn Bimini, producing a rhythmic cadence on the hanging solar panel. Damp sea spray fills the cockpit. The motor groans unevenly with each wave.

The engine temperature gauge straddles the red zone. Hand steering against the wind and current, I try to push our speed without damaging the engine. After three hours of my hand steering, straining against the force of the wheel, Dennis takes the helm. I slump next to him on the cockpit seat. Lauren emerges from below and hooks in by my side.

A red light flashes. The mic on the radio jumps to life. It vibrates with a static shudder like a hissing snake. I flinch at the sound.

"Sécurité, sécurité, sécurité. This is the United States Coast Guard with a NOAA emergency weather alert. All vessels should seek immediate shelter. Repeat. All vessels seek immediate shelter. Extreme weather, lightning, and tornadoes move across the entire Hatteras region at nineteen hundred hours."

Nineteen hundred hours, 7:00 p.m., earlier than Ken's forecast.

We are sailing at two and a half knots; the storm approaches us at thirty-five knots. Immediate shelter is six to eight hours away in the same direction as the storm. The Gulf Stream air is warm, yet I'm shaking.

We are the only boat as far as I can see. Our mast, a fifty-eight-foot aluminum pole, is a lightning rod rising high to tempt fate.

"Fuck. I hate lightning," I say.

"What?" Dennis asks, as the sea slams the hull.

"Lightning. What should I do?" I yell.

"We're gonna be okay. *Centime* is strong. Put the handheld electronics in the oven in case lightning hits."

"I'll plot our dead-reckoning course on a paper chart in case we lose our electronics."

"Good idea." He pauses, staring at me under his wet, yellow slicker, hair pasted to the side of his face, droplets of water running down his cheek. "I love you, honey." Dennis reaches out and touches my shoulder and then grabs the wheel again.

"I love you too."

I unhook one end of the tether of my life vest, then re-hook it on a metal ring near the hatch that leads inside the boat. As the boat pitches from side to side, I hold on with both hands and stagger across the cockpit. I clamber around Lauren, duck under the broken solar panel, and free one hand to push open the hatch. It doesn't budge. Shoving my full body against it, I create a small opening and crawl through. Trying to block out the storm, I slam the hatch closed.

Below, a closet door bangs in a jarring, unsteady rhythm. On the floor, cans roll about with a scattering of tea bags, raisins, nuts, bags of pasta, and Chinese noodles. Books are everywhere. Cushions have fallen off the cabin sofas.

The boat slams from side to side in an erratic motion, as I wade through the debris. I grip an overhead railing to steady my progress. Stumbling across the cabin benches, I re-latch the banging cabinet door.

Our handheld radio and GPS fit snugly in the oven, yet Faraday's notion that a metal cage might possibly redirect lightning around this precious cargo offers little comfort. After checking the emergency ditch bag to make sure our locating emergency beacon, handheld radio, wallets, and passports are inside, I secure it near the companionway stairs. I rope together two extra gallons of fresh water for the life raft.

Lightning streaks across the porthole and floods the dim cabin with bright light. A sharp thunderclap follows. My head jerks backward. Our metal mast stands tall. I'm clammy under my foul-weather gear.

My mind races through what needs to be done, thoughts clear and focused, my body filled with adrenaline. Opening the top of the desk, I find my reading glasses, a sharp pencil, ruler, and a rolled-up chart for Cape Hatteras. Spreading the large unruly paper across our salon table, I pinpoint our latitude and longitude and mark our heading and speed. An area dense with symbols of reefs and shipwrecks lies between my mark and the shore.

I contemplate what could happen if we lose our electronic charts, GPS position, and visibility. I've had a good life, as has Dennis. We have shared incredible moments together. Dennis's older children, my two stepchildren, are happy and settled in their California lives and will be okay. Nico, the youngest, is a strong and stable young man yet he is having a rough start in his first semester at a demanding college, living abroad with classes harder than any he's encountered. He's grappling with a long-distance relationship with his girlfriend 1,500 miles away and worried that this relationship might be over. Our last phone conversation was difficult. I had wanted to reach out and hold him.

I consider a worst-case scenario: lightning strikes our mast, blows a hole in the hull, water pours in and the emergency position indicating radio beacon (EPIRB) signals the Coast Guard. Flying a helicopter in lightning to rescue a sinking boat seems near impossible. The Coast Guard would contact brother Vern, and he would call Nico. I picture Nico's tiny student housing room and the twin bed where he sits as he answers the call, alone. My breathing becomes shallow.

Staring blankly through the porthole, tears begin to flow. My head hangs low; my body collapses inward. My own conflicts get tangled up with what I imagine his could become. I feel the pain he might feel along with the emotions I'm experiencing. In the past, whenever Nico struggled, I felt that struggle deep inside myself. Like many parents, I want to carry my child's pain.

Memories of Mother, and the vow I made as a preteen to be different from her, cloud my thoughts. My longing to be a near-perfect mom for Nico has, at times, been obsessive. My failure to do so feels shameful. Being a bad mother is my greatest fear—my worst failure.

(Trigger Warning) My hand wraps around my throat. My stability is gone. My body pitches in an uneven motion as *Centime* lurches forward and back. The pencil falls to the floor. The cabin blurs.

The storm overtakes me. Lightning flashes through the porthole. We are one small boat alone in a sea of lightning. I have felt small and alone before.

An immediate, electric crack of thunder sends vibrations through my body.

Orange-brown eyeglasses appear before me. In an instant a familiar man towers over me. I choke back vomit as I fall to the floor. He's here in the cabin.

I'm trapped with my back on the floor, pinned under my assailant. His adult frame crushes my childlike body.

My heart races as I struggle to escape, shifting from side to side. Nothing is clear except a heavy weight on my chest and the rage in his eyes, framed by orange-brown glasses.

My breathing is strained. I smell his sweat, the alcohol on his breath. My throat burns. I hate him. I hate myself.

Tears well up in my eyes knowing what it feels like to want to survive.

I am eleven years old.

CHAPTER 4

Torment

*The more you approach infinity,
the deeper you penetrate terror.*

Gustave Flaubert

Philadelphia, Pennsylvania, May 1967

The door slowly opens.

I smile at the creaking sound, still hoping that Terry might bound through, ready to play.

She and I are both small, under five feet, weighing less than 100 pounds. Though some of my friends have started to mature, I'm still one of the smallest in my sixth-grade class.

I stretch, looking up at the door.

(Trigger Warning) Mr. Hart's orange-brown eyeglasses appear in the crack. His expression is hard to read. He's never paid any attention to me. He doesn't like me very much. In the past he often seemed to have a permanent scowl, yet today he stares directly into my eyes. I bite my lip, uncertain of what to say or do.

"Is Terry home?" I whisper.

Terry's father is angular and bony, in his forties perhaps, with a narrow stern face and short, thinning, reddish-brown hair. He's wearing a well-worn sleeveless undershirt tucked into brown slacks. I notice a tan stain on his shirt and a thin black belt holding up his pants. His feet are bare.

Mother has warned me several times to stay out of Mr. Hart's way, especially if he's stumbling down the street or parking his car. Dad says he drinks too much. Although we're next-door neighbors, we have mostly avoided one another.

"Terry is visiting her aunt. She'll be home soon," he says, and then, after some hesitation, he opens the door wider. "Come inside and wait."

Mother taught me to do as I am told. For the first time in my life, I enter the brick house next door. The bright sun lights up the entryway creating a path forward, yet most of the living room is dim and quiet; no one else appears to
be home.

The layout of the Harts' living room is a mirror image of my own family's living room with a different ambience. I think of Terry being my twin, our houses being twins, and smile for a moment.

The beige curtains are drawn, and the room is musty with a faint stale smell. The rug is brown and worn. The furnishings are sparse: no plants, pictures, knickknacks, throws, or sofa pillows. The brown sofa, the most prominent feature, is old with assorted clumps of pet fur. It sits alone in the middle of the room, blocking the direct path to the stairs and the dining room.

In contrast, our living room is open and airy. My mother arranges our furniture to give it a spacious feel. When it's warm outside, she keeps the windows open to draw in fresh air. She decorates our home in white and yellow fabrics, wallpapers, and paints. The pieces of art on our wall are cardboard reproductions that Mother found in our grocery store, yet she framed and placed them with care. The prints were my first introduction to Renaissance masters, and I love them.

(Trigger Warning) "Let's play a game," Mr. Hart says. "Whadda you want to play?"

I stare at him. I've never played with a grown man, except rare games of catch with Dad. I know that Terry owns a Barbie doll. "Can we play with Terry's Barbie?" I ask.

"Come upstairs," he says. "She keeps her dolls upstairs."

I hesitate and then cross the room behind him. Mr. Hart climbs the stairs at a slow, unnatural pace. With each step a voice sounds in my head. Don't go! It is as if someone is calling out to stop me. Something I can't name is wrong. My heart speeds up as my climbing slows.

Halfway up I turn around and scamper down the stairs. "I'll wait for Terry down here."

I don't want to disobey Mr. Hart or sit on his fur-coated brown sofa. I stand in the middle of Terry's living room, feeling queasy.

Mr. Hart follows me back to the living room. He isn't running, yet he walks faster. "Come with me," he says. He grabs my hand and yanks me off-balance toward the middle room of the first floor. My arm aches.

The middle room in my home next door is a light-filled dining room. My mother has a large formal table in the center with a yellow tablecloth covered with spring flowers. We have long, bright white curtains that she pulls back with thick golden ropes to let the sun pour through the ample side windows.

The middle room at the Harts' home is a downstairs bedroom. The bed and nightstand are large, crowding the space. I wonder if Terry has a sick grandmother like I do; if so, where is she? The curtains are closed, and the room has a distinct smell reminding me of Grandpa Lloyd. The bed is unmade. The sheets are stained. Magazines are scattered across the top. My eye catches a large-breasted woman on one cover.

"We're going to play a new game," he says.

My body stiffens. He forces my light frame backward onto the dirty mattress between the magazines. He is thin, wiry, and strong, smaller than my dad. Throwing off his clothes, he exposes his chest, sparsely covered with auburn hair. He stands above me.

A peculiar pair of eyeglasses are the only item adorning his body. They aren't the wire spectacles that my New Jersey grandfather, Pop Pop Malin, had, or the serious black style my dad wore; instead, they are an opaque orange-brown, the color of burnt maple.

As I try to rise, his hands press against my shoulders. His gestures are commanding. He pins me beneath him. I am a live butterfly impaled on a waxed scientific tray. His face is so near I can feel his heavy breathing and smell sickly sweet alcohol and butterscotch on his breath.

The long oval orange-brown glasses frame his eyes. I stare at the frame and then look through his eyeglass lenses. Time slows as his myopic eyes penetrate mine. I sink deeper into the mattress. His leer overpowers me. I am surrounded by something I have never seen or felt. He looks through me as if the body beneath him, my body, is everything he has ever hated in his life.

He tears at my clothes, pulling off my shorts and my favorite shirt—white cotton, short-sleeved with pink fish swimming across the front.

Stabbing pain sears through me. I cry, "Stop!" The ache continues as he finishes what he intends and collapses on top.

He's heavy and his body is covered with sweat. The hair on his chest covers my mouth and my breathing is labored. The gasps of air I take in are foul.

Mr. Hart is a sleeping monster that I don't want to disturb. Lying paralyzed under him on the bed, not daring to move, I try not to gag. Tears roll down my cheeks. I believe with total certainty he will kill me. I saw it earlier in his eyes framed by his glasses.

I'm aware of every second, every move. I hold my breath as I carefully squeeze from beneath him, his large body stuck to mine. Uncoupled, I spring to my feet and rush to the door as he stumbles behind me. He reaches out to grab me.

"Nooo!" I scream. "Please, God, let me out. Please! Please! Please!"

I reach the door first, tear it open and slam it hard in his face. Startled by the bright sun, I stumble off his porch.

I am alive. I am alive.

My legs buckle under me as I run toward home. Then fragments of images shatter like glass.

CHAPTER 5

Defeat

*Learn to lose your destiny to
find where it leads you.*

Munia Khan

The North Atlantic Ocean, November 2011

    Thunder cracks overhead. Mr. Hart is gone. I'm no longer eleven.

    My PTSD flashback has left me crumpled and beaten on *Centime*'s floor. Hyperventilating, I curl into a ball. My body tumbles side to side in the cramped space under the wooden table, synchronized with the erratic rhythm of disturbed waves.

    As my mind clears, a singular idea comes into focus. It would be easy to climb to the cockpit and slide overboard in darkness. There would be no trace. I have lived too long with secrets and shame. My loved ones are better off without me.

    I plot my course. The route toward the companionway hatch is still littered with books and loose shelf-stable food. The large paper chart is on the floor ahead. *Centime* continues to move with fits of jarring, side-to-side rolls. I crawl uneasily over detritus toward the cockpit. Concentrating on the sea, I long for an end of my torment—the end of the torment I must cause others.

    Forward progress is an ordeal, my movements sluggish. My legs are heavy, almost unresponsive. Pushing aside the chart and debris, I crawl, dragging my weight and using my arms to pull myself ahead.

A can of black beans collides with my head, and I collapse again flat on the floor. My face, wet with tears, brushes against the faux leather cover of the logbook. I stare at the brown cover. It is an immediate and present reminder of Dennis, Lauren … and Nico. My head pounds. The weight of obligation is heavy.

Looking back, I remember a shift in my mental state when I encountered the logbook: from tormented feelings of shame to an awareness of responsibility. The logbook reminded me of the fragility of Dennis's and Lauren's safety, and the hurt I would cause Nico if I slipped over the side. Some say suicide is a selfish act, others argue against that. For me, mental anguish instantly twisted my perspective, setting a dangerous course. I was overwhelmed by warped feelings that I was so horrible that loved ones were better off if I didn't exist, then concern for Nico and Dennis brought back my sanity.

Perhaps if I hadn't seen the logbook, I would have reached the cockpit, seen Dennis, and changed my mind, or perhaps not. In the end, I dragged myself up to the navigation table, retrieved the log and paper from the cabin floor, found a new pencil, and stared at a blurry map. There, uncontrolled tears streamed down my face.

Gray daylight fades in the cabin, accentuated by lightning flashes. The overhead lamp glares red in night vision mode. I rub my eyes and peer at our latest position on the instruments and mark it on the chart. The new distance to shore is less than a half of an inch from our old position.

The VHF radio in the cabin hisses with static. The clock shows 16:45. Dennis's voice crackles over the radio from the cockpit above me as if he were miles away.

"Morehead Marina, this is sailing vessel *Centime*. Do you read?"

"This is Morehead Marina." The voice is a tenuous connection, a lifeline to land and hope. I strain my neck to listen.

"I called earlier. Can you accommodate *Centime* after closing?" Dennis says.

The marina manager repeats his earlier warning. "There is a big storm coming!" I taste the remnants of vomit in my mouth. "Call Frank on the VHF when you arrive. He's a cruiser on the outer dock and can help guide you in. What's your ETA?"

"Midnight."

Lightning flashes. Hours pass. At every loud crack I repeat: if I can hear it, I'm still alive.

As *Centime* rocks, the porthole shifts from sea black, with her side angled toward the ocean, to a sky aflame when she rocks back.

A bright line on the LED radar screen sweeps in a circle like a racing second hand of a watch. Squalls appear as menacing ink blots, populating the display at a furious pace. We are surrounded. I relay their positions to Dennis. He tries to maneuver around the worst squalls since we can't outrun them.

Gripped by emotions, I work in slow motion to plot the course. The storm and heavy rain continue. By 00:20, just after midnight, the wave bashing subsides. I leave the shelter of the cabin and my role reading the radar and climb on deck.

"I'm heading forward," I say into the wind, my head low.

Grasping the lifelines, I move methodically toward the bow, hooking and unhooking my tether, my body stiff, my legs shaking, willing my hands to hold tight to a thin veneer of safety.

The sea and sky blend in obscure darkness, black waves indistinguishable from a murky horizon. Intermittent lightning strikes provide glimpses of obstacles as we limp toward the channel. I flinch with every flash of light and clap of thunder. If I can hear it, I'm still alive. Channel markers and hazards emerge ghostlike, eerie images appear and then fade from view. My reality is suspect. I question what is real, what is imagined. I'm afraid of what, or whom, I might see in the shadows.

I switch on the floodlight and we are bathed in amber light. Stretching my neck and arms, I search back and forth with the light, making a pattern through gloom to mark the route for Dennis and Lauren. My face and body are wet inside and out. The light flickers across obstacles. My voice falters as I try to shout directions and warnings to Dennis into a handheld radio. Finally, I catch a glimpse of the shore. I lick the salt from my lips and wipe water from my face and eyes.

Frank answers our hail and uses his handheld radio and flashlight to guide us. The dark night and a power blackout at the marina conceal the slip. He outlines the edge of the dock with his light.

I throw the bow line to Frank, stagger past Lauren at the beam, and then jump to shore with a stern line. My legs collapse under me. Falling, then rolling, I stretch and tie the docking line lying down. The wooden planks are solid under my hips and shaking hands as I spread my fingers across them, feeling every inch of dock under me. I lie in the dark rain, nearly invisible, and sob, my body convulsing.

I am alive. I am alive.

The next day, in Morehead City, North Carolina, Lauren flies home. Dennis and I register *Centime* with the marina manager. "I'm glad you're safe. I was worried," he says. "Several people died last night in the tornadoes; one man came in before you with broken ribs and torn sails."

On the boat, gear is strewn in every corner: life jackets, charts, cans of food, pencils, books, and rubber boots. Wet rain slickers and pants hang over our food hammock. Dirty dishes and food scraps are piled in the sink. Clearing a body-sized space, I collapse amid the debris and sleep through the day. By early evening, I awake to a growling stomach.

At the local fish restaurant, shiny blue oilcloths cover each table. Sea shanties play through speakers, filling the room. The dining room is deserted except for a bartender wiping down his counter in the far corner. The off-season tourist town appears empty after the storm. Dennis sits across from me. On the table are two empty wine glasses, a cup of tea, and a large plate, half-filled with fried fish and french fries.

Tears pool in my eyes. "When I heard the storm warning and you wanted our electronics in the oven, I imagined lightning hitting the mast and blowing a hole through our hull," I say. I hold my teacup in both hands, absorbing the warmth. The hot liquid spills onto my fingers as they shake. Dennis stops eating and scans my face and hands. The cup clinks as I return it to its saucer. After wiping the spill with my napkin, I hold my hand on my stomach. He reaches across the table and holds onto my elbow.

"I thought we might die. You and I have had good lives, your kids are doing well on their own; they'd be okay. When I thought about what our deaths would do to Nico, then I felt like a bad mom … ashamed that I shouldn't be taking this risk. I don't want to hurt him or have him experience the grief I've felt.

"I've told you about my mother. I've always wanted to be different than her. My mother passed her trauma on to me. She was hurt herself and hurt me badly too. Dennis, it's my worst failure to be like her, to be a bad mom. It triggers every fear I've ever had. When I feel like I'm her, my PTSD starts."

Dennis stares, his eyes wide. "Oh, honey, I had no idea. I was so busy dodging squalls, I didn't think of what was happening below. You gave me positions, guided us into the harbor, did everything we needed." He reaches across the table and grabs my arms.

"When I saw the lightning, I had … I had …" I say, lowering my voice to a whisper and looking at the bartender to see if he is listening, "… a flashback … like soldiers have after combat." I slump down in my chair.

Dennis's mouth falls open. "What?" he stammers. I've never shared my full trauma. I've tried to hide my flashbacks and my shame.

"Every day, I remember pieces of my childhood trauma, but they're just bad memories. Yet sometimes I have real flashbacks. This was real. Mr. Hart was right there in the boat with me. I saw him. He … he … was … there. I smelled him. I mean … I know now he couldn't have been there, but at the time I thought he was on the boat, Dennis, he really was. I … I … saw him." I cry, my body shaking. "He will never stop raping me."

Dennis pushes his chair away from the table. He walks to my side and pulls me up to give me a strong hug, holding me tight. All my strength falls away, and I collapse in his arms like a rag doll.

"I feel like such a … bad … mother, leaving Nico." I sob. His arms tighten around me. "What if we had died out there? What would that do to him?" I grab a napkin to wipe my face. I take a deep breath. "I don't know if I can go on. What if I stay behind and don't sail to the Caribbean?"

He pushes me back to see my eyes while holding my arms tight. "You are not a bad mom."

Hanging my head, I stare at the floor as he continues.

"Look at me, Heidi. You're not a bad mom. You love Nico fully and have done a tremendous job for eighteen years of his life. He's a grown man, ready for independence. I know life is challenging him right now, but he's smart and capable. You and his dad have raised him to be strong. If you don't want to continue, you don't have to. You're far more important to me than sailing. I love you so much. I can find crew and meet you there, or we can both stop sailing right here, right now. Why don't we get the boat fixed and you can take your time to think about what's next? No matter what, you and I are together. And Heidi, you're not a bad mom."

A few weeks later, after Thanksgiving, we complete the final repairs. With her solar panels bolted into a new sturdy aluminum frame, *Centime* is ready to go. I'm not sure if I am. I'm sleeping in the cabin when the phone rings. It's close to midnight.

"Mom," Nico says. "I'm sick."

"What's wrong?" My breath quickens.

"My stomach hurts. It's intense. It might be food poisoning."

"If it's intense, you need to call the hospital, in case it's your appendix." Nico has a high threshold for pain and rarely complains. After breaking his leg in a ski accident a few years earlier he'd told me, "It's not bad."

"If it is your appendix and it ruptures, it will be very serious," I say.

"I'm already at the hospital. It hurt so bad, I just went. The doctor said it might be food poisoning. She just released me. Now I need to walk home."

"If you're sure you're okay, buddy, call Uber. I'll fly up in the morning, or tonight if I can find a way."

"No, I'll be okay. I just need to sleep."

"Take a taxi home on your credit card and rest. Let's talk in the morning. Promise me you'll call me if anything changes in the night. I love you."

By morning, Nico is still ill but recovering. I long to be close in case he needs me. My decision is clear. I will not sail *Centime* to the Virgin Islands. I also know that I'm not ready, and may never be ready, to sail again.

Dennis supports my decision. He emails Lauren and finds she is willing to try the crossing again. He finds two more sailors excited for a trip. I will track Dennis and his crew every step of the way. I'll look into flights to Montreal and talk more with Nico to see if he changes his mind about a visit. I love Dennis and Nico and will try to be my best for both of them.

Looming large in the background of this decision is a deep sense of failure.

It is thirty-eight degrees at 6:00 a.m. on a late November day in North Carolina. Dennis and his new crew are dressed in long johns and full foul-weather gear. The sky glows red in the east, a few faint stars are visible. Ken, our weather advisor, has given Dennis the recommendation to leave today.

I untie their lines and shove them away from the narrow wooden dock, while waving goodbye and wishing them a safe journey. A cold wind blows. I place my arms across my chest and lean against the piling. Small waves lap against the dock. The air smells of brine. *Centime* appears smaller and smaller, and then disappears beyond the horizon.

Alone, I stare at the empty harbor. A mist forms on my face and yellow rain slicker. I rub my eyes and force myself to look away from the empty sea. My head hangs low, and I trace the lines of white salt that have marred my leather boat shoes.

CHAPTER 6

Sisterhood

*Sisters are like flowers in the garden of life,
they bring beauty and joy wherever they grow.*

Louisa May Alcott, *Little Women*

Beaufort, North Carolina, November 2011

Dennis and his crew are gone.

It's early morning. The quaint streets of Beaufort are deserted. The moisture-laden breeze smells like seaweed and wood smoke. I sit on a white wicker rocking chair with a crimson blanket wrapped around me. Dennis and I had rented a second-floor condo with a boat slip for a few days, waiting for his new crew to arrive. Now the slip is empty. Beyond the porch, an expansive gray sea fuses with an endless gray sky. Dennis is out there, somewhere, in the Atlantic. I'm here, alone.

A nearby wicker table holds a paper chart weighted down with smooth sea stones. Scribbled across are speeds, distances, weather, ETAs, and a penciled-in route. Next to it my MacBook glows with an electronic chart revealing a pulsating red dot, *Centime*'s current position. Her route trails in yellow behind her, like a raindrop wiggling down a windowpane. Late last night, her path turned north for over an hour, and I wondered if she was in trouble. By 3:00 a.m. she had returned to her correct course toward the British Virgin Islands; I returned to sleep. Now large spaces behind the flashing dot indicate fast movement, consistent with strong winds. I bite my lips as I check again for a satellite generated email from Dennis and weather forecasts from Ken.

The wind in Beaufort has died. The rising sun begins to illuminate the sea that stretches for thousands of miles. I hold my coffee mug with both hands, trying to absorb its warmth.

My phone interrupts the quiet with a jarring ring. My heart beats faster than normal as I grab it. Please don't be the Coast Guard.

"Hi, Mom," Nico says. A smile breaks across my face. It's been three days since he left the hospital.

"It's great to hear your voice, buddy. How are you?" I ask.

"I'm good. Tired. My stomach is better. Thanks for sending the soup and bread. I was starving."

"You're welcome. I told the restaurant to choose something easy on the stomach."

"It was full of vegetables. You would have liked it."

"Would you like some company in Montreal? Why don't I stay at a hotel for a few days, shop for food, and cook for you? Fill up your fridge and freezer."

"I'm okay. I have two papers due and finals start next week. I'll have a break after that. Then I'll come down to the boat. How's Dennis?"

"He's sailing fast. He should be there in six more days. If you're sure you don't want me to come up, I'll fly to Tortola and meet him."

"Yep, I'm good. When he finishes the passage tell him congrats for me. I'll see you soon. I have class. I better go."

"Okay. Call me anytime."

"Yep. Love you, Mom."

"I love you too, to the moon and back."

Later that week, I fly to the British Virgins and connect with sailing friends I had met earlier, at the start of the Virginia rally. I had attended a workshop called "Women at Sea." The instructor told us to look around the room. She said some of the women near us would become best friends for life.

The adventurous woman sitting next to me in class was Danielle. She and her partner Michel have a forty-six-foot French sloop called *Nyctea*, meaning snowy owl. Danielle was afraid of the dark, like me, and loved the owl as a symbol of courage and strength through the night. Finally arriving in Tortola and climbing aboard *Nyctea*, I can't stop smiling.

Danielle and I sail *Nyctea* toward the harbor where Dennis hopes to make landfall. The wind powers the sails as I take the helm. Tropical winds blow through my hair. Adrenaline streams through my body. I sing aloud.

After anchoring and enjoying a pasta primavera with an abundance of wine, Danielle and Michel retire. I wait, anxious, for Dennis's arrival. *Nyctea*'s cockpit is large, more spacious and modern than *Centime*'s. As hours drag on, I write about my journey over the past month. Alone in the cockpit, I find a thickness in my throat. I miss Dennis and have been worried about his safety. Though he had supported my decision to remain behind, I can't shake the feeling that I let him down, let myself down.

At 2:00 a.m., I stretch my legs across the seat and elevate my head on a blue-and-white-striped cushion. The red blinking dot on my laptop's chart, *Centime*'s position, is getting closer to our anchorage, closer to me. A thousand stars and a sky full of beauty surround me. I close my eyes, let my head fall back and feel the wind dance on my cheeks.

At first, dawn's radiance masks *Centime*'s light when she rounds the distant point, then a faint glow on the horizon matches the position that blinks on the computer. The slow-moving light approaches like an apparition, and *Centime*'s shape begins to reveal itself. For over an hour she sails in the gentle breeze toward the quiet harbor. Using Danielle's binoculars, I can see Lauren pick up a mooring not far from *Nyctea*. I wake Michel and Danielle and we row over in their small dinghy. Scurrying on board, I fall into Dennis's long, strong embrace.

"I'm so proud of you," I say, a large grin across my face.

"I missed you, honey." His eyes scan my face as if he's memorizing it. "It was challenging. Your emails every day and night helped."

"Even though I didn't sail, I wanted to support you. When you were leaving the Gulf Stream, I watched you sail north for over an hour; I knew something was wrong."

"Wow, you saw that? We lost a batten in the mainsail, and we had to head into the wind to reef her. You were watching that close?"

"Yes, I was worried that I couldn't help you."

"It was rough out there, but now it's odd to be here, after being so long at sea. I missed you, but I'm not ready for it to end."

"The journey doesn't have to end," I say, taking a deep breath, hoping I have the courage to continue sailing. How will Dennis feel about us if I don't?

Our Caribbean sailing season starts with tropical sunshine and star-filled nights. My anxiety and fear lie dormant as Nico arrives for winter break. Though he showed up exhausted from his studies and needing sleep, he is the first to suggest a multitude of adventures. Every day we sail to a different island, explore, swim, and snorkel. Nico enjoys fishing, swimming, and sailing, taking the helm at every opportunity. On his last evening I find him lounging at the bow under a moon-lit sky.

"I love being here, Mom," he says.

"I love having you. I'm proud of you for your work at school. You're a good sailor too."

"Yeah, I totally get why you wanted to do this. When you first took off, I resented being left. It didn't seem normal or anything like my friend's moms were doing. Now I understand more about why you had to go. Someday, if you don't want the boat anymore, I could totally take her off your hands. I could live like this." An engaging smile spreads across his face.

"I hope someday life offers you ways to follow your dreams, sailing or anywhere they lead."

After Nico departs for Montreal, Dennis and I sail south to the Caribbean Island of Dominica. The high peaks of the lush, green island pierce the clouds and disappear from view. The native Kalingo call Dominica "Waitukubuli," meaning "tall is her body." She rises in a series of abrupt vertical ridges, four to five thousand feet from the sea. Every spine is crowded with rainforest. Myriad palms and ancient tree ferns provide the texture of her woven canopy.

Her wilderness holds nine active volcanoes or "devil's peaks," geothermal springs, and a unique boiling lake. As nature's jewel her forests accommodate beautiful flowering plants, fifty-five kinds of butterflies, giant frogs called mountain chickens, and the largest of all Amazonian parrots.

Her vibrant tapestry flows beyond the wilderness to the colorful diversity on her shores. Scattered along the edges are bright pink, yellow, red, purple, and lime-green huts. Each hut mimics its surroundings, where a profusion of flowering shrubs and fruit trees abound. Her people are gracious, generous, and welcoming, with European and African ancestries, and some mixed with deeper pre-Colombian indigenous roots.

Rickety wooden docks protrude into a clear, azure Caribbean Sea, where the enchantment continues. The harbor holds dozens of small, colorful powerboats painted with names: *Rainbow*, *Lawrence of Arabia*, *Cobra*, and *Sexy Bones*. Strong, dark-skinned island men with broad smiles and bright white teeth race their small power boats toward *Centime*. The air is filled with laughter, greetings of welcome, and offerings of produce, moorings, and boat help.

As I greet our island hosts, buying grapefruits, limes, and bananas, I hear women singing. Sounds of reggae drift through the air. I look to the source. A small, white boat, with the name *Providence* painted in green across her side, carries four beautiful women. They are friends from home: Bonita, Annie, Layne, and Judy. This is the start of our "Strong Sisters' Sailing Tour."

We planned this rendezvous months ago, hoping to start a tradition of friendship and celebrate our feminine energy. We chose Dominica for her raw beauty. Our guidebook states, "If Christopher Columbus came back today, Dominica is the only Caribbean Island he would recognize." She does not disappoint.

"Ahoy, *Centime*. I have brought you melodious, exotic birds," says Martin, the boat driver.

He lifts up my friends' precious possessions as they scramble on board. They giggle as they try to gain footholds on the narrow ladder of our rocking boat and fall into hugs and kisses when they make it on deck. Setting duffel bags aside, we toast with rum punch. To sisters!

Dennis has offered his space to my friends and will spend a few evenings ashore. This time is for female energy.

Bonita is a generous woman with a small frame, short-cropped hair and a broad smile. She runs a nonprofit that supports education in Belize. Reaching into a large, woven bag she pulls out handmade bracelets, symbols of connection.

"These were made by my friend, Elvira, in Punta Gorda," she says, holding up a handful. "They're for you."

"Oh, they're beautiful!" Annie replies, the sun at a low angle highlighting her joyful face, and long red-blonde hair.

"Aren't they?" Bonita asks. "Which do you want?"

"Could we choose for each other and tie them as a symbol of our sisterhood?" I ask.

"Oooh, great idea. Why don't you choose for Annie?" Layne says. She runs a nonprofit too, working to reduce gender-based violence.

I find a bracelet with earth tones, symbolic of Annie's love of gardening and Mother Earth. Its rich shades of brown, rust, and gold complement her beautiful hair. "How about this one, Annie?" I ask. She nods her approval and I tie it around her wrist.

Around the cockpit we go, selecting ties for one another. Judy, a talented artist and graphic designer with long black hair, chooses one for me: blue, edged in yellow. Blue is my favorite color.

"This reminds me of your connection to the sea. The yellow represents the warmth of the sun. May it bring you fair weather," Judy says.

"May it bring us all fair weather," Annie laughs. "I'm nervous about the big, bad ocean."

I take her hand. "Look at the sun and sky and these strong women surrounding you, Annie. You will have amazing weather and capable sisters to sail with you."

A soft splash interrupts the discussion. Annie jumps. "What was that?" she asks.

We peer over the side into the blue-green sea. "Could it be a shark or a barracuda?" Judy says, leaning over the lifeline while Annie retreats.

"It must be a turtle, a mother turtle, honoring us," I say, smiling. "She's a sign from the sea of feminine connection."

The tying of wristbands among friends and the drinking of rum and mango juice seal our bond. We are now "turtle sisters." The sun sets with vibrant colors and the sky fills with stars.

"May the turtle-sister-sailing tour begin," Bonita says.

After midnight, we retire, and I lock the hatch at the entrance to the cockpit.

"You aren't really going to lock that, are you?" Annie asks.

"I always lock it to feel safe," I reply.

"We'll keep you safe, sister," Bonita says. "Let's leave it open."

"No, I'd be afraid to NOT be locked in," I say, my voice louder than I expect.

"I'd be afraid TO be locked in. What if we sink? We couldn't get out," Annie says.

Annie and I were both violated by men and our opposite phobias linger. I feel more protected when I'm locked inside; she feels safer outdoors. We've had this conversation before. She leaves the doors and windows to her home unlocked day and night. She once broke down in her car at night and wasn't able to get help right away. She climbed a tree and spent time in the upper branches until help came, feeling safer in a tree than in her car.

"What could happen if we keep it open?" Layne asks. Working with boys, she is an experienced mediator.

My breathing accelerates. "We could get boarded by a strong man and—"

"I'll sleep outside in the cockpit, sister," Bonita interrupts. "No one will get in. I want to sleep under the stars. Would that be okay?"

Annie joins. "Me too. I'd like to sleep under the stars. It is such a beautiful night."

I begin to rub my throat. They watch, wait, and stare. I'm not ready to relinquish the constraints I place around myself. The tension builds.

"Look, I lock the door even when Dennis is here. You don't know this harbor. Someone could swim here from shore or another boat. How about tomorrow night? Give me one single night to get ready," I plead.

They look at each other and then we all look at Annie who nods a tentative approval.

"Okay, one night with the lock, if you promise we won't sink. Tomorrow, it stays open," Annie replies. My shoulders relax. I will be safe one more night.

Lying in bed I wonder if I will ever feel totally safe. Who are these two women I have become? One side of me is adventurous and radiates boundless energy and courage; the other shrinks back, paralyzed in fear. I am my parents' daughter.

York, Maine, November 1987

My hands were clammy as I unlocked the door.

The year was 1987, and my husband, who had yet to become Nico's dad, had left three days before on a business trip. Our neighborhood in Maine was friendly. The town's crime reports were mostly filled with traffic violations; the thirty-five-mph speed limit of the town's straightaway was lucrative for the local cops.

I'd left work early in hopes of being home before dark. I was afraid of being alone and I hated the dark. As I scurried inside my house, my Dalmatian, Tasha, bounded up to my chest, licking my face and wagging her tail. I let her out and back in, quickly locked the door behind her, and cautiously moved through my home inspecting every room, window, closet, and under our bed to convince myself that the rooms were safe and secure.

I could smell my sweat in spite of my deodorant. I was desperate for a shower and change of clothes but was frightened to undress without my husband at home. As a total wimp, I'd slept in my work clothes for two nights to avoid undressing. I could no longer abstain from showering or changing my clothes. I needed to be clean for a work meeting the following day.

The heat came on and I flinched at the sound. I grabbed our largest kitchen knife and headed toward the bathroom. Inside I placed the knife and a pile of clean clothes next to the bathroom sink. Grabbing a heavy living room chair, I dragged it into the bathroom, and called Tasha.

The narrow bathroom was crowded with the chair barricading the door and Tasha lying on the bathmat. My towel was on top of my clothes that were stacked in the exact order of how I would put them on. I moved the knife to the edge of the bathtub. I felt a bit dizzy and sat down on the chair, my head in my hands, my heart racing.

It's only a brief shower. You don't have to wash your hair. You're safe with Tasha. I stood up next to the bathtub for several minutes, fully dressed, and then turned on the water.

"We can do this, Tasha," I said aloud, my heart pounding; her tail thumped against the bathmat. Taking a deep breath, I threw off my shoes, skirt, blouse, and stockings in a few quick sweeps, and jumped into the shower, keeping on my underwear.

After a few seconds I jumped out of the shower, grabbed the towel, wiped off the soap under my arms and wrapped the towel around me. As I rushed to put on pajamas, I felt my wet underwear soak through.

What if someone came into the house while I was in the shower? What if a man is outside the bathroom door? How can I protect myself? I hyperventilated. Clutching the kitchen knife in one hand, I reached for the lock, but couldn't unlock it. My hand was shaking. I stood frozen at the door, Tasha by my side, staring up at me.

I collapsed in the chair. My chest convulsed as I sobbed, my tears falling on to my pajamas. The water from my undergarments seeped onto the chair.

I knew I must leave the bathroom, but it was challenging.

Several years later when Nico was three, I separated from his dad and sought out a therapist.

"Why are you here?" the therapist asked.

"I'm afraid," I replied, squirming in my chair, trying to a fake a smile.

"What are you afraid of?"

"I'm afraid of being alone without a man to protect me," I said, surprising myself with this answer. Is this my voice talking? I don't like this voice. I sound like my mother.

"What scares you about being alone?"

(Trigger Warning) My body stiffened and I crossed my arms. My breathing grew faster. Looking toward the exit, I wanted to run. I slid my hips toward the edge of the seat, then forced myself to stay rooted to the chair. I studied the pattern in the rug on the floor.

"That a horrible man will hurt me," I whispered.

"Let's forget about being alone for a moment and imagine something lovely, something safe and fun. What if you had a man to protect you? What would you do next month if everything was perfect, you had a wonderful man in your life, and you could do anything you wanted?"

My shoulders loosened and I sat up straighter. "I'd go to Europe. I'd take Nico to Paris. We'd climb the Eiffel Tower, eat baguettes, cheese, and chocolates. We'd stroll along the Seine and walk through the Tuileries Garden. I want him to explore different worlds, to open his mind, to be filled with life."

"What's stopping you? What would happen if you and Nico went to Paris—alone?"

I held my breath. The room was hot, closing in. Sweat formed on my brow. I tried to picture Paris's Champs Elysée. A large, multistory, granite hotel, old and gray, appeared. I became trapped in an image of a huge, stone mausoleum with men traipsing in and out, laughing at the bloody mess left behind. Nico was crying. I couldn't protect him.

The therapist's door was a few steps across the room. I stared at it. My throat hurt. The words choked me as I answered.

"I would be raped ... again."

On *Centime*, lying near Annie in the forward cabin, I wake in the middle of the night screaming. It is only a nightmare. Annie awakes in fright. She rushes to the stern of the boat, unlocks the hatch and retreats to the cockpit. Soon, Bonita joins her.

The next morning, I apologize to Annie, and we hug. Neither of us want to talk about our fears. The door lock remains off. I remain uneasy.

After breakfast, my four sisters and I venture to Spanny Falls with Dennis and Paul, a Dominican guide. Jungle roads snake up the mountain as overhanging branches brush the side of the van. Mountain peaks rise at sharp angles, their darkness in dramatic contrast with the white clouds that settle in their midst. We stop at an unmarked path, a small tunnel in the vegetation. Paul leads us up a long, dirt trail laden with palm trees, fragrant herbs, and colorful flowers.

A powerful waterfall cascades sixty feet into a cool jungle pool. The force of the falls spreads tangible energy around us. Large leaves flutter and water sprays high into the air. We snap pictures, breathe in fresh, humid air, and continue hiking. A steep path ahead has sections of old knotted ropes, hanging from above. We ascend into the rainforest, holding the ropes. At the top of the ridge an overgrown path continues. Hand over hand on the climbing rope, cautious with our footing, we reach the base of the secluded upper falls.

Torrents of water thunder off a jagged mountain peak, seventy-five feet, into a wild pool. The area is surrounded by lush jungle forest. We are alone in this part of the rainforest. We strip to bathing suits and dive into the sparkling, clean water. It's cool and refreshing on our hot bodies. One by one we swim against the forceful current to rocks directly under the falls. We stand underneath, five strong women, holding hands, slipping on algae-covered rocks, catching and supporting one another and laughing with delight. On the sidelines, Paul and Dennis laugh too, taking photos of our playful behavior. I'm breathless under this cold waterfall in this rainforest Shangri-La.

That evening, we sit in the cockpit under a canopy of stars. I pass around a bottle of bordeaux and another of sauvignon blanc. Bright orange bird-of-paradise flowers that Paul picked fill the cockpit, highlighted by twinkling solar lights that Judy brought. Layne and Annie pass around a dinner of fresh breadfruit, potatoes, onions, peppers, garlic, ginger, and noodles. The tropical air holds a hint of coolness.

We empty the two bottles of wine and open another red.

"Thanks for inviting us. It's been so busy at work, and I haven't taken a break since my mom passed," Judy says, her voice dropping in volume as she grasps my hand.

"How are you, Jude?" I ask. Her alabaster skin has red splotches. "I know you were close to your mom."

"I'm okay …" she says and looks down. "It's just that … death is really final. I was closer to my mom, yet her passing was easier than Dad's, because we had time to say goodbye, to say we loved one another. With my dad, there was … unfinished business. When someone takes their own life, it never … leaves you." I squeeze her hand, pull it tight against my heart and feel it shake. She fans her face with her free hand and then wipes her eyes. Annie passes her a travel pack of tissues.

"Judy, I'm so sorry that happened," Bonita says, rubbing Judy's shoulders. "We've all had major losses, yet with your dad, it was harder than anyone should have to go through. When Matt was diagnosed with cancer, even though we were divorced, he came home. We'd shared so much life together:

meeting in college, raising two kids. I felt blessed to share his last days, to get closure on our lives. Not having closure seems hard."

Bonita grabs the bordeaux from the cockpit table and tops off our glasses. "And Heidi, I'm thankful to be here too, with my true sisters. This is amazing."

Lush vegetation and colorful boats surround the large harbor. The sun is low in the sky painting the clouds with a pink tinge. A cooling breeze ruffles Judy's hair.

"I'm grateful you're here, and that we keep in touch through hard times," I say. "This may sound odd; I've wanted close girlfriends since I was a kid. I had a best friend, Terry, when I was young. We did everything together for years until my family moved away. Then I never saw her again."

"Haven't you tried to find her?" Judy asks.

"No, I'm afraid. Anything could have happened to her. I'd rather not know. When I lived in Philadelphia my friends had tough lives. I suspect many have died. One girl was brought to school by a truant officer after missing months of school; she didn't have any shoes. She was disheveled and malnourished. Imagine an eleven-year-old child in the US too poor to have shoes. I don't even know what emotional and physical challenges she endured.

"My grade school friends were at such a disadvantage growing up poor in Philadelphia. Later, I became a supporter of programs that gave children from under-resourced communities a chance to succeed. I got into an argument with a white, conservative politician who was angry that certain groups might be given what he called an unfair advantage over him. I don't know what he went through to be successful, yet I did know some of the hardships my Philadelphia friends had to overcome.

"The politician tried to shut me up. He said my friends are 'probably all dead.' Even if Terry is still alive and I found her, do you think she'd want to be reacquainted with the woman who put her father in jail? Her dad … hurt me. I don't want to face her. I ruined her life."

Annie leans forward and embraces me. They all stare.

"Did any of you have a best friend you lost?" I ask.

"Our losses are hard," Annie says, looking into each of our faces. "Heidi, you didn't put her father in jail, and you didn't ruin your friend's life. It was all her father's doing. We need to stop carrying guilt that doesn't belong to us."

"I'll second that," Layne says. "You can dump that guilt into the sea."

"I know how you feel losing Terry," says Annie. "My sister and I were very close. She was homeschooled and we fantasized about the world around us. We had our own secret world of adventures. We shared so much. She passed away when I was thirteen. There wasn't any closure."

Annie pauses and places a hand on her chest. I grab her hand and she takes a deep breath before continuing. "She was so courageous and I really … miss her. Now I need tissues … and rum," she laughs, as Judy passes the Kleenex.

"Okay, sisters, hug time," Judy says, reaching out to Annie. "This is such a stunning place, how about we turn this sorrow into joy? Best friends cry together, but they also get to celebrate friendship and life!"

"To friendship, life, and this gorgeous evening," I say raising my glass to a chorus of "cheers."

Through the week we hike, sail, snorkel, laugh, and share more stories. Annie and I spy an octopus among coral, Layne and Judy point out constellations, and Bonita sings, dances, and makes us tropical drinks. As the sun rises on the last day, my sisters embrace. After they climb into Martin's boat and wave goodbye, they again break into song.

"Martin row your boat ashore, hallelu … jah … Milk and honey on the other side, hallelu … u … jah."

Martin creates his own verse and sings in a deep, clear voice. "Dom … ahh … nee … ka is green and nice."

"Hallelujah."

"A sea and mountain in par … a … dise, hallelujah."

Bonita, the only single woman, joins in. "Bonita likes the island men."

"Hallelujah."

"She will love them until the end."

Laughter fills the air as their boat recedes toward the shore. A part of me longs to head back with them; another part is content to stay. I smile, wave, and take a deep full breath.

Dennis and I leave Dominica by the end of March for a two-month sail toward Grenada. We visit the "oh so French" island of Martinique where we splurge on cheese, pate, and fresh warm baguettes. We choose a spectacular anchorage at the base of the Pitons in St. Lucia, near Danielle's *Nytea*, where two verdant green pinnacles rise over a thousand feet from the sea. We stop at the small whaling village of Bequia, south of St. Lucia, where I had sailed with two professors thirty years earlier.

The sea surrounding the Tobago Cays is as clear as stained glass. Every shade of azure, turquoise, and bright blue glisten as light for the soul. Spotted eagle rays, two and a half feet long, glide with grace past our boat. A large area of the bay is a protected turtle sanctuary, and we swim and glide next to three- and four-foot turtles. Dennis and I scuba dive through a wall of hundreds of bright blue wrasses swimming above crimson coral fans, purple sponges, and resting sharks. Floating in this natural wonderland brings me peace.

By May, Nico has finished his first year at McGill University. He is starting a summer job as a lifeguard in Portsmouth, New Hampshire. When he was at school, I wanted him to have freedom and independence; now that he is home, I ache to see him. Dennis and I secure a house-sitting opportunity, leave the boat in Grenada, and fly back for three months of summer in Portsmouth. I smile as our plane lands.

CHAPTER 7

Shadows

*There is no light without shadow,
just as there is no happiness without pain.*

Isabel Allende, *Portrait in Sepia*

Portsmouth, New Hampshire, June 2012

Historic brick and clapboard buildings crowd a lively New England seaport. *Centime* remains in Grenada for hurricane season while we summer in New Hampshire. Having sold our Maine home before we went sailing, Dennis and I are caretaking a small historic home built in the 1700s. It rests on an old, narrow street close to a harborside park with fountains and bountiful gardens with flowering, ancient Chinese cherry trees. On summer nights, music, dance, and theatrical performances on an open-air stage liven the air.

Every Saturday there is a farmers' market a few blocks away. It overflows with stands of bright red heirloom tomatoes, colorful vegetables, fragrant flowers, and dozens of baskets of corn on the cob, my favorite with a sign boasting "picked this morning by Zack." Vendors serve organic iced tea and free-trade coffee. Small children dance while local musicians play guitars and sing folk songs. Artists display watercolors, pottery, hand-dyed wool, and assorted crafts.

Nico's summer job is near where we're staying. I stock the pantry and refrigerator with his favorite foods: Vermont cheeses, rosemary crackers, Sicilian olives, and locally smoked fish. He sends regular texts asking if I might like to bring lunch to his work. I treat him with thick sandwiches on fresh bakery bread, blue cheese, succulent tomatoes, locally made salty chips, and homemade iced tea the way my mother made it. I don't have a car, so I take his lunch bags and cold drinks to him on my bike. It's a huge pleasure to feed and nourish him and see him happy. His texts bring me joy.

"Mommm," he writes.

"Hi, buddy, what's up?" I ask.

"I didn't have time to make lunch, and I don't have any food at work. Do you think you could bring lunch to the pool? Pleeeeeease."

"I'd love to. What would you like?"

"Anything. I didn't eat breakfast, and I'm really hungry."

"I have leftover eggplant parmesan. Do you want a sub?"

"That would be amazing."

"Okay. I'll ride over in twenty."

"And can you bring me a smoothie? Chips too? And a snack for later?"

"Sure. Hey, would you be available Saturday night for mom-son sushi dinner with Alex, Max, and Evan?"

For seven years, we have had a tradition of mother and son gatherings with three other mothers and their sons and daughters. We have enjoyed these outings since the boys became friends in sixth grade. We hike and ski together and take trips to Boston and the White Mountains. The mothers are best friends, and the boys are like brothers.

The teens have a special fondness for sushi. Saturday arrives and we sit tatami-style at a low Japanese table. The small room is crowded with my girlfriends and our four nineteen-year-old sons and two younger daughters. The table overflows with a wide assortment of sushi, sashimi, a large bowl of edamame, cups of tea, and glasses of beer. Laughter abounds.

My friend Lynn reaches over to Nico and runs her hand through his dark brown curly hair. He smiles.

"I've been wanting to do that for almost a year, Nico," she says.

"Me too," says Joan as she runs her hand through his hair too. "I've missed all of our boys."

"It's good to be home. I've missed you too," he replies. "And it's great to not have to cook or do laundry."

"Did you ever actually do laundry at school?" I tease. "I got the impression it just piled up through the semester."

"Funny, that was my impression too, with Alex. Tell me again, Nico, what are you studying?" Joan asks.

"I'm studying political science and economics. I want to travel internationally, learn about other cultures, and support people in developing countries," he says.

"He's a bit like both of his grandfathers and even one of his great-grandfathers," I say. "Two were sailors and another an adventurer and humanitarian. They all died before he got to know them, yet I suspect he carries some of each," I say.

"You're no couch potato, girl. I wouldn't mind joining one of your adventures," Lynn says to me.

"Would you really come? To French Polynesia?" I reply.

"I'm in," Max and Alex say together, laughing.

Too soon the bright, fleeting days of summer darken to fall. Cool temperatures sit at my doorstep, unwelcome. While adventures on *Centime* beckon, saying goodbye is hard. I drive Nico five hours to Montreal for his sophomore year. Before I leave, he lifts me off the ground, and twirls me around until I laugh and scream with joy.

Later, a heaviness closes in, as I return over the White Mountains alone, driving in the rain.

Before Nico was born, I became anxious thinking about having a child. I had an irrational fear that traces of evil had been forced inside me when I was eleven. I worried that strands of Mr. Hart's DNA, and his vileness, lay dormant inside me. I worried that if I became pregnant, they could seep into my womb and poison my fetus. While the idea was absurd and scientifically impossible, the thoughts tormented me.

On the surface my life was manageable. My husband at the time knew of the rape, yet he was less aware of the depths of my internal struggles and didn't know of my flashbacks. I never told anyone except my therapist. I was worried I would be labeled as crazy.

I was afraid to be like Mother.

Issues festered in my thirties. Doctors at the time warned against having children after the age of thirty-five, with increased risks of damaged chromosomes. I was desperate to have a healthy child before time ran out yet scared to be pregnant.

The more I kept fear inside, the more it consumed me. I dreamed that unsaid words lodged in my throat, choking me. In my dreams I inhaled olive pits, swallowed pearls, and choked on semen. In these nightmares, I could no longer breathe and no one could hear my screams.

One day, my throat physically swelled. It hurt to swallow and talk. Hormones flooded through my body. I couldn't sit still. My hands trembled; my heart pounded like I was running in a marathon. I had hyperthyroid disease. For several days I was delirious, my throat swollen; my supercharged body had electric currents coursing through.

At the height of my delirium, I believed that everything feminine was vile and weak. The more I rejected my femininity, the sicker I became.

After my body recovered, I tried to heal my mind and get pregnant. Hoping to rejuvenate my spirit, I went on solitary walks in a nearby marsh. As I got to the farthest edge of the marsh, crashing waves cleared my soul. I would sit on a large boulder to write and reflect. The sea was healing.

A year later, I was pregnant. I invited Mother to visit, hoping she might reveal stories of her own pregnancy and our early days together. Though I was still afraid, by then I was excited to be carrying a child, hoping to share a deeper connection with Mother.

We were walking down a quiet street near my home when I asked, "What was it like when Vern and I were young?"

"Oh, Heidi, I don't remember a thing," she replied.

"You've told me about ice skating as a teenager, cutting people's hair when you were single, making crab cakes and iced tea with your mother-in-law. How can you remember those earlier times and not remember Vern or me?" I asked.

"It was long ago. Stop asking. Well ... I do remember one thing," she said. "I was pregnant with you in Alaska. I saw my doctor and he told me he needed to induce labor because I was long overdue. It was just before the Fourth of July picnic. I argued with him. I wasn't going to miss that picnic. And I didn't.

That's why you weren't born until July sixth. I wanted to attend the picnic. That was important."

Heaviness surrounded me. Uncertain if I should continue, my voice soft, I asked, "What else do you remember?"

"Nothing. Not a thing."

By January 2013, Dennis and I had fly back to Grenada and sail north. As we approach Barbuda, my phone springs to life. There's an email from Vern: Mother is sick. Father had passed decades earlier and Mother lives in a nursing home near Vern.

I fly to New York and, wearing a flimsy sailing windbreaker, drive a rental car through the snow. Without gloves or a scraper, I use my bare hands to wipe ice from the windshield. My body shivers. The heat is on high, but I can't get warm.

Mother's nursing home is bleak. The grayness of the day seeps into group living spaces, where busy caregivers rush past residents as if their clients are invisible. Staleness fills the air. Elderly people sit together in communal spaces staring into spaces in front of them; most are alone.

When I'd visited the past summer, Mother sat by a large, outdoor goldfish pond near her room, her favorite place to soak up the sun and fresh air. Today, the pond is iced over, the glass door locked.

Now she sits in an overstuffed chair, with a dozen other residents, the TV blaring. I face her and put my hand on her shoulder, and she smiles.

"Do you know who I am?" I ask.

"Louise," she replies. I flinch. My hand drops away from her shoulder, and I place it on my chest. I don't know anyone in her life named Louise. I get closer to her face, look into her eyes and try again.

"Don't you know me?" I ask, urging her to remember. "I came a long way to see you."

She shakes her head slowly. No.

My throat begins to swell. I put my hand over hers and hold it tight, blinking back tears. A part of her has been erased. A part of my history, and the memories she held for me, is fading too, with her. Aspects of my childhood trauma that only she might know remain unclear, acknowledgments of shared pain and sorrow not spoken. Am I losing pieces of myself that I've never owned, never knew? Is it too late to recover them? Will she pass from this life taking our secrets with her? I tell her my name, and for a moment she smiles, as she did for Louise, then she stares ahead at the oversized television screen.

Generations of life and death pass before me: Grandma Katie, pregnant while Edgar died at sea; my mother, pregnant with me in Alaska; Dad, long gone; my pregnancy with Nico; Mother's pending demise. I rub my eyes and squeeze her hand. She doesn't squeeze back.

We've struggled to connect over the last three decades. I lived and worked four hundred miles away before sailing *Centime*. She wanted me physically closer, but not emotionally close and never alone with her. I had an advanced degree and a creative, lucrative job; she said it was not enough. She asked for items I couldn't or wouldn't give her: a Mercedes, a trip to Hawaii, frequent visits, a permanent room in my home. I want treasures she can't provide: memories of us, greater clarity around her life, her pain, and our collective pain; I wish she could heal her own wounds, and help heal mine. We both want greater love—under our own terms.

Mother and I visit through the week. I take her to the community restaurant every day where she eats potato chips and ice cream for lunch, leaving her sandwiches untouched. We make cookies together and mail them in to Nico's college housing. I push her wheelchair through the hall and show her the view out every window. Vern, Sarah, and their children visit, and we share stories of our youth, hoping she might remember a few. One day, Nico calls her from his university, and I relay his messages.

At the end of my week's visit, she sits in a reclining chair in the corner of her shared bedroom. She is ninety-two. Her time left on this earth is short. Her face, with its many wrinkles, holds ageless beauty, goodness, and hardship. I bend down in front of her where she can best hear, and also read my lips. "Mom, I love you!"

It's a powerful statement, hard for me to say. I haven't said it for years. As my tears well up, I find it hard to talk. Holding my throat, I tell her, "You were a good mother." I hope after ninety-two years, after all her suffering, she finds peace.

She stares with intensity, her vibrant blue eyes penetrating mine. She has a questioning look on her face as if trying hard to remember. She tugs at my shirt as she stares.

The room is quiet, and then she clears her throat and speaks. "Important! Important!" I put my face right in front of hers.

"What is it, Mother? What's important?"

She holds my hand and squeezes. I wait. Silence hangs between us.

"Buy your brother a dog," she says.

I look at her with narrowed eyes. My brother owns two cats; he doesn't want a dog. Was I hoping for some slight recognition of her place in the tragedy we shared? Tears stream down my face for the many missed opportunities that might have healed the heartbreak that stands between us. It is too late. It will never be.

"I love you, Mom."

"Buy him a dog."

I drive slowly to Vern's house. Dad passed away thirty years earlier, yet I long for his comfort and insight. I want to know why Mother is odd. I wonder how he might respond if he were sitting next to me. I remember Dad's huge sense of humor, and it then becomes clear; he would make a joke.

With his heart full of love for both of us he might say, "Heidi looks for love; Mom says, 'Buy a dog!' Ha ha ha."

The irony rushes in, and I find it really funny. I laugh hard, out loud, an uncontrolled release of the tension I'd built through life with Mother. I pull to the side of the road and call Vern; we both laugh. It is time to stop wanting my mother's apology and her love; it's time to enjoy whatever laughter we have shared as a family.

The next day, I head back to Dennis and *Centime*, feeling lighter.

Two weeks later, Vern and his wife Sarah arrive in the British Virgin Islands to sail with us. The wind blows from the west and we head toward Norman Island. Vern takes the wheel, the boat heels. A broad smile spreads across his face.

By evening we are nestled at anchor in a small cove. The sea is calm, the island is fringed with palm trees and tropical vegetation. The sky is tinged with red, and welcoming winds blow through our hair. Vern, Sarah, and I lounge in the cockpit, enjoying fresh breezes and sipping rum punch while Dennis grills fresh Mahi Mahi smothered in mango sauce. Pungent fragrances permeate the air. The night descends and the sky fills with bright stars.

"Do you ever miss Dad?" Vern asks.

"Sure I do," I reply. "He was a great man with high integrity, and he loved us. I love him deeply."

"Me too," Vern agrees. "I was angry when he died. It was like he spent his whole life doing great, selfless deeds, dedicating himself to God, and as soon as he started to plan one thing for himself, he was cut short. I used to go to church. Before Dad died, I was a strong believer in God, and then I started to question everything. I don't know about church anymore. I'm not sure what I believe. I wonder why Dad had to die young. He was younger than I am right now."

"That's because you're an old man," I tease. "At least he had a happy life. What I remember most is the joy he got in helping people, and his corny jokes. They still make me smile." I pause and ask, "Are you still angry?"

"Not really, just confused," Vern answers. "I mean … mostly about what's up with Mom. She has always had such volatile reactions. I wish Dad were here to help us understand. He must have known why she is so strange."

"Ha, do you want to hear a funny story?" I ask.

"Sure," he says.

"When I was eleven and we left Philadelphia, I was in a bad place. After the assault I felt that I had lost my childhood and my friends."

"Is this supposed to be funny?" Sarah asks.

"Just wait," I say. "I had nightmares and started sleepwalking and wetting the bed. Mother was good at helping me get back to bed and changing soiled sheets, yet every time I had a nightmare she would say, 'You ate too many mashed potatoes tonight. Stop eating mashed potatoes. They make you wet the bed.'"

"What?" Sarah says, her eyes wide.

"She even said it when I hadn't eaten any potatoes. It took me years to realize that mashed potatoes don't cause people to wet their beds."

"You always were a slow learner," Vern teases, shaking his head. "Mom sure did have crazy ideas. She always wanted us to be perfect, and I did okay … but you were a challenge."

"Me? You were the one who thought you were an Italian chef and threw the pizza dough so high it stuck to the ceiling."

"Yeah, but you opened the grape soda so that it sprayed purple fizz all over her brand-new yellow curtains."

"Who shook the can for their unsuspecting, innocent sister?"

"Innocent? Heidi?" Dennis joins. "Were you ever innocent?"

"Well, it wasn't me," Vern says. "I never did anything wrong. I was perfect."

"What do you remember from Alaska?" I ask.

"I remember Anna. She took care of us. Do you remember her?"

"Not really. I met her briefly when she visited after she got married, but Mom seemed mad at her."

"When you were born, Dad brought Anna from the orphanage to live with us. Mother couldn't care for two kids. Anna took care of us while we were in Alaska and then Dad brought her back to Pennsylvania."

"Wait. What do you mean, Mother couldn't care for us?"

"Yeah, she said we were too much for her."

"There were only two of us, and she didn't have a job outside of our home. Why couldn't she take care of us?"

"I don't remember why."

"That's strange. I remember so many details, so many feelings."

"Like what?"

"The constant tug-of-war between Mother and me. She would dole out love and take it away. I know now it's not true, but then I felt like I was in charge of her every mood: I made her happy, and if she was upset, it was my fault. At times she adored me and later she would say, 'You're disgusting,' because I scraped my knee, spilled a drink—or even when I sat quietly reading a library book. I don't mean to make her sound like a monster; she wasn't. At times she really seemed to love us. It was just that everything revolved around her. I don't think she could help it. You must remember more."

"I don't want to remember. Maybe I've blocked it out on purpose. I didn't have a childhood I want to remember."

Vern, Sarah, and Dennis head below after dinner while I linger in the cockpit and ponder Mother's inability to care for us. I slump down on the bench. I know what broken feels like: a broken body, a broken child, broken love. My throat feels thick as if I'm fighting a cold. Mother's ups and downs, her violent outbursts, her unhinged mood swings had created a need. I wanted her love, and to feel safe. I yearned too for an acknowledgment of our shared pain.

Once, in my forties, before Mother went to the nursing home, the events of my past slipped out. In a conversation with her. I was making huge strides with my therapist. Speeding down Highway 95 in my blue Mini Cooper, I was feeling more courageous than most days. I spoke on the phone with Mother about a trip to an out-of-bounds Canadian snowfield where Nico and I skied.

"Aren't you ever afraid?" she asked.

"After what happened to me when I was eleven, it takes a lot to scare me." The words tumbled out of my mouth and presented themselves to Mother, for the first and only time in my life. It was too late to put them back. I held my breath for her response.

"Nothing happened when you were eleven," she said, her voice sounding robotic.

My mouth fell open. I pulled the car to the breakdown lane. I felt sweat on my hands as I clutched the wheel.

"You remember, don't you ... the terrible thing that happened ... in Philadelphia in sixth grade ... the violence?"

"Nothing terrible ever happened to you."

"You remember why we moved away from Philadelphia ... because of our neighbor ..." My heart pounded. "Mr. Hart?"

My heart raced. I reached into my glove compartment, pulled out a bottle of pills I used to control panic attacks, and swallowed a small white pill.

"Nothing bad ever happened. There is no Mr. Hart." The conversation was over. I waited for her to ask who Mr. Hart was or about what had happened. I couldn't imagine Nico telling me that something violent had happened and not asking him dozens of questions to learn every detail and confirm he was okay.

Mother didn't appear upset. It was as if she had no recollection and didn't care for one. I could have told her everything at that moment, yet somehow it seemed wrong. Why upset her after all these years?

The silence rested between us. How could she not remember? I thought about having been raped every day.

As the tears fell, I hung up the phone. We never discussed it again.

After a restful sleep on *Centime*, we awake to a clear dawn. The wind beckons and Vern wants to sail. I take the wheel as Dennis pulls up the anchor. We raise the mainsail, unfurl the genoa, and then head toward the British island of Jost Van Dyke to the northwest. It starts out as the classic sail, wind off the starboard quarter, shifting to a run through the Narrows. The sun glistens off the spray as *Centime* slices at an angle to the sea.

Sailing past Tortola, we're close enough to town for cell phone connections to kick in. A ding announces a new email from Amy, Vern's daughter. I hand the phone to Vern and he opens the email.

"Mom died," he says.

Silence fills the cockpit. We stare at one another and out to sea. No one says a word.

"Dennis, please steer," I whisper. He grabs the wheel, turns on the autopilot, and puts a hand on my shoulder. I fall into his arms and then drop onto the seat cushion. Tears fall.

"What did Amy say?" Sarah asks.

Vern clears his throat and reads, "Grammy died in her sleep last night. I spoke with the funeral director and he's taking care of her. He says to finish your vacation because everything will wait until you get home. We all agree. You never get away and you've wanted to do this for a long time. We have everything covered." Vern stares out to sea. Sarah puts her arm around his shoulder, and he slumps into her arms. His body shudders. It is the first time and only time I remember seeing him cry.

I grab his hand and he shifts to wrap his arms around me, holding tight. We sail to a nearby harbor and sit for a few hours in Soper's Hole, arrange flights to Pennsylvania for the following week, and then continue on in silence to the island of Jost.

After anchoring and sharing a somber night on the boat, we take the dinghy to shore. On the far side of the island, the Bubbly Pool at Jost is a natural land formation where a narrow rock passage opens to the Atlantic. When strong northerly waves squeeze through the slot, they tower high as they reach land, and crash into the natural pool. We hike a half mile over rough rock formations, through mangroves, skirting a salt pond, and then arrive.

The four of us wade to our chests only to get "bubbled" as the foam and current, stronger than any Jacuzzi, carry us back to shore. I scream underwater, releasing pent-up tensions. Over and over, we wade out and the sea carries us back. It is a cathartic way to grieve and to connect with my only sibling.

Back on the boat, I cook pasta and a red sauce. Vern comes down to the galley while Sarah and Dennis relax above. "Can I ask you something?" he says.

"Sure."

"When Mom was sick, why did you tell her she was a good mom, after all she's done to you?" he asks.

I pause for a moment and reply, "I just wanted her to have peace. When I visited her last summer, she seemed afraid to die. It surprised me, given her strong faith, her age, her suffering, especially with Dad gone. I had expected she might want to be with him, yet she seemed to hang on. It made me wonder if she thought she might not go to heaven. In my own head I questioned if there might be something deep inside her that she couldn't let go. I analyze way too much, and I'm likely wrong, but maybe she felt … ruined.

"Have you ever seen that black-and-white picture of her when she was about five years old? She has bangs and a magical smile. Somewhere deep inside her was that joyful girl. I just wonder if someone stole that from her; if she struggled through the years trying to get it back, struggled with her sanity. When I looked at her that day in the nursing home, I was trying to find that little girl."

"Wow."

I study his face. "After all her years of suffering and all the good things she's tried to do, how she cared for hundreds of people, street people, church folks, orphans, friends, her mother-in-law, and Dad's brother when he was arrested—trying to love us and her grandkids the best she could—she deserves peace. We all deserve peace."

"Maybe," he says. "I just don't understand her, why she did what she did."

"Maybe we never will."

A week later, we fly to Pennsylvania and meet with Nico, Adam, and Amy. It's a cold February. I shiver in my sailing jacket.

At the church I walk slowly to the front. I give a eulogy about the love she had for her grandchildren and the funny antics Vern and I pulled: the pizza tossed to the ceiling, grape soda sprayed over yellow curtains, silly putty stuck to the couch. I say a tearful goodbye and return to my seat between Nico and Dennis. They each grab a hand and hold it through the rest of the service.

As we lay Mother in the ground, next to Dad, Grandma Katie, and Lloyd, I notice a fifth headstone for Grandfather Edgar, the sailor Dad said I took after. It reads "Edgar Vernon Hendricks, 1893–1918." With his body lost at sea, his spirit is here with us.

That evening, Vern's kitchen is warm and bright. Amy pulls out food: cold chicken, macaroni salad, and homemade cookies. Vern opens bottles of sauvignon blanc and hands full glasses around the room. We laugh about our childhood and play 1960s songs from Motown Records, listening to the smooth voice of Smokey Robinson singing "My Girl," and our favorite tunes from the Temptations, the Jackson Five, and the Supremes. The days of our youth in Philadelphia seem close. In his living room, the tunes blaring, we dance and sing, releasing joy and sorrow.

We laugh, remember Mom, and wish her peace.

CHAPTER 8

It's Not Your Fault

*A sister is a gift to the heart,
a friend to the spirit, a golden thread
to the meaning of life.*

Isadora James, *My Sister, My Friend*

Culebra, Puerto Rico, February 2013

Let the second annual "Turtle Sisters' Sailing Tour" begin!

The Culebra ferry arrives from mainland Puerto Rico. Annie, Bonita, and Judy bounce down the gangway laughing, excitement in each step. Bonita drops her bags on the gangway and runs to embrace me. Judy and Annie follow. The air is warm and fragrant with flowering shrubs and rotting fruit. Embarking from the over-air-conditioned ferry, they race to strip down to shorts and T-shirts, extra layers of clothes falling to the ground in a heap.

Culebra, 20 nautical miles west of bustling St. Thomas, has twenty-three cays, mostly uninhabited, and scenery that beckons the wild of spirit. Surrounding each cay is water of every shade of blue, teeming with sea life: turtles, dolphins, fish, and coral.

A marine sanctuary protects loggerhead, leatherback, hawksbill, and green turtles. We spot our first green turtle welcoming us at the anchorage. She's over three feet long and matronly with her broad, patterned shell. This is the second time a turtle has welcomed the arriving sisters.

Fifteen years ago, after divorcing Nico's dad, Annie gave me a stone turtle to remind me of what is important in life. I gave the same turtle back to her when her young son was having open-heart surgery. We have passed that turtle back and forth through the years, staying connected through important moments in our lives.

On *Centime*'s deck we share laughter and gifts. Annie offers five small, wooden turtles and passes them around the cockpit. I pass out black T-shirts with bold, white letters proclaiming "Chicas Rule!"

The evening begins with music and dance. We take our dinghy to the Dinghy Dock, a waterfront café. A group of conga drummers are in town. Bonita is our group's prime dancer with swiveling hips and a contagious smile. Soon she is in the front of the crowd, swaying with the music. Judy is at the dock, amazed to see a school of tarpon, each four to six feet long, swirling around the underwater light near her feet. As she moves to conga rhythms, it looks like she is charming the tarpon under the moon. Annie, Dennis, and I snap photos to send to Layne, who couldn't make this trip.

To our surprise, Dutch sailing friends Irene and Theo arrive at the café. Sailors often stop at the same protected harbors. It is not uncommon to make great friends and then see them again and again as years and islands pass. It's also common to make great friends around the world and never meet again.

As the energy of the night builds, and the music drowns out our conversation, we join Bonita, dancing near the drummers. She weaves in and out of our group in night rhythms. At the end of the evening, a local artist awards her a bracelet for her dancing.

The next morning, we circumnavigate the seven-mile island, sailing past verdant cays with white strips of sand. We skirt crashing waves, exposed reefs and jagged rocks. As we round the northwestern point, waves pound the boat from the fury of the open Atlantic. Large swells give us a wild, rolling ride. *Centime* takes it in stride, riding up and down steep waves.

"Hold on, Annie," I say. "The big bad ocean is rough on this side."

"I'm fine," she says. "With all these turtles around, she's no longer the big, bad ocean. She's the big, beautiful mother ocean, and I'm loving her. Sometimes it's good to shift perceptions."

We anchor in a quiet bay ringed with mangroves. Judy and Bonita create a fresh fish dinner with local bok choy and rice.

"Sorry to hear about your mom," Judy says to me. "How are you? Were you able to make things right with her? I know you two had a rough time."

"I'm at peace. I hope she is too," I reply. "I saw her two weeks before she died and told her I loved her. At first, I was disappointed that we couldn't connect. Then memories of my dad just made it right. I'm trying to love her the way he did ... but it's not easy. She haunts me when I'm scared. But tonight, I'm with you, my sisters. Thanks for coming." Judy squeezes my hand.

On Sunday, we sail to a small island, Culebrita, off the northeast corner of Culebra. It is a lush, uninhabited island. Diving into the clear blue water, we spot a loggerhead turtle with intricate brown and white patterns on her shell. Annie swims underwater with the turtle, diving below with grace. Judy, always the artist, snaps photos with her underwater camera. A large blue and green parrotfish and bright yellow damselfish glide past. We swim from the boat over a coral reef and onto a long, white sand beach.

Hiking across the island to the east, we find a second beach on the windward side—deserted, windblown, with loud, crashing waves. We climb on jagged rocks that extend into the sea, as waves spray over us.

An old, abandoned, stone lighthouse stands on the top of the island. Encircling the structure is a wire fence, torn away, where people have ignored a "keep out" sign and have created a path through. We scramble under the fence and climb the rickety, circular stairs that wind through the tower to a broken, three-foot platform at the top. Squeezing together we look at the 360-degree view. *Centime* bobbles about, like a small toy, anchored in the distant cove. We are alone on the island.

This moment, this paradise, is ours. Later, a full moon brightens the evening sky. Phosphorescence sparkles through the water with each stroke of the oars as I row our dinghy across the bay.

Irene and Theo have invited us to their boat for a Greek dinner. The sisters have agreed in secret to induct Irene into our turtle sisterhood. We arrive with a canvas bag holding wine, a Belizean bracelet and a small stone turtle for the induction ceremony. Theo brings out glasses and Judy pours the wine as we relax in their cockpit. Clink ... clink ... clink. She taps a spoon against her glass to signal a special announcement.

I stand and raise my glass. "Under this full moon, in a bay filled with turtles, sisters unite with a special toast," I say. "Tonight, we have all agreed to induct a very special woman, a turtle sister, Irene the Siren, into the sisterhood."

"What?" Irene says with her thick Dutch accent. "Me? I'm to be a turtle sister? I'm honored. Wait, what do I have to do to prove myself?"

"You have already proven yourself worthy as a sister," Bonita says. "Like many turtles, you have journeyed thousands of miles through the sea, and through life, to bring joy, wisdom, and love to others." She pulls a purple and gold bracelet from the bag and ties it on Irene's wrist. Annie gives her one of her small stone turtles and then a hug.

Judy finishes the toast. "To Irene and her journeys. May you always travel safely through adventure and keep us close in your heart."

"To Irene!" we say, clinking glasses.

"This is magical," Irene replies. "I was just with turtles a few months ago, in Trinidad. Look—I will show you." She grabs her computer and we gather around it. She plays a video of a beach filled with turtles hatching under a full moon.

We eat and drink, sing and dance. Dennis opens a special bottle of Vin Santo, a dessert wine that we had been saving from our Greek honeymoon. Theo pulls out marimbas and drumsticks, and we dance and sing through the evening's magic.

As the days pass, we rent bikes and ride to Playa Flamenco where pristine white sand extends for more than a mile. On the way, a giant iguana, three feet long, darts across the road in front of me. I almost collide, first with the iguana and then with Annie, my heart beating fast.

At the beach, Dennis and I splash in the cool water, Judy does a headstand on the beach, and Annie sleeps under a palm tree wearing a big floppy hat.

Farther down the beach, Bonita is talking with a thin man. We join them and meet Ranthy, a local guide. He tells us of a cove on our return route where turtles travel to lay their eggs under full winter moons.

As we head to the cove, the bike route that winds over the top ridge of the island rewards us with a long, fast ride down. No iguanas challenge my ride this time.

Later, we snorkel over immense, golden brain coral and tall, orange staghorn coral. The reef is home to hundreds of colorful fish and countless invertebrates: red sponges, black spiny sea urchins, banded shrimp, and squirting tunicates. A large school of bright blue tangs weave through the soft, purple sea fans that sway with the current like a wheat field in a gentle wind.

We follow Ranthy's instructions and swim across the bay in search of turtles. Confused by a large, muddy brown shape of disturbed water, we swim ahead with quiet care. Beds of long, thin strands of turtle grass undulate with the current. Beyond the churned-up mud, dozens of green turtles eat the grass. Annie catches up with a large female and we watch as the sun sparkles off the turtle's back, revealing an intricate shell pattern with shades of red, cream and brown, contrasting with her green skin. Annie's long, red-blonde hair flows behind her like a magnificent mermaid.

On our last day at the anchorage, Annie, Judy, Bonita, and I are lined up at the edge of *Centime*'s deck. The azure water blends seamlessly with the sky. Judy's yellow bikini and my cobalt blue and pink tankini contrast with Annie's and Bonita's animal-print swimsuits. Our matching Belizean woven bracelets unify our group.

Dennis rows our dingy alongside. He points his camera, adjusts the lens. "Ready?" he asks.

"How are we doing this?" asks Bonita.

"Climb over the lifeline and grab hands. I'll count to three and say 'go,'" I say.

We hurdle the lifeline and balance at the rail.

"Oh my," says Annie, unsteadily, and Judy grabs her hand. We giggle like children.

I count fast, "One, two, three … Whooohooo," as we jump in together. We splash each other in the turquoise waters, bubbles all around: mermaids laughing in the sea.

That night, *Centime* rests at anchor, sheltered from the wind and waves. Judy and Bonita are drinking rum in the cabin as they sauté fresh island vegetables. Annie is at the bow, her body flowing with the gentle rock of the boat. A soft, cooling breeze ripples the still water. A chorus of tree frogs adds soothing harmony.

Gloam is a word used by the Scots to describe the magic light before sunset that glitters and sparkles, illuminating all it touches with soft, golden light. Annie's presence radiates as if she has a visible aura surrounding her. Her hair glows like falling autumn leaves, her freckles dance across her pale Scottish skin. Far from the Northern Isles, she is bathed in gloam.

I toss a blue seat cushion next to her and sit. Her eyes stay closed but she smiles, hearing my approach.

"You're aglow," I whisper.

"Am I?"

"Yes. You're beautiful. It was magical to watch you swim with the sea turtle, like a mermaid. And now you look puzzled. What are you thinking?"

"I was feeling the colors of the sunset ... and ... wondering if I can talk to you?"

"You can always talk to me. What's up?" I say, feeling my body stiffen.

"I haven't talked much about this to anyone. It's time," she says, sitting up, eyes staring out to sea.

(Trigger Warning) ("Heidi, I told you that when I was in high school, I had a boyfriend. I was always hanging out with him. His mom wasn't married. She had a boyfriend too, an adult her own age. My boyfriend would bring me to his house after school and sometimes his mom and her friends would be there, partying. It was his mom's boyfriend who encouraged me to try alcohol and drugs. At times I saw guns, needles, and people tripping at the house, but I felt safe with my boyfriend."

She stops and clears her throat and then coughs as I wait for her to continue. "Then it ... happened ... it was the mom's friend," she says, slumping forward and looking down at her hands. They start to shake. I hold her hands in mine to still them and my hands shake too.

Staring at our hands, I have one urge to hold her and another to run. Black thoughts swirl through my brain and I bite my lip. I can feel her pain.

"... He gave me a drink. I got a little drunk. He was strong. I had no way to fight back," she whispers. I lean in to listen. "It was long ago but I still feel ... guilty like I shouldn't have been there. Like it was ... my fault for being in the house." I loosen one hand from her grip, wipe a tear from the corner of my eye, and put my arm around her shoulder. I feel her body convulsing.

"Annie, look at me." She lifts her head, and her cheeks are wet with tears. I imagine how she looked as a teenager. "It was not your fault. An older man forced you after getting you drunk. Just because someone is drunk it doesn't give anyone the right to assault them; you were a child. He was twice your age, and it was horrible and illegal what he did. He, not you. Remember what you said to me in Dominica last year ... that it wasn't my fault? It is always easier to have compassion for others than for ourselves. For years I felt like I was bad for putting my best friend's father in jail and maybe I still feel guilty. That little girl who still lives inside you, like the one inside me, is ready to be forgiven for something she never did. She needs to be hugged and to be loved. I love her, and I love you fully."

Her body falls against mine and I hold her tight as she sobs, rocking in my arms.

"It was never your fault," I whisper, stroking her hair.

CHAPTER 9

Alone

*Sometimes you can't fight.
Sometimes you can only survive.*

Alix E. Harrow, *The Once and Future Witches*

Philadelphia, Pennsylvania, May 1967

Dad runs, carrying me. His breathing is loud in my ear. My body jerks up and down in his grasp, hurting with his every step. I'm wrapped in a rough, gray wool blanket, my arms and hands wedged underneath as if I were in a straightjacket. I'm locked within his grip.

He hasn't carried me for years. It's like a dream. Nothing is clear except the throbbing pain between my legs, yet I can't reach it, or soothe it.

A siren blares. Doors open and he runs through the entrance of Germantown hospital. The large space has a dozen men sitting and standing; they all stare.

Dad sets me down on a wooden chair and pulls the blanket higher. The wool wrap is scratchy on my neck. He darts across the room and disappears.

Curling myself into a ball with my knees at my chest, I reach down to hold the place where it hurts and am startled with how it feels.

"I'm bleeding," I say, breathing hard, holding my wound. "Help me! I'm bleeding!"

A man sitting on a bench across from me stares right through me as if the blanket isn't there. He has cuts and dried blood on his unshaven face and his clothes are torn. I stop crying and bite my lip. I hold the blanket tighter at my neck. A bad taste in my mouth and soreness at my neck distract me.

Other men, with scruffy beards and disheveled clothing, sit on benches too. No one is smiling. I close my eyes so I can't see them stare. I float into a blurry place filled with shadows, someone undressing me, grabbing at my clothes.

"Wait here."

I wake up alone in a long, cold hall. Sitting on a hard wooden bench against the wall, I watch a nurse scurry away.

The wool blanket is gone. My body shakes under a thin hospital gown, which is faded green with brown smudges. It's dirty like me. I'm too thin and small for the loose oversized gown.

Bringing my knees up to my chin and holding my arms around them, I wrap the flimsy gown tight. I'm not wearing underwear; Mother always insists I wear clean underwear. I have one pair for each day of the week. Today is Saturday. Where are Saturday's panties? I rock back and forth on the bench. Warm tears roll down my face.

Doctors hurry past in dull blue uniforms.

What will happen to me? Dad is gone. Will he ever come back? Will he and Mother abandon me? Mother hates me. No one will adopt me because I'm very, very bad … ruined forever.

I plot how I might live. I'm familiar with Philadelphia's homeless. Beggars and homeless men had often frequented my porch at Wayne Avenue asking for food. My mother and I made bologna and cheese sandwiches and offered iced tea. I served them on our porch, and I liked the men. They were always kind, yet different from my dad and his friends. They enjoyed my company and liked to hear what I had to say; I never felt threatened. If I stayed out too long, Mother would yell at me to come in. Though she always served them, I don't think she liked having them close to home.

At the hospital, I plan a life without parents. I imagine finding a large cardboard box in a dumpster, behind our grocery store. Perhaps I can take the box apart and refold it into a large flat strip, making an arch over my head. With my back against a wall, I can sit where no one can grab me from behind. The cardboard arch can cover my head and sides, and keep out rain and dirt.

Years later, in my forties, a therapist asks me to draw myself at age eleven. I draw a girl in rags, sitting on the ground, curled up with her knees to her chin, her back resting against a dirt-streaked wall, and a strip of cardboard over her head. Above the cardboard it's dark and raining, yet below the cardboard there's a rainbow surrounding the girl. I wanted to believe a cardboard strip would magically protect me. I wanted to be wrapped in a rainbow.

In the hospital hall, an aide arrives. He's wearing a light blue smock and the top of his head is covered with the same blue fabric. He has gloves on his hands and a white mask over his mouth. He stares at me. He pulls his mask down for a moment and it hangs at his neck.

"Can you walk?" he asks. As I stand, my legs shake. "Come with me."

With each step, pain cuts like a razor. I want to sit on the floor, yet I keep moving, following him, holding myself below my belly.

The room we enter is white, with an overhead light and a metal table bed covered by a white paper sheet. A doctor helps me climb onto the metal and guides me to lie under a glaring white light. Other men enter the room and stare. Their blue coverings and masks are the same as the first man. No one talks to me. They seem like faceless, voiceless men. They stare at my body, but they don't see me.

(Trigger Warning) A man slides me toward the edge of the table and puts my feet in cold metal holders. Another man pulls up my gown and spreads my legs apart. I jerk them back together. Two men force them apart again, holding them there, pinning me down, while a third probes where it hurts the most. Tears form in my eyes, and I blink them back. Still, no one says anything to me. They push a cold, metal instrument inside me and the pain increases. I try to be very still because it hurts when I move.

I close my eyes tight and pray in silence. *Please don't hurt me, please, please, please.* I miss my dad and think of the treats he used to give me when I was sad: his chocolate pudding and homemade apple dumplings. I bite my lip hard. I can no longer stop the tears.

"I WANT MY DAD!" I cry.

CHAPTER 10

Providencia Means Heaven

But in the morning everything can, and must, be seen.

Amy Bloom, *Away*

The Caribbean Sea, March 2013

With the turtle sisters gone, Dennis and I are alone on a 1,000-nautical-mile open-water passage that stretches southwest from the Dominican Republic to Panama. It is our fourth night away from land and we've sailed over 400 nautical miles. Rotating four-hour shifts day and night is exhausting. I take fitful naps on our rolling boat.

Alone, on my night watch, *Centime* pitches over seven-foot seas. The wind blows at twenty-one knots. An uncanny, high-pitched whirling sound of our wind generator fills the air. Clouds obscure the moon and stars. We race through the night in inky blackness.

At night, I worry about losing Dennis overboard. I'm scared about the weather and the large waves that smack the sides of our small craft. I shudder thinking about what might happen if we hit a reef, a whale, or a container. Large merchant ships carry containers, with goods that travel the world, which can weigh up to 68,000 pounds each. Every year five thousand or more are lost at sea, metal time bombs that can float for months, a few inches below the water's surface. One hit to our fiberglass hull could sink us in minutes.

Below the surface of these thoughts are ever-present concerns about flashbacks. The more I try to dismiss Mr. Hart, the more he intrudes. Like a ghostly apparition, he haunts my darkness when I'm alone and afraid.

The following day is brighter with perfect sunshine and moderate winds. In the late afternoon, Dennis takes over the watch. He smiles as he grabs the wheel. *Centime*'s bright white sails are full. Her hull is angled toward the sea as she surges through cobalt blue waves.

The sun begins to descend, painting the horizon with layers of apricot, melon, and papaya. The ocean becomes darker, appearing more agitated in the diminishing light. White sea spray flies off waves that smack our hull. A glare of light flashes on the sea, and I grab the rail and scan the surface.

"There's something out there. I'm going to look," I say, securing my tether to the safety line. I scramble forward, holding tight to the lifelines on the angled deck as *Centime* speeds through the water.

Suddenly, a dolphin jumps high in the air, then another, and another. They dive into the boat's bow waves. Dennis joins me at the bow while *Centime* sails on autopilot into the sunset. The bow rides up and down six-foot waves as we hold on tight. I lie down on the bowsprit to try to get a front row view, as close as I can to these brilliant creatures. Dennis hooks in, lying above me, giving the moment an even more exciting and romantic edge.

All around us, more than a dozen dolphins cavort. They race to catch the waves off our bow, crossing one another in intricate patterns, with the grace and skill of trapeze artists. They get very close to each other and to us, at high speeds. Their silver underbellies sparkle as they twist by, illuminated by the thousands of bubbles they create.

A few jump high with their tails fully out of the water. An aura of dazzling low sunlight encircles each dolphin as it soars through spray. They create ten- to twelve-foot plumes through the sky's shifting palette from soft orange to deep red and purple. As the sun sets, bodies become silhouettes against a neon sky just before they disappear. Dennis returns to the wheel. I breathe deep, warmth radiating through my body. As I turn to head back to the cockpit, a low, enormous, full moon sits behind us, just above the sea in near-perfect symmetry with the setting sun.

There is an old saying among sailors: life on land ranks five out of ten; life at sea is a nine or ten on good days and one when death is near. At sea there is little middle ground.

The fifth night turns into the sixth morning and the weather deteriorates. I am on watch alone from 4:30 a.m. to 8:30 a.m. while Dennis sleeps below. The wind direction has shifted north, gusting over thirty knots. The seas slap us broadside. The boat jolts with each wave, and water flows in and out of the cockpit over my blue-and-white-striped rubber boots. I steer *Centime* a few degrees closer to the wind to take the waves at a better angle. The electric winch motor growls as I reef or shorten the mainsail and pull in a bit of genoa. Dennis appears and studies the new sail configuration. He disappears below as *Centime* races at top speeds.

Reappearing with his life vest on, he hooks in, rubs his neck, and stares at me.

"How are you doing?" he asks.

"The winds have picked up, but she's handling them well."

"I got an email from Ken. He says the weather is going to get worse over the next few days. If we can't get to the canal within two days, we could hit some nasty squalls and poor visibility."

I check the chart plotter to read the distance. "We're 293 nautical miles away. That's cutting it close." I grip the wheel harder. "There's probably going to be merchant traffic as we get near the canal. Not ideal if the visibility sucks."

"Yeah, that's what I thought. Do you want me to look for alternatives, or take the helm while you look?"

"I'll see what I can find."

"Look for places that are protected from north winds."

I head below and find my binder of printed cruising information. I read a warning about Nicaragua, the closest coast. The government is apparently known for confiscating foreign vessels. I also see a shallow reef encrusting much of Nicaragua's Caribbean coast that appears challenging to navigate.

An offshore Colombian island lies ahead. Isla Providencia is riddled with reefs, and I read that charts in the region are notoriously inaccurate. Navigators warn Providencia's charts, including the harbor entrance, can be off by two hundred meters and should not be entered in the dark. I find conflicting information on which direction they might be off. A two-hundred-meter mistake in a field of coral can sink a boat. If we, instead, attempt to lie outside the harbor until dawn, the wind and seas could push us toward the shallows off Nicaragua, where we could be grounded.

We could stay up and drive her in circles through the night, yet fatigue is another complicating factor. Dennis is able to sleep off watch. I'm having difficulty getting enough rest. The rougher the seas, the harder it is to sleep.

When entering Providencia at night, it is safest to anchor in the lee of the uninhabited northern reef, rather than attempt to enter the narrow passage to the harbor. Though the reef does nothing to diminish the wind, it typically flattens the sea. It is large enough that even if our chart is off by two hundred meters we can still navigate safely. We decide to try the northern reef. If it feels unsafe, we will abort our attempt to anchor and continue toward Panama.

We race toward Providencia as the sea builds. *Centime* hobbyhorses, slams, and careens through each wave. Hour after hour my stomach churns. I force down dry crackers and drink sweet warm tea.

Dusk arrives. A lone dim navigation light appears. I pinpoint a lighthouse on the chart and sail *Centime* around the top of the reef as the sky turns black. Rounding the top, I start the engine, I point her into the wind so that Dennis can take down our sails. The engine roars as I move the throttle back and forth to try to keep her steady in the wind. She hurls up and down with every wave. I push the throttle close to full and grip the wheel with both hands.

Dennis strains to pull in the genoa. It is a slow process and hard for me to help, given the pressure on the wheel. Finally, he secures the forward sail and moves to the mast, dropping the mainsail. It flaps loud and hard in the wind, and the boom crashes back and forth within the limit of its sheets like a wild horse resisting capture. Dennis secures the boom and mainsail. He moves to the bow, unhooking and re-hooking the two safety tethers on his life vest to reach and prepare the anchor. I watch him, glancing back and forth from him to the electronic chart, to the wind gauge, to the waves, doing my best to hold the boat steady and keep *Centime* off the unseen island.

By 8:00 p.m. our electronic chart shows that we have entered the bay in front of the reef. The reef is invisible in total darkness. Howling winds carry the roar of waves. *Centime* heaves up and down with fury. Alone in the cockpit, I clutch the wheel. My heart pounds as I navigate blindly, with only the electronic chart, inside a semi-circular hellhole that I can hear yet not see.

My imagination expands as I consider unlikely yet possible consequences: the boat could hit the reef, Dennis and I fall overboard and wash hundreds of miles away toward Nicaragua. Or perhaps our bodies might be thrown into the hard coral beds, attracting sharks.

Shame seeps through my pores knowing my anxiety makes these projections worse. *We'll be fine.* I try unsuccessfully to calm myself.

The safety of our boat is dependent on our precise coordination. Dennis is directing from the bow. It is all I can do to follow his orders while wondering whether they might lead to our demise.

Gusts of wind continue. The boat pitches like a frightened stallion. Breaking waves echo in my brain. I drive the boat slowly forward in the dark toward the reef. I yell, "Fuck. Fuck. Fuck," into the wind. Dennis doesn't respond. Every second stretches out. I move the engine's throttle to inch closer and closer to the blackness that obscures the reef.

My face is caked in salt spray, my vision periodically blocked. At the bow, Dennis is a dark blur moving up and down as he motions me forward with a large sweep of his hand.

"Depth?" he yells, his voice carried by the wind.

"Twenty-three feet," I yell as loud as I can into the wind. Again, he motions to move *Centime* forward.

"Depth?"

"Seventeen." My body stiffens as I hold the wheel hard against a pitching sea. I strain my eyes to try to keep Dennis's arm and hand visible. My breathing is loud, fast, and shallow.

"Depth?"

"Fourteen!"

He motions again. I rev the engine and can smell diesel fumes. Wave sounds intensify.

Orange-brown glasses with rage-filled eyes flash before me. I choke on bile.

"Abort! Abort!" Dennis yells. "Turn the boat around now!"

I swing her away from the reef too fast. She pitches through the confusion of her own wake. She rocks hard to her starboard side. Dennis is flung off his feet with both hands holding the forward stay, held to the boat by his life jacket's tether. He scrambles to return to the cockpit, hooking in along the way. Breathing heavily, he collapses on the bench. My hands gripping the wheel, I motor *Centime* back to deep water.

"What happened? It felt like hell," I say.

"I kept expecting the waves to diminish when we got inside the reef, but they never did. They must be crashing high over the reef. It's too rough and dangerous to put the anchor out. She wouldn't have held under this force, and there's no room to drag without hitting the reef."

"It's good you didn't deploy the anchor. It would have been impossible to get it back up. What do we do now?" The question hangs in the air. "Dennis … I'm really scared."

"I don't know. Let's get outta here first."

I turn *Centime* south into the lee of the island; the wind and waves start to diminish. Conditions improve as we leave the wild reef. The island's height blocks the heaviest winds. The sound of breaking waves lessens. My breathing slows.

Within minutes, a most beautiful, full, red-orange moon appears on the horizon and illuminates the sky. I burst into tears. We're propelled from the darkest night to a glorious moon-filled vault of heaven. It's a powerful, life-affirming spectacle.

The diminished wind and seas now come from behind *Centime* and I motor ahead with more control and slower speed. We need to decide whether we will navigate through a difficult channel into the main harbor of Providencia with our unreliable charts, try to steady her through the night in a holding pattern off the lee of Providencia, fighting exhaustion, or continue the long distance to Panama through deteriorating weather.

"Let's try to go into the harbor," Dennis says. "We're exhausted, and it's calmer here. It will be rough if we leave this side of the island and continue to Panama."

"What about the charts? What if they are really off by two hundred meters? We don't know which direction they're off by and the entrance is narrow. How do we avoid the reefs?"

"Slow the boat down now. Let's wait until the moon is higher. We'll have better visibility. Maybe I can contact someone in the harbor who can guide us in. If we start toward the harbor and it's not right, we'll turn around again. We have to try."

I slow *Centime* down. The full moon rises and brightens the sky. As we near the harbor's entrance a large, well-lit freighter appears inside of the reef. Dennis turns on the VHF radio and calls for any vessel in the harbor to respond. The captain of the freighter answers. He can see us under the full moon and begins to guide us through and around the encroaching coral reefs. Dennis takes the wheel. I grasp the iPad with its electronic chart. Our GPS boat symbol shows us directly on the shallow reef. If the iPad is correct, we will go aground in minutes.

"Head to starboard, now," the captain says. "You're too close to the reef on my AIS."

My body stiffens. I make quick glances around the cockpit checking the locations of the life ring and horn, and then watch the depth meter as it teeters back and forth between five and three feet below our keel. Though I'm not religious, I pray.

Finally, we arrive in the middle of the calm harbor under a bright moon and drop our hook. I press my hand to my chest. Dennis opens a beer. I drink a full glass of water, trying to wash away the bad taste in my mouth. Exhausted, I collapse in the cockpit.

The island's name, Providencia, means heaven. Arriving in this peaceful harbor, the name fits. It is a haven from squalls, and a deep anchorage after hazardous shallow reefs. Yet, as the night progresses, I sit alone in a corner of the cockpit, unable to sleep while Dennis snores below. My nerves remain taut as I reflect on the near debilitating fear I encountered.

Why do I torture myself when I'm afraid? Is my imagination hardwired to conjure up the worst of the past and future? There was real danger in entering that dark reef, yet the visions I created of being tossed into the coral and shredded by sharks made it worse. Memories of Mr. Hart impaired my abilities when clarity was crucial. Our safety was compromised. Attempts to calm myself failed.

The bench is hard; the cushions remain below. Bringing my knees up to my chest I make myself smaller and begin to rock.

I have decided. I will never go on a long passage again. I will not sail to Fatu Hiva. I will never find my cleansing waterfall in the Bay of Virgins. I will help Dennis get the boat to Panama, and then I'm through. He can sail without me or throw away his own dreams.

My eyes fill with tears, and I cover my face with my hands. My body slumps farther forward. A torrent of body-wrenching sobs flows through me. It's hard to breathe.

(Trigger Warning) I know where my deepest fear lies. Images surround me: the blackness of the reef, the darkness of rape, the haunting look of Mr. Hart's eyes, the rage beneath orange-brown glasses. At times I live deep inside my fear—Mr. Hart lives deep inside me—I don't know how to stop him. I can't stop him. After forty years of trying to overcome trauma, I have become my own tormentor. When my fears arise, my mind takes over and I remember. He raped me once, yet I am the one who has relived it thousands of times. All my attempts to escape have brought me nowhere.

I'm finished, spent.

The rapist is now me and she has won.

CHAPTER 11

Seeking Courage

They came to sit and dangle their feet off the edge of the world and after awhile they forgot everything but the good and true things they would do someday.

Brian Andreas

Portsmouth, New Hampshire, June 2013

    Camp Four on Mount Everest—the Death Zone—is where climbers stop before their final ascent. The air is thin. It is perhaps the world's hardest place to breathe.

    My new therapist is a climber who understands breathing and conquering fear. If anyone can help me get back on the boat and achieve my dreams of sailing to the Galapagos and Fatu Hiva it will be her.

    A few months earlier, after the weather had cleared, Dennis and I sailed the final two days to Panama. We left the boat in Bocas del Toro for the rainy season and flew to New Hampshire.

    My ordeal in Providencia, while crushing, had been a revelation. I understood, at a deeper level, my own participation in the violation of my body, mind, and spirit. I couldn't stop myself. Like all trauma survivors, a part of my brain was automatically triggered whenever I felt fear.

    For over forty years, countless times, I had perpetuated the image of violation. It's not that I was responsible for the rape; I was absolutely not. If, however, my mind and body recreated images and feelings from that event, then perhaps I could learn to manage them differently. I had to move my therapy beyond talking about what happened and the feelings that arose and learn how to stop the rapid downward spiral between seeing the glasses and having full-blown PTSD flashbacks.

Although I didn't know it at the time, the idea that I held some responsibility for reliving the trauma was the first of several revelations. It would take two more years and the insight of three strong women to determine whether a full transformation might be possible. I wasn't sure if I could ever rise above the silenced child or the traumatized woman I had become. All I knew was that I needed professional support.

My new therapist's office is close to our condo in Portsmouth, NH. It's at the top of a building, a small room in the loft with a sofa and chair, . Next to the sofa is a table with a glass of water and a box of tissues. On the wall hangs a photo of Everest.

"When I do anything frightening, I hold courage close," she says. "I do this with techniques, like breathing, and tangible, physical items like pieces of clothing. I'll wear the climbing bra that I wore on Everest because it helps me to feel powerful. You can wear a special shirt or carry a calming essence with a powerful fragrance, hold a symbolic stone in your pocket or a note of love from a friend… anything to give you strength. I chant Buddhist mantras and sing powerful songs. Do you have a song that makes you feel powerful?"

"When Nico was little, he used to sing 'I Believe I Can Fly' from the Space Jam movie, and it helped him ski hard slopes. I could use that."

"You could. Do you have any of your own songs, or powerful images?"

"Well … there's Rocky. There's a scene in the first *Rocky* movie that's powerful. He rises up from the streets, working harder and harder, and when he runs up the steps of the Philadelphia Museum of Art, he gives me the sense that anything is possible."

"Take Rocky with you," she says.

Friends ask for stories and photos of my journey. I recount gorgeous places, amazing people, and fabulous adventures. I don't talk about flashbacks, visions of Providencia's reef, or feeling worthless. On land, with the help of my therapist, my fears subside, and my wanderlust reappears, with trepidation.

Can I overcome fear? Can I reclaim my lost dreams? Am I going to let Mr. Hart haunt me for the rest of my life? Will my voice ever be strong again?

After one of many sessions with my therapist, I come home to one of Dennis's generous dinners. With a passion for cooking, he enjoys finding new recipes and surprising me with creative meals. He moves through the kitchen with ease, chopping herbs on a wooden cutting board, tossing the contents in a frying pan, and sipping red wine. Energetic blues play over our sound system.

Our small dining room is surrounded by windows and opens to a tiny living room. The table is solid wood. Both of my feet rest on the floor's firm surface while windows block out bad weather and doors hold back intruders. I relax in my chair. At this moment, I feel safe.

He places our dinner on the table: fresh fish tacos, fried corn tortillas filled with cabbage, cilantro-chipotle sauce, and a Spanish tempranillo. The tacos are warm and spicy and the wine is smooth and full-bodied. As we finish our meal, Dennis pours me a second glass. My throat is warm as I swallow the wine.

I clear my throat and ask, "What do you think of me taking an advanced sailing class in Port Townsend, Washington, this fall? There's a woman, Marina, with a thirty-eight-foot boat, who takes women sailing. She teaches storm tactics, person overboard, and emergency preparedness while we're at sea on her boat. If I can get more experience, maybe I can lose some of my fear."

Dennis's face lights up; his eyes are wide as he stares at me. "Wow, honey, that would be incredible. Would you consider going out to sea again? I thought you were done with sailing. Do you think you might get back on our boat?"

I clear my throat. "I'm not committing, just looking at ways to be braver… and healthier. My therapist is great at helping with my emotions. If I could improve my sailing, too, maybe that will help."

"You're already a great sailor. You could probably teach a course yourself. What you really need is confidence."

"Marina has circumnavigated twice with all-women crew. If anyone can help me build sailing confidence, it's her."

"Two circumnavigations! Definitely do it." He pauses and covers my hand with his. "Heidi, stop for a moment. Just think of this. Regardless of whether you make it happen, it's a huge step. Do you think you might really try again? Is there any hope of you crossing the Pacific?"

I squirm in my seat. "Whoa! Not yet. Don't put me in the middle of the ocean."

"Ah honey, I don't mean to push you. Whatever happens, happens. Know that I love you to the ends of the Earth, darlin', and I'm sticking with you, wherever." He pulls out his chair, moves to my side, and puts his arms around me.

Marina asks if I want to invite anyone on our three-women at-sea course. I wonder if Eileen will be interested.

I first encountered Eileen at the start of the Virginia rally two years earlier. One afternoon, she left the marina's public shower and was drying her hair in the wind. She had a lively spark, and her long, wavy red hair was wild and beautiful. Eileen is a nurse and her husband Mark is a doctor. They have a regal ketch, *Wavelength*. It's a forty-four-foot Cherubini with classic lines, reflective of *Centime*'s. We became fast friends.

It's a long shot for Eileen to come; I send an email anyway. I pour a glass of cabernet sauvignon. Fifty-five minutes pass, and my computer dings, announcing an email: "I'm definitely coming!"

Then my phone rings. "This is so exciting. I'm in! I'm in!" Eileen exclaims. "Every time our friends ask Mark what's next, he tells them, 'We're sailing to French Polynesia with our friends Heidi and Dennis.'"

"You're what?"

I set down my wine. I never imagined them joining us for a sail across the South Pacific. She didn't want to sail on long passages, and I guessed they would stay in the Caribbean. Confusion, excitement, and overriding nervousness surround me. I put my right hand on my throat. I haven't told Eileen about my flashbacks or my plan to quit sailing. After giving up in Providencia, am I strong enough, brave enough, to sail to French Polynesia?

If Eileen sails to the South Pacific, do I want to be left behind?

The summer passes quickly. I take Nico back to Montreal with trailing tears, and join Marina, Eileen, and a third friend, Sharon, for our sailing challenge.

Marina is a short woman, strong and capable. I feel an immediate connection. Her boat, *Athena*, appears strong and capable, too. *Athena* reminds me of *Centime* with her size and traditional lines; her heavier full keel makes her slower and more stable. Like *Centime* and *Wavelength*, she's a great ship to sail the world.

"Ladies, we'll leave tomorrow at 10:00 a.m.," Marina says. "If we delay, currents will be against us. There's a gale on the way. It's predicted to be the worst of the season. We want to be safely across the sound and anchored in a protected harbor before the weather gets bad. The harbor we're going to is better to enter in daylight, because it has a narrow, winding, unlit channel with several rock hazards. We need to leave on time." My breath quickens. I remember my therapist's lessons: breathe … breathe. I will wear my *Rocky* shirt tomorrow.

Before heading to sea the next morning, we shop for a weeks' worth of provisions. Marina is excited to share her favorite stores, and it's fun to linger over choices of wine, fish, cheese, produce, and chocolates. We lose track of time. Checking my watch, I doubt we will leave by 10:00 a.m. I seem to be the only one concerned. By noon we're at the dock, loading food. A steady breeze causes the metal shrouds that hold the mast to clink like disharmonic wind chimes.

"Breathe … breathe," I tell myself. "Marina, shouldn't we wait? The current has turned against us. The wind's getting stronger. We don't want to arrive in the dark."

"We'll be fine," she replies.

"What if the harbor is crowded and there's no place to anchor? With the gale coming, what will we do?"

"There will be space. We'll be okay."

The boat is sluggish as we first leave the dock. Eileen and I set smaller reefed sails knowing the wind will build.

"Please take the helm," Marina says to me, and I smile. *Athena* has a long, handcrafted, wooden tiller to steer rather than a wheel. It's solid, satisfying. As I pull the tiller toward me on the high, windward side, I feel *Athena*'s energy course through my hand. She heels over and her speed increases as the sea rushes past. She is powerful and free. We sail together as one. Images of my seafaring grandfather surge through my brain, yet this time they are welcoming images. I wonder if the sea is in my genes, my destiny.

Through the afternoon, the sky darkens. The wind increases, gusting over twenty knots. Light rain falls. The horizon is a dark uniform gray.

The VHF radio jumps to life, first with static and then a raspy robotic male voice. "Sécurité. Sécurité. Sécurité. This is the United States Coast Guard with a special NOAA weather bulletin. Gale warnings are in effect from the Straits of Juan De Fuca to the Canadian border. All small craft should seek immediate shelter."

My body tenses. Chaotic thoughts rush through my brain. Where are we? Where are the Straits? How long will it take for gale-force winds to arrive? Will there be lightning? Why did I do this?

Marina is calm. Her confidence and apparent lack of fear reminds me of Dennis's when a squall approaches. The power and freedom I felt earlier are gone. Now I feel trapped on the boat. It reminds me of Philadelphia.

"Marina, do you want to take the helm?" I ask, gripping the tiller.

"Nope, you're doing fine," she replies.

"But …"

"You're a good sailor," she says with a stern voice.

The light fades. The rain is cold. Sharon, sitting at my side, begins to shiver. She arrived from the south without warm clothes. Marina takes Sharon below and later pops up.

"Eileen, I want you to navigate for Heidi," Marina says. "Sharon is overchilled. She's shaking, so I've wrapped her in a wool blanket, and I'm making her tea. The stove will warm up the cabin for her. Let me know if you need anything."

"Okay," Eileen says in a cheery voice. "Tell her we're thinking of her." She moves to the companionway where she can see the electronic chart, hidden from the cockpit.

The sky and sea are dark after another hour of sailing. The wind howls and the boat flies. No ships or land are visible, just blackness. I hate blackness. The feeling is surreal, speeding through the dark. The only light is a distant, dim, green flasher.

"Eileen, can you find that flasher on the chart?" I ask. "It's green, two-second intervals."

Eileen studies the chart as *Athena* speeds ahead. "I don't see any lighted buoys near us," she replies.

"Look over there. It's right there at 11:00 slightly off to port," I say.

"I just don't see any lights on the chart near our position," Eileen says.

Marina's head appears and she looks over Eileen's shoulder at the electronic chart. "We're right where we need to be," she says. "There aren't any lighted navigation buoys in this area." She disappears below.

I strain my eyes and count the flashes. We sail on.

"Eileen. Look over there and then please look again on the chart," I plead. "Are you sure it's not there?"

"I'll look again," she says. *Athena* cuts through the sea, waves pound a rhythm on her hull. The wind howls.

"I can't find one," she says.

"Marina, I'm one hundred percent sure there's a two-second, green flasher ahead," I yell and then repeat the mariner's rule. "Marina, is it 'red, right, return'? Green stays to the left ... if ... if we're returning .... With all these islands, which way is returning?" I bite my lip.

"Huh?" she replies.

The installed electronic chart is too far away to see, and I can't let go of the tiller in these strong winds. Islands are everywhere, invisible in the dark. When I sail in Maine, I use the Coast Guard's red-green light system going in and out of harbors, going away from and returning to land using the red-right-return rule. Here, near the Canadian border, sailing between so many islands, I don't understand if I'm heading toward, returning to the harbor, or sailing away from the harbor. I'm confused which side to take the flasher on. I've never sailed in these waters; I can't see the chart or land, and I no longer remember the complete rule. I only see a green flasher ahead.

"Marina we're returning, aren't we?" I yell. "Are we returning or heading out?"

"What?" she replies again. She appears to be busy below with Sharon and uncertain of my cryptic message.

The flashing green light gets closer; my brain mimics its warning signal. My skin tingles. I'm hot. I unsnap the top of my yellow foul-weather slicker and cold air rushes past my throat and chest and I shiver. The wind is strong. I recheck the sails, the course, and the light. I strain my eyes to see through the black ink of night.

"We're going toward an island, a harbor, right? Which way is returning? You know the rule … red, right, return?" I ask again, trying to be clearer.

She looks over Eileen's shoulder again. "You're doing fine, there are no navigation lights here," she replies, unconcerned—she's worked with incompetent beginners before.

Often buoys mark rocks and navigation hazards. Taking one on the wrong side can be dangerous. Hitting a rock in these cold waters could be catastrophic.

"Marina, will you please take the helm?" I ask in a quiet voice.

"Just keep moving straight ahead on your course. I know exactly where we are and there's nothing to worry about. You're doing great."

I want to run away, but I can't leave the tiller. My head is pounding. With no lighted buoys in this area, why am I seeing one? Maybe we're not where Marina and Eileen think we are? A gale is on the way, and I'm heading us toward an unknown flashing buoy, in an area with numerous rocky outcrops, uncertain where we are. If we hit a rock, we might sink. It won't take much time in this cold water to become hypothermic and die. It could happen any minute. If we're going down, I don't want it to be my fault. I clutch the tiller with one hand, grabbing my throat with the other.

"Breathe … breathe … take Rocky with you," I murmur to the wind. "What would Rocky do?"

Though I am trained to always obey the captain, there is also a navigation rule to avoid immediate danger. My best instincts are that the light is marking a rock or shoal; not knowing which side to take it on appears to give me a 50 percent chance of hitting it. I let out the sails. *Athena* responds with an abrupt stall as her sails flap loudly in the wind. I let go of the tiller. "Captain! I need you! Now!" I yell.

Marina runs up on deck, grabs the tiller and pulls in the genoa. *Athena* surges forward under perfect control. I sit, watching, waiting. No one says a word. We immediately pass the green flasher close to port, nearly close enough to touch it.

"This is new," she says. "Number three doesn't have a light on either chart. Interesting." Feeling the heat rise in my face, I avoid looking at her, and slowly exhale.

Beyond the green light we're in total darkness. She pulls out a floodlight from under her seat. As we enter a channel, the flashlight illuminates rock outcrops close on either side. She steers us with competence through a narrow winding passage. The harbor opens ahead. The floodlight reveals a harbor filled with boats. We drop anchor and settle into the night. All is safe.

"We're here!" Eileen says, euphoric. I give her a strong hug. I'm shaking in the cool night wind.

Snug and secure, we have a delicious dinner of wild sockeye salmon and several glasses of chardonnay. Sharon has recovered her warmth and is bundled in Marina's wool sweater. We relax below, while the gale blows outside.

The cabin is small, cozy, and warm, filled with varnished wood. We sit around a mahogany table. "Tell me more about what you specifically want to learn on *Athena*," Marina says.

Eileen brushes back her long hair with a flick of her hand. "Mark wants to sail to French Polynesia, just the two of us. Much of it will be downwind. We haven't sailed much downwind. I'd like to learn a good way to raise and set a spinnaker and anything else to make us safer on a long open-ocean passage."

"I want to learn everything: sail trim, knots, how to have great meals when you're at sea for three weeks," Sharon says.

I clear my voice. "I want to build my skills so I'm not afraid anymore. I was scared tonight, and you and Eileen were unconcerned."

"You're already a competent sailor," Marina says, cocking her head to the side. "I would never have left you alone sailing while I was below if you weren't. Although you may not have been aware, I was constantly checking on you and the chart. You did a perfect job."

"But Marina," I say, raising my voice, "when I get scared, I think of all the disasters that might happen. Tonight, when I saw the buoy light that wasn't on the chart, I thought we could be lost … I could take it on the wrong side and hit a rock … we could get hypothermia in minutes. I prepared for the worst in my head. I located your life raft. I reviewed my lifeboat training. I refused to continue sailing. I shouldn't have let out the sails, but I didn't know what else to do to keep us from possibly hitting rocks. You were calm the whole time, while my fears and emotions took over."

"I trusted you and my boat. I knew where we were the entire time. You didn't. I knew you were confused and pissed at me, but we were safe and I wanted you to have the chance to figure it out under pressure. It was my way to help you experience uncertainty at sea, while knowing we were safe. It's that uncertainty that you're trying to handle. The green flasher threw you off. There will always be contingencies as you sail—weather changes, the unexpected happens. A really good sailor will do what-if scenarios like you did to determine the possible risks and outcomes of their decisions. Heidi, you have a keen ability to consider issues that may arise and talk through preparations to reduce risk."

"But Marina, I can't make my fear go away." I place my head in my hands.

"Fear can be a good thing that helps you prepare for potential challenges," she replies. "You don't want to get rid of fear."

"I was really afraid my first season," Eileen says. "When the winds and sea would pick up, my heart would race, my palms would sweat, and I'd curl up in a fetal position. Last summer, I worked on breathing techniques that helped. I have some great books you can have when we get back. I'm still afraid at times but it's not as debilitating."

"Heidi, you can't rationalize away emotions." Sharon is a therapist with a doctorate in psychology. "You can build your confidence and you can try mindfulness exercises to calm and better manage fear. But you can't think your way through fear or have any success telling yourself not to be afraid. Don't even try."

"Remember you are competent," Marina says. "Fear helps you get through the tough stuff. When I started, there were many things I was worried about. Hardly any of them happened. It was a total waste of energy. And the things that were really frightening, I would have never anticipated.

"Once, a minister in Sudan offered me forty camels for one of my crew members. He wanted her as his fourth wife. He had our passports. I was scared because I didn't know what might happen. I didn't sit down in his office when he asked, and I didn't leave room for negotiations. I just stood strong and told him I needed her to sail the boat, thanked him, and left quickly. It all ended well. We got our passports back and were able to leave together. I found out later forty camels was a damn good price," she joked.

"Another scare was when we sailed the north coast of Australia at night. Something strange was happening on the surface of the sea so we got out a floodlight to look. There were hundreds of deadly Australian sea snakes mating under a full moon. The floodlight attracted them and they tried to climb on board. They were everywhere and they were aggressive. My heart was racing. Virtually all sea snakes are venomous; they're some of the most venomous animals in the world. Somehow, we pushed them off with boathooks, but it was frightening.

"Funny though, in eleven years of sailing and two circumnavigations, I can count on my two hands the number of times it's been really icky."

As I write this scene by my fireplace in Maine, I remember Marina as having been a wonderful, compassionate teacher who would not have been apt to leave me alone, had she been aware of the fear I was experiencing. I suspect that at the time, my sailing concerns grew larger for me than they might have for many experienced sailors, and my inability to express myself properly grew along with my fear. I also find it true in my life. In the past, the more fearful I became the more I would shrink back in fear and in silence.

We ride out the gale at anchor and then sail north, improving skills and building confidence. We anchor in a pretty cove surrounded by tall, imposing pines. The mist settles in the treetops like an illustration in a magical storybook. Marina relives her South Pacific crossings. I want to hear about the Marquesas and the cove of my dreams, the Bay of Virgins.

"Tell us about Fatu Hiva, Marina," I say. "It's been my lifelong dream to go."

"The island is magnificent, volcanic, lush, and the people have a generous spirit. They smile often and wear flowers in their hair."

"Did you see a tall, gorgeous waterfall there?" I ask.

"There were rumors about a waterfall; we never found it, but the bay is stunning. The cove you'll anchor in is narrow, steep-edged with high rock pinnacles. They used to call them penises. That's where we renamed *Athena*'s cockpit," she says, her eyes sparkling.

"What do you mean?" Sharon asks.

Marina looks at each of us, and smiles a slow smile. "We were sitting on the boat under the stars and moon. We could see those pinnacles, those giant penises, and we wanted female strength. That is where we decided to no longer have a cockpit on *Athena*. We now have a clitpit instead!"

Laughter fills the air. I pledge to bring strong female energy aboard *Centime*; maybe she needs a clitpit too. Being near Marina, I hope some of her well-earned bravado and expertise will rub off on me. She's a great sailor, a great teacher. I will miss her. I pledge to take her, my therapist, and Rocky with me in my travels, wherever I go.

On our last evening, we go ashore. Sharon and Eileen take a walk while Marina and I head to the restaurant at the harbor. A gentle breeze blows across an expansive wood deck where we share glasses of wine.

"You're a great helmsperson," Marina says. "You have skills to catch the wind and sail. You know what to do to reduce risk. As a sailor, just remember, you're a natural. When you let go and trust yourself you can sail with the best of them. Heidi, I would be honored to have you as a first mate, anytime." I renew my promise to pursue my dreams: to try to sail to the Bay of Virgins in Fatu Hiva.

At the end of our sailing week, Dennis meets me with a rental car, and we drive south. We're flying to Panama soon and are still uncertain about where we will sail this season. Will we stay in the Caribbean, sail home, or cross the canal to the Pacific?

"How was it out there? Were you in the gale they predicted?" he asks.

"We were at anchor in a protected cove when the full gale hit. When we did sail, *Athena* handled the wind and seas well. She's a heavier boat than *Cen-*

time and Marina is extremely capable."

"How about you? How did you handle the bad weather?" he asks, taking his eyes off the road to glance at me.

"At the start, I was anxious. Talking through my anxiety helped. Marina said I was a natural and that she'd be honored to have me as her first mate."

"That's great, honey. I'm proud of you."

I take a deep breath and look down at my hands. "I want to sail to Fatu Hiva. I'm still afraid … I might change my mind … who knows where life will lead … if you think I can …"

"I know you can!" Dennis says, a broad smile across his face. He places his hand on my knee. "You're an amazing sailor. You have good instincts. I've seen it."

"It's a matter of changing my attitude. When I'm positive, I think of sailing *Centime* to tropical islands and I get excited. When I'm afraid, I imagine dying in huge storms."

"Remember the saying, 'What you focus on expands'?"

"Yeah, so I'm saying it: I want to sail to Fatu Hiva."

We stop that night at the Martine, a historic, Victorian bed and breakfast in Monteray, California, built in 1899. She's an elegant lady perched on a small cliff overlooking the ocean. Our seaside room has flowered wallpaper and two tall floor lamps made in 1910. Dennis moves about, unpacking his suitcase and hanging his coat in an antique armoire. I sit in a blue upholstered rocker. If we were wearing different clothes it would appear like we've stepped back in time.

Our bedroom window is large, wrapping around the corner, capturing an expansive view of the sea. I imagine turn-of-the-century women gazing out of these windows, watching for husbands, sons, and lovers, wondering if they will return from the sea. Grandfather Edgar never made it home. Grandma Katie never had a home like this, or one near the sea, yet she must have imagined him returning.

Dennis pauses and stands behind me.

"What are you thinking?" he asks.

"I feel like I'm in an Andrew Wyeth painting where the viewer is in a room, looking out, searching," I say.

"What are you searching for?"

"My restless soul," I say, laughing. "The sea is beautiful. I missed you and our boat. It's been a long time since I've sailed without you."

"I missed you too," he replies.

"Did you know Gauguin created a painting called *Where Do We Come From? Where Are We Going?* It was his favorite. It makes me wonder what I'm searching for, who I want to be. I know I want to be a great mom, wife, and friend. I know I need to heal my PTSD. If I can make it across 3,000 nautical miles of wild, open ocean to that beautiful island, maybe I'll learn how to manage my fear, figure out where I'm going and why. Maybe I'll find paradise…and peace."

He pulls me up out of the chair and holds me in his arms. "I remember our first date when you told me about your dream. Did you ever see the movie *Shall We Dance* with Susan Sarandon?"

"Sure, I loved that movie."

"There's a line in it where she talks about there being a billion people on the Earth and she questions what life really means. She says in a marriage you promise to care for one another through the good and bad, that part of marriage is to be a witness to someone's life. Your life won't go unnoticed. I love being your witness and having you as mine."

My heart swells. Standing on my toes, I stretch my body to reach his and we embrace. "Maybe we've already found paradise," I say.

"Maybe we have. I'd love to sail with you to Fatu Hiva … to sit at the edge of the Earth with you." He pushes back to look into my eyes. "Feet hanging over."

CHAPTER 12

Dios Se Vie De Ti

*There is no greater hell than
to be a prisoner of fear.*

Ben Jonson

Santa Fe, Panama, October 2013

His new name is "Guapo," Spanish for handsome. He's a brown and white gelding, a speckled horse from Santa Fe in Central Panama.

Dennis and I had stopped at a farm in Santa Fe, a small rural village on our three-day trip from Panama City to Bocas del Toro. We had left *Centime* in Bocas, Panama for hurricane season after the nerve-racking sail to Providencia.

The gelding doesn't have a name, so I call him Guapo, hoping the compliment will bring me favor. He licks the brown sugar I have cupped in my hand, saved from my morning coffee. Dennis has ridden before; I'm a beginner.

Our guide, Erec, is a vaquero, a cowboy. He is a sturdy man in his early forties, with faded, well-worn blue jeans and black boots. He looks natural and happy riding his brown stallion, like a Panamanian Marlboro Man. His dark hair and eyes, and close-to-perfect white teeth compliment his tan leathery face. He will take us to the Bermejo waterfall at the foothills of the Santa Fe National Reserve, an area far away from tourist towns. It isn't the Polynesian waterfall I'm trying to find, yet I hope it to be an interesting diversion en route.

Erec leads Guapo at first, riding slowly ahead, holding his reins. Dennis follows on his own larger stallion. As Guapo and I become familiar, Erec hands me his reins, and I guide my horse on a dirt path past flowers of every shape and hue: yellow, orange, pink, red, and deep purple. Fruit trees are abundant, heavy with mangoes, papayas, avocados, limes, and grapefruit. Dramatic hills and green valleys are to the left of the path. Majestic mountains rise behind. Bushes with bright red coffee beans are abundant across the landscape.

Soon, the path becomes steep and Guapo slows and snorts, shaking his head from side to side. Dennis's older horse stops abruptly. Erec dismounts, ties the three horses to a shady tree and gives them water from an old metal tray from inside a worn leather pack. He gestures that we will travel ahead on foot.

The walk to the waterfall is downhill. The footholds on the steep, narrow path are muddy and scattered with rocks and roots. The thick vegetation of the jungle closes in. It's hot and humid. Clear-throated birds and sounds of cascading water fill the air.

Rounding a bend, we get a dazzling glimpse of a thunderous fall, divided into two sections by an outcropping of large boulders. Hiking through overgrown bushes and over steep rocks, we reach the lower section. Erec and Dennis drop their gear on a large flat rock and wade in the lower falls. I put down my pack and search, alone, for the concealed upper falls.

Lush vegetation and hanging vines surround the chiseled rocks. Scrambling over slippery moss-covered river rocks, I sit and slide on my backside when I can't find a good handhold. As a child with Terry, I loved climbing and finding ways to scamper around obstacles. The way forward is through knee-deep water. My hiking boots and the bottom of my jeans are already soaked. Hidden from Erec and the world below, I leave my boots and jeans behind and continue barefooted, wearing only under garments and a sweat-streaked T-shirt.

Clouds gather, obscuring the sun. The roar of the falls becomes louder. A sheer rock wall, black with a scattering of wet moss, defines the right side of the river's edge. It has a narrow shoulder-high ledge, just wide enough for my hand. The now thigh-deep river flows fast below the ledge. Wading over slick rocks, I test each step for a possible foothold. Watching my feet, I feel for handholds along the ledge.

My eyes catch a flash movement, a trick of light. A giant black spider, with long hairy legs and a swollen body, is next to my fingers. He's almost as large as my hand. He moves fast along the edge of my fingers and my heart races. Screaming, I yank my hand away from a tarantula. I fall over rocks, drenching my body and cutting my knee.

Free of the spider, I wash mud and blood off my knee and start again. I can hear the close thunder of the waterfall.

As I continue around the bend, an opening in the thick of the jungle reveals the falls. It cascades forty or fifty feet above me into to a once-hidden cerulean pool. I let out a loud whoop, splashing my hand through the cool water. At the source of the falls is a rock crevice in the shape of a large V. Water shoots through its narrow cleft. The sun breaks through the clouds. The powerful rush of water is near blindingly white. The air is filled with mist, and beads of water sparkle in the bright sun.

My body tingles as a large, vivid blue butterfly appears and dances in the sunlight, framed by the V of the cleft. The cobalt wings of a blue morpho shimmer in the light like a dozen prisms, catching my eye with iridescent intensity. I feel a surge of electric energy and raise both hands to my heart.

It takes a full day to travel by bus on the narrow, winding roads from Santa Fe to Boquete, the next mountainous town in Panama's Chiriquí Highlands. We arrive in a cloud forest, a moist, drippy, high-elevation forest filled with an abundance of diverse plants and animals.

The sun is low in the sky. River rapids rush over rocks. Hundreds of frogs chirp in harmony with the river. Wind whistles through the trees. Melodic birds sing. I close my eyes, absorbing the complex patterns.

As I open my eyes, the view unfolds beyond the river. Lush mountains rise to meet the clouds with myriad textures in shades of green, woven across the valley. Soft tall grasses intertwine with large-leafed banana plants and red-berried coffee bushes. Moss-covered trees dot the lower elevations. An abundance of orchids hangs from nearby tree branches. The thick canopy blankets every inch of space, reaching up to the heavy clouds that have settled among steep peaks. A dark hawk soars majestically in the white gray mist, stretching its wings to ride the thermals.

At the inn's lush garden, blue and green hummingbirds shimmer. Darting from one flower to the next, they appear inches away from my eyes. Every color and shade of flower abound, in bright contrast to the leafy greens throughout the garden. An archaic stone sculpture draws my eyes deep into the thick vegetation. Who created it? What stories does it hold? It appears to be an ancient god of fertility, grounded in the earth. If so, it has blessed this garden.

The inn's Spanish architecture complements the setting. Three modest buildings, of faded orange stucco and terra cotta roof tiles, sit in tranquil accord with the river tributary that curves among them. A secluded terrace, a small fireplace, and a few lounge chairs offer warm refuge from the cool jungle.

While I am drawn to linger in this magical place, darkness has set in; the nearby restaurant will soon stop serving. Sauntering a mile down the road, Dennis and I come to a low stone wall with a handwritten sign, George's. Near the entrance a friendly man, George himself, greets us with a broad smile and an outstretched hand, beckoning us to enter. He's a sturdy man with weathered skin and dark hair.

The rustic structure with its open stone and bamboo walls uses the mountains, river, and gardens for ambience. Arranged across a stone floor are a half-dozen thick, handmade, wooden tables. A stone fireplace vents out of the high-pitched ceiling. George tells us he built the two-sided fireplace to have one side to warm the guests and the other to serve as his grill. The light fragrance of wood smoke mingles with heavier fragrances of grilled meats and peppery sauces.

In the far corner, a family of seven, with distinct features of the indigenous Ngäbe Indians, sits at a long table. They wave and greet us with "Buenas," smiling and laughing as they eat and drink. The youngest, a teenage girl in a traditional bright orange dress with ribbons of colorful rickrack, has beautiful, thick black hair plaited in a long ponytail that reaches the full length of her back. Sitting next to her in a purple dress is a short, plump woman with wrinkled brown skin. She gives the girl hugs throughout the evening and with each hug the girl falls into the older woman's chest like a beloved child.

We order steaks and ask George to bring red wine. As Dennis fills our glasses there is a slight shuffle at the family's table. Two men bring out guitars and adjust chairs, getting ready to play. Soon the place is awash in song. A third man joins in with his deep, strong voice and though we don't know much Spanish, we can make out a few words: corazón and amor … heart and love. He looks across to the plump woman and places his hand across his chest, singing directly to her.

Song after song, the three men serenade their loved ones and us. The closest guitar player, dressed in black, plucks his strings through complex rhythms. He joins his compadre in song. He looks up occasionally toward our table, being sure we are engaged in his music, and smiles. The second guitarist, with white hair and a red plaid shirt, has an expressive face as he sings.

Our steaks arrive smothered in a red wine, butter, and rosemary sauce. I savor each bite as I do each note. The flavors are rich, the music luscious. Some songs are slow, deep, and romantic. Others are lively and I clap my hands while Dennis drums out the rhythm on our wooden table.

During a break in the music, George asks if we would like to try his famous pineapple cake. The fancy, decorative cake arrives smothered in a sweet white sauce and fresh pineapple, and covered with piles of vanilla ice cream. I ask George if he can make a second plate for the musicians and their families as our small gift for their lovely singing. A clamor arises when George delivers their cake. They smile, surprised, and wave "gracias" across the room. The evening winds down, the cake is long finished, and the musicians stop playing. No money cans or requests for contributions appear. It was a simple time for sharing joy.

Setting instruments aside, they each come to our table in a line, elders first, and shake hands with us. The man in black talks in Spanish to Dennis and George, while the one with the red plaid shirt kisses me lightly on my cheek. Next, the plump woman looks in my eyes, places both hands on my shoulder, and offers a nod and a broad smile. She is less than five feet tall and has a strong, warm presence. The only language we share is friendship. They have given us a gift greater than a few songs, a gift of connection, a lasting memory.

The following morning, Dennis and I wake early. We travel for miles in the front of an old pickup truck, up a rutted road to visit a zipline that crisscrosses the jungle. The overgrown vegetation slaps the truck, leaving tracks of sap and water on the windshield. Flowers and huge Panamanian cedars with long, wide buttress roots crowd the dirt road. Behind us, the colorful village disappears and the rugged mountains dominate.

At the top of the road, a dark mountain peak hovers, suspended over bright, white cumulus clouds. Vulcán Barú is the highest point in La Amistad, a thirty-five-thousand-acre national park that stretches from Panama to Costa Rica. The peak rises above the clouds at 11,400 feet. We stop at five thousand feet.

The area is quiet except for natural sounds: a rushing mountain stream, bird songs, and the whisper of light breezes. A new wooden building nestles next to the river. Fresh-brewed coffee fills the air. High-bush coffee plants heavy with beans, surround us.

A fit man in his twenties appears from the back of the building. He's wearing jeans and a brown short-sleeved shirt that stretches tight across large, well-defined muscles. He reaches to shake our hands. "Bienvenido. Me llamo Isasios." Isasios will be our guide on the mountain zipline. Two more guides, Carlos and Jonanton appear, schlepping helmets, harnesses, safety lines, and gloves. We are the only guests and have scored three excited, handsome guides.

Carlos, a teen, puts on safety equipment, hooks onto a sample line, and flies by. His demonstration, a few feet off the ground, looks easy. At the end of the demonstration, we don gear and walk on a narrow path through bountiful gardens toward the first platform.

"A few of these trees are over two hundred years old," Carlos says. He points to a white flower, its bloom smaller than the eraser on the end of a pencil. "This orchid is the world's smallest."

"Look!" Isasios shows us one tiny, yellow flower in a large group of green. "These orchids bloom only once every two years, for only one day. Today it blooms for you," he says. His cheeks are red.

He points across the deep valley, where a heavy steel cable terminates at a wooden platform that surrounds a large tree. The gap between where we stand and the tree appears bottomless. "The number two platform is 180 feet high," Isasios says. My eyes follow the cables across the valley. Excitement and trepidation fight in my stomach as we climb up onto the first canopy platform. We start at six thousand feet above sea level, one thousand feet above the lodge. Arriving at the first platform, I'm breathless.

"If I fly from the first to the second platform and I'm afraid, can I stop at the second platform and walk back?" I ask Isasios.

"Oh, no! Once you start you can't go back. Impossible," he says.

"How many platforms do we cross?" I ask.

"Thirteen."

I wonder if the Panamanians have the same superstitions we have. I try my therapist's breathing techniques.

Carlos and Dennis head across first, speeding out of the gate like hawks. Hooked on and in position—I'm off! I soar, gliding over the treetops. I am a small speck high above green valleys, with rivers spilling over their banks. I fly over cascading waterfalls, past mountains and through the lush "cloud forest," across the steep ravine.

Legs crossed, feet tucked under, I hold one gloved hand on the harness rope and the other behind me on the cable, streaming through the air. At 240 feet above the valley, adrenaline pulses through my veins. Using the thick glove, I try to brake at just the right moment so I don't crash into the platform, or slow down too soon. Anxious, I stop short, a few meters before the platform, hundreds of feet above the ground, and dangle like a spider on a thin strand of web. I'm out of the reach of the guides.

"Do you need help?" Carlos shouts.

"I can do this," I reply. Breathe ... breathe ...

I turn myself around, swinging on rusty wire and try not to look down. I pull myself up the ascending cable at a slow pace, hand over hand, until Carlos grabs me. We move on.

At each section my skills improve. I marvel at the valleys and waterfalls below, and look across to the mountains, clouds, and Vulcán Barú. I sing at the top of my lungs where no one can hear. I am free as I soar.

At the seventh section, the longest and fastest, I leap off the platform and glide high through the shade of the canopy. Dark clouds gather and the wind picks up. I descend across the vast open valley, floating like a fallen leaf at the mercy of the gusting wind. Suddenly, the sun breaks through. The cloud forest is alight with hundreds of streams of sunbeams. When I reach the platform Isasios is there. His cheeks are red, and his face and body animated as he exclaims, "Dios se vie de ti! God smiles on you. Look up. The sun is on your face, just your face alone." Bursting into a broad smile, I laugh hard.

It seemed like heaven opened in that sunlit zipline moment. I didn't know then if I believed in heaven or God. I wanted to believe in the God who smiled on me as I soared through the jungle.

I no longer believed in the God I'd prayed to when I was eleven. As a child in Philadelphia, my father a pastor, I grew up with religion. I read the Bible, knew many biblical stories, and believed, without question, God would protect me if I were a good girl. When I was raped, afraid Mr. Hart would kill me, I had pleaded and prayed to God to be saved. The more I prayed, the worse my situation became. I escaped Mr. Hart's rage and fell straight into hell.

CHAPTER 13

A Whiter Shade of Pale

*I am not what happened to me,
I am what I choose to become.*

Carl Gustav Jung

Bocas del Toro, Panama, October 2013

It's a new sailing season. Piles of cardboard boxes, suitcases, and backpacks spill over *Centime*'s bench sofas, crowding the cabin floor. A narrow path marks the way through gear to the forward berth. This berth is the only place of refuge, away from clutter, where cool breezes blow through the portholes and invite a less frenzied pace. As I pause for a moment between tasks, music floats on the wind.

"Are you excited to be back?" Dennis asks.

"Very," I say. "It feels like a new and different season after working with Marina and my Mt. Everest therapist. Once we get all this gear and food put away, *Centime* will seem like she's ready to go too."

As the sun sets, Dennis and I stroll over to the Calypso Cantina, the marina's funky, open-air restaurant. The cantina, with its separate protruding dock space, sits on a narrow edge of the marina surrounded by water on three sides. It offers an oasis from the hot town. Sailors of many nationalities jostle around wooden tables painted in almost every color from leftover boat paint. Old boat flags from several countries and boat clubs hang below her eaves.

Jasleen, our favorite server, weaves through the patrons. Her hips sway to music under her wide, colorful skirt as she serves beer and steaming plates of spicy fish and plantains.

Live rock music fills the air as musicians jam. Patrick, the guitar player, sings, and Andy matches his beat, tapping out frenetic rhythms on bongos. Patrons sing along, dance, and share the mic.

Dark, fast-moving clouds roll across the distant sky. Lightning flashes as rain begins to tap on the cantina's metal roof. There's a buzz of energy in the air and rumors from sailors abound: a monsoon trough is heading our way. We struggle with other sailors to unroll and fasten the clear plastic walls that hang from the ceiling, as they whip in the wind. It takes four of us to stabilize each small panel.

As the rain strengthens, the duo inch closer to the dry center. The frenzy of the music increases as water begins to run into the drier parts of the cantina. Soon, Patrick unplugs speakers and amplifiers while Andy pulls out a plastic tarp and covers the instruments.

Palm trees bend and sway, branches break and scatter. The wind gusts over twenty-five knots. *Centime* is tucked away in a semi-protected slip in the marina; however, numerous sailboats are anchored in the exposed bay. We watch them pitch about through plastic windows, and check for signs of dragging anchors. One man jumps up from a table and runs through the rain to his dinghy. He drives his small tender with its underpowered outboard across a sea streaked with lightning. Three more follow, rushing to secure their boats. Ten minutes later a sailor returns, maneuvering his small rubber boat through the waves and wind like he's a cowboy on a bucking bronco.

As fast as the squall started, it's over. The wind calms, the lightning is gone, and the rain stops. Waves continue to crash on the shore. Patrick dries his chair, removes the tarp, and plugs in his equipment. Andy looks on, finishing his beer.

Patrick starts with a quiet song. I recognize the very first chords, feeling the power of a lifelong emotional trigger. He is singing my song: "A Whiter Shade of Pale."

Dennis squeezes my hand as I stand to leave, trembling. I walk alone to a quiet neighboring pier.

The song was released in 1967—the "Summer of Love." That summer was famous for hippies and flower children; race riots and anti-government protests; battles and unspeakable horrors in Vietnam. Marked by war, social unrest, and cultural upheaval, the world was changing. My childhood had already changed in its own ways. Hearing the song at age eleven, shortly before my twelfth birthday n July, started a cascade of emotion, moving me from a state of shock and numbness to one consumed with deep grief and anguish. It was perhaps the first time after the rape's initial aftermath that I relived the traumatic torment.

My family had moved out of Philadelphia, abruptly leaving our home which stood next door to the house of my best friend, Terry Hart. My paternal grandmother was in a nursing home, unable to speak after a stroke. Dad, a kindhearted family man, social worker, and minister, was preoccupied with a new job and the demands of caring for my dying grandmother.

Mother was different then, too. Her Sunday dinners shifted from large gatherings with suppers of roast beef or turkey and all the fixings to solitary frozen dinners and canned soup. She slept late and went to bed early, rarely talking to anyone. The dirty clothes piled up in our damp basement. She no longer gave me chores, checked my homework, or told me it was time to sleep. I felt invisible when I was with her.

I found a summer job at Zoe's Café, near my grandmother's empty cottage, in a seaside New Jersey town. My boss required that I work on weekends. I pleaded with Dad to let me stay there alone when he and my mother would return to the city for his Sunday church obligations. It had been our family tradition, before Grandmother's illness, to spend summer weekdays at the seashore away from the heat in Philadelphia, and commute to the city on weekends. I loved the shore, and longed to escape the new suburban neighborhood and my altered, detached life. Mother didn't appear to care where I was, so Dad relented.

It's a moonless night at the seashore.

As I walk home from work alone, I stifle yawns. The red front door of the empty white cottage is locked. My parents have left for the weekend. Around back, a glass slider opens to what my grandfather had built as the "kids' room." It's a small room that was once outside space between two sides of a previously u-shaped house.

Twin folding beds sit on either side of the room against opposing walls, each with a small table at one end. A tube of Coppertone and my brother Vern's cast-off transistor radio are on the table next to my cot. A damp musty smell penetrates the room as if the night has crept in.

I change out of my Zoe's uniform into pink-striped pj bottoms and a white T-shirt, grab a dog-eared *Seventeen* magazine, and flop onto the bed. Stretching my arms, I flip on the radio.

The first song is one I've never heard. The musical intro is mysterious and engaging.

Once the lyrics start, the singer tells a story; I sit up, spellbound, trying to decipher this enigmatic song. I feel as if I'm the main character brought into a café.

Turning up the volume, I stare at the radio, mesmerized, straining to hear and understand each word.

And then the triggering starts with two profound words: "vestal virgins."

I suck in my breath. Virgin. I am no longer a virgin.

I begin to hyperventilate.

(Trigger Warning) Two words have unleashed a torrent of emotions, feelings I had locked away, words that were silenced. I feel a slow, overwhelming progression. Images appear: his orange-brown glasses and piercing eyes. An enormous upwelling builds and breaks over me. My body shrinks. If I hadn't understood the enormity of what happened on that sunny Saturday in May, two months earlier, I understand it now.

Everything I was is now gone. Not just gone. Taken. I feel weight on my chest. I curl into myself, my hands on my throat, my nose to my knees, crumpling my body into the sheets. I begin to rock.

The walls of the room tighten. I jump off the cot, grab my flip-flops, stumble to the glass slider, fling it wide open, and bolt into the dark night. I run in bare feet, clutching my sandals, faster and faster, toward the beach. Tears obstruct my vision. I don't slow down until I reach the shore four blocks away.

Collapsing in the sand, buttressed against a locked shack that holds beach umbrellas, I sit in darkness. The cool wind blows from the ocean. I feel hot and cold at the same time, my arms shivering, my thoughts whirling. I cry until numbness sets in.

Steady winds amplify the sounds of the surf, bringing comfort. My breathing slows as I sit alone on the empty beach.

Loud voices approach from farther down the beach. I dive into a ten-inch crawl space below the umbrella shack. I'm hidden, ensconced within a narrow gap between sand and wood, between freedom and danger. Above me is the bottom of the wooden shack. Below where I lay, soft cold sand contours to my body and the side of my face. Raucous laughter breaks the night's stillness. My body stiffens. A pair of shoes walks close to my head. I am as alert as a hunted fox.

I used to sleep soundly under a quilt of butterflies next to a large blue teddy bear and wallpaper with pink rosebuds; now I am in a bed of damp sand that reeks of tobacco and urine.

Beyond the crawl space, the man's shoes point toward me. I hear the sound of a zipper followed by liquid hitting the wood shack. I can't stop the images storming through my brain. I stifle a cry. Zipper sounds repeat. The shoes turn, heels toward my face. I watch the play unfold concealed below the shack.

"Hey Johnny, check this out," the man yells. My heart pounds.

"What'd ya find, dumbass?" a second man replies, his voice loud.

I can barely make out a large hand near my head. It grabs one of my rubber flip-flops I left behind before my quick escape under the shack.

"Ya forget ya slippers, princess?" he asks.

One of my sandals flies toward the second man. He hurls it back, hard against the shack.

A third voice, husky, joins in. "What've we got here?"

I push myself farther from the gap, without a sound, and bring my left hand to my neck.

"Johnny's pretty yellow thongs."

More laughter. A pair of dark sneakers kicks up sand as they run toward the shoes. A body slams against the shack and groans.

"Hey. Watch it."

"You two boys cut your fighting. Leave him be, Johnny," the husky voice says. "I'm outta beer."

Glass shatters against a metal can. The shoes disappear. Voices fade. I remain still, below the shack. Only the roar of the ocean remains.

I crawl out of hiding, find my flip-flops, and sit with my back between a corner post and a trash can. Sand drops onto my face and eyes as I shake out my hair using my fingers as a comb. Clouds continue to obscure the moon and stars, and I can barely see the crests of large white caps. I wonder how it would feel to sail away, far from here, beyond the waves.

The men, now at a distance, blur into the darkness of the long beach. I stretch, mesmerized by the repetitive cadence of waves, crashing to shore and receding, crashing and receding. The sea works its magic, carrying me away. Yawning, I close my eyes and the song returns. Visions of young virgins in white communion dresses merge with taunting dark shadows.

Someone shakes my shoulder. I flinch at his touch and stare at hairy hands and a dark blue uniform. I had encountered policemen before, two months earlier. My stomach churns.

"You okay?" he asks.

I nod yes.

"What's your name?" he asks.

"Heidi," I reply, my voice cracking.

"How old are you, Heidi?"

"Eleven." I whisper … and no longer a virgin.

I heard Procol Harum's song throughout that summer as it climbed the charts. The first chords of music brought immediate recognition of who I was not—a virgin. I slept fitfully many nights that summer, waking with haunting visions of rage-filled eyes, shattered burnt-orange glasses, and virgins taunting me in white communion dresses and being set on fire. That's when I'd run. I'd try to hide where no one would find me, if anyone were to look, under the boardwalk or under the wooden beach umbrella stands. I'd turn inside myself to plot my disappearance, to calm my breathing. It was another of many secrets I would keep.

One day, I would disappear. It was my obsession. I just didn't know where to go where no one would find me.

Decades later, in Panama, I sit on the dock, straining to listen to the lyrics. I already know every word.

"Vestal." I'd looked it up when I was twelve. Vestal virgins: pure, undefiled, untainted. In Roman times, if vestals were found to no longer be virgins, they were burned alive and on occasion had molten lead poured down their throat. I imagined the hot lead burning my throat. The words remain emotional triggers.

I close my eyes and listen to the crashing waves. Breathe … breathe … you're strong … carry Rocky with you. My body begins to relax. Tonight, the song and my breathing evoke a strange mix of emotions: raw and ugly, yet also releasing and evolving.

Walking along the Bocas pier away from the cantina, I face the sea. A man runs past, from the far end of the pier toward the cantina, as if I were invisible. I have felt invisible before. My song stops abruptly. The man who had ran past talks through the microphone.

"Can anyone help? Billy needs help with his boat!" he says.

The men in the cantina jump up and run past me on the pier. The women stay behind. At first, I hold back; I'm not needed with all these men. Then, I think of Marina, rise up straighter, and follow. It's a role shift for me, to stand in my own power and to join the men.

The sea is roiling from the remains of the squall. An old fifty-foot schooner seesaws through surging waves. One single taut line at her bow is all that is left to restrain her. Her long bowsprit points to the dock. Her stern, once alongside the dock, now fights to be at sea. A broken line dangles off the dock as sea spray fills the air. Billy, a frail man with white hair, is on board the schooner, his eyes wide as he grips the lifeline. He grabs a new line, tosses it to the men on shore, and ties his end around a stern cleat. There is no room for me, in the midst of the chain of men, to grab the rope.

"Ready on three: one, two, heave …" Six men pull hard on the new rope attached to the schooner's stern. Their bodies are angled against the tight line, like a game of tug-of-war. The schooner's stern moves a few yards toward the dock as the men struggle to bring her back. Waves hit the schooner, pushing it partway over, its mast angled to the sea. Billy falls on the slanted deck.

"One, two, heave!" Groans and loud creaking rise above the sounds of the waves.

She barely moves, straining at the line.

"Fuck, pull harder, one, two, heave!" Two of the men at the far end of the line lose their footing, fall, and quickly line up again.

"She must be aground!" one yells. "Look at her angle." The men pull harder in an effort to free her.

I walk past for a different perspective. The creaking at the bow becomes louder as they pull. Then I see it: the dolphin striker, the schooner's metal strut that attaches to the front of the boat from the bowsprit to the hull, is stuck on a wooden piling on the dock. If they keep pulling, it will bend or break.

"The dolphin striker is stuck on the piling," I yell. "We need to release it!"

No one notices.

I yell again as loud as I can with all of my force, "Stop now! You're breaking the striker!"

Most of the men ignore my plea. A burly man, Tony, saunters over to look while the others continue to tug at the stern. As soon as Tony sees the striker he yells, "Stop! We have to release her up here first."

The men stop and stare. Dennis runs over to join us, and the three of us rock the bow of the schooner up and down until her dolphin striker clears the low piling. Once the bow is free, the remaining men on the stern line pull her with minimal effort. She was not aground.

"I guess you need a deep man's voice to be heard," I say to Tony, shaking my head.

"Yep, that seems to be the way the world works," he replies.

But I wonder, does it have to be that way? Can I change my world? I ask the wind.

The words "vestal virgins" tonight had at first dampened my spirit as they intertwined with images from long ago. Yet my role with Billy's boat has given me added strength.

Back in *Centime*'s cockpit I look up the band's name, Procol Harum, on my computer. It means "beyond that which is." Gusts of change swirl around me. I feel destined for a journey "beyond what is."

CHAPTER 14

Guna Wisdom

When all else fails, look for the turtles.

Guna Art Society Member

Playón Chico, Guna Yala, Panama, January 2014

My body is awash in sweat, my heart hammering. I'm choking. Rising up on all fours like a dog, I hit my head on something in the dark. I shift the angle of my neck, to stretch my throat to clear the obstruction. I cough, suck in air with a low groan and cough again. The obstruction dislodges, sliding, sliding, down.

Choking … dying … have … to … get … away.

Arms grab! I struggle. Held in a stranglehold, I can't breathe! I force my escape, hitting my head again, hard. Coughing. Must … get … out! Trapped … choking … blackness.

"What's wrong?!" Dennis yells, his eyes wide as I straddle him, gasping for air. He shakes me hard. "Wake up!"

I collapse on top of him in *Centime*'s cramped sleeping berth.

Years earlier, when Nico was young and I had left his father, I spoke with my therapist about my night experiences. "They're called night terrors," she said. "They're rare in kids, very rare in adults, although I suspect they may be more prevalent than reported. They come before the REM cycle so they're different from nightmares. It's hard to wake a person up. Although they're terrifying when they happen, they're only dangerous when paired with sleepwalking. That's when people get hurt. Do you ever sleepwalk?"

"I run in my sleep and wake up downstairs," I replied.

"That could be dangerous," she says. "Night terrors occur after deep trauma. We can't take the trauma away, but we can work on the healing. Where did the first one happen and how old were you?"

"Philadelphia. I was eleven. I fell down the stairs trying to run away in my sleep."

It's 4:07 a.m.; Dennis gently puts his arms around me as I lay on top of him. He rubs my back and strokes my hair.

"You're safe, honey," he says, in a quiet, steady voice. "It's okay."

My breathing slows. I clear my throat; the rawness feels like I have a bad cold. There's a ringing in my ears. The cabin is still. My body is heavy as if I'd run ten kilometers, carrying a load that doesn't belong to me.

Dennis falls asleep underneath me. His chest rises and falls with an even rhythm; his breathing is loud, close to my ears. He sleeps more easily than I.

Every muscle I have is tight, sore. I stretch my neck trying not to disturb him. I shift my weight to lie next to him, near the cabin door, pushing him toward my side of our small berth. Half awake, I climb out of the berth with care. I grab a blue wool blanket and stumble to the cockpit for fresh air, hoping to shake the remnants of my night terror.

Centime swings on her anchor in a bay in eastern Panama. Small waves rock her. The air is filled with a salty dampness. The night is dark without stars or the moon.

A phenomenon occurs in aviation called the death spiral. It happens in darkness when the pilot can't see the horizon and loses her sense of equilibrium. The pilot mistakenly believes she's flying with her wings level when the plane is actually at an angle. The angle causes the plane to fly in a circle. If the plane's altimeter shows that the plane is falling, the pilot pulls back on the controls to bring the plane up. Her actions tighten the circle and cause the plane to lose altitude at an increasing rate, like water swirling down a drain.

The plane and pilot spin out of control.

Am I spinning out of control? Have I lost my equilibrium? Acts of violence at age eleven have become a lifetime of clutching for control.

Shivering under my blanket, I curl into my seat, knees to my chest, and rub my arms. What is this imagined blockage in my throat that terrifies me? It is the same vision in every night terror, a pearl slowly traveling into my throat where it will choke me. I don't understand its significance. Light breezes cool my wet cheeks. Rain patters against the plastic cockpit windows. I listen to the rain for hours through the night, without answers, as numbness sets in.

We had left Bocas del Toro, Panama, sailing east toward Colombia for two months, passing remote jungles. We will soon turn back before reaching FARC territory, where a revolutionary army hides in the Darien jungle from the Colombian government. We've heard that cruisers who sail too far east have been fired at.

Yesterday we anchored in a deserted bay surrounded by an isolated cluster of islands, fifty miles from the border. This is a peaceful region of Panama known as Guna Yala, an archipelago of 378 islands, self-governed by an indigenous people, the Guna. The mountains, or Yala, are among the world's most undisturbed tropical forests in the northern part of the remote Darien Gap.

The dark of the night turns into a watercolor dawn as I remain in the cockpit. The anchorage is calm. As the sky brightens with oranges and reds, I hear doors bang and the tick, tick, tick of the spark as Dennis lights the propane stove. The kettle whistles and the aroma of fresh coffee fills the air.

Every morning, Dennis makes two pots. It is a ritual, his morning gift to me. He drinks a strong, dark roast. I drink decaf; otherwise, I'm jumpy. Nico's dad, my ex-husband, used to say I had two speeds: "fast" and "off."

Dennis climbs the companionway stairs, holding two travel mugs of steaming coffee, and hands me the pink one. It warms my hands, and I breathe in the delicious aroma.

"Sorry about last night." I pull my blanket tighter and stare into my coffee. My face is bathed with steam from the mug like a facial.

"Don't even think about it." He reaches down, grabs my mug, setting it in one of *Centime*'s cupholders, and pulls me up into his arms.

I stand on my toes, stretching my body.

"What happened?" he asks.

"The doctor calls them night terrors. I haven't had one since I met you. I thought they were over."

"Was it a bad dream?"

"No. I can't wake up, I just run in my sleep. When I crawled over you last night, I thought I was choking on a large, slippery pearl and only had a minute to live. It's always the same: a blockage in my throat, choking, and running."

I sit down on the bench, and take a sip of coffee. He sits next to me, his hand on my shoulder.

"When Nico was little, I imagined dying in my sleep and didn't want him to find my dead body. I was afraid of being a bad mother. I'd try to run out of the house. I thought if he woke up alone and the police found me in the woods that would be better than him finding me. I often woke up on the kitchen floor. I could never unlock the sliding glass kitchen door in my sleep.

"When I had night terrors in Philadelphia, there were two of me. One was innocent and the other evil. The innocent me ran away from the evil me. Now there's only one but the choking is the same. When you tried to wake me last night, I was choking on a pearl."

Dennis squeezes my shoulder. "Why did you have one after all these years?"

"Maybe I was afraid in yesterday's storm."

"Heidi, it wasn't a storm, only a squall. The boat was fine. What were you afraid of?"

"I was worried I might do something wrong, and we'd lose our boat."

"Is there anything I can do? Anything that would help?"

"Just hold me a few minutes more."

Centime swings in a gentle motion as the sun rises across a calm bay. Waves break over an outer reef echoing a distant roar. Light dances over a tiny island of pure white sand. Beyond the island, verdant mountains pierce thick, dark clouds that feed the lush rainforest: the Yala. The vista offers layers of beauty: golden light above stripes of jungle green and dark charcoal, framed by a turquoise sea.

A bright white egret stands tall and still in the shallows. The Guna people say large crocodiles live here. I scan the water's surface for hints of movement; no eyes return my gaze. Impenetrable mangroves reveal sea green bushes held above tubular roots of burnt umber, reflective of jungle homes on stilts.

A lone man paddles his ulu, a canoe made from a hollowed-out tree. He glides toward *Centime* with slow, quiet strokes. Each stroke ripples on the calm sea. I marvel at how adept he is at maneuvering his small boat. He is old, handsome with dark, weathered skin that hangs loose from bony arms and legs, yet the muscles in his arms reveal lasting strength. He smiles, showing only two front teeth.

"Nuedi. An nuga, Heidi." I greet him and ask his name. "Igui ben nuga?"

"Gonzales," he says, with a large smile.

He is an elder tasked to greet us and register our boat into his village. His paddling took an hour or more. I offer him water, fresh pineapple, and rum cake. He smiles again and tells me in a mix of English, Spanish, and Guna that I can stay in his bay for as long as I like.

His granddaughter will soon give birth. He faces the mountains of Yala, praying for his great grandchild's well-being, giving thanks for the continuity of life.

Another ulu arrives. This man offers a papaya and fresh-baked rolls. I buy twenty rolls for one dollar. They are soft and warm, with a hint of cinnamon and sugarcane. The papaya is a gift. I give the man my baseball cap he has been eyeing. He laughs and accepts the hat. Before placing it on his head, he looks inside and points to a "Made in America" tag with an American flag.

"Norte Americano—bueno," he says and gestures a thumbs-up.

A third boat approaches. Our boat, the only foreign boat for miles, has become a trading hub. We are offered more coconuts, bananas, fish, lobsters, and crabs than we can possibly eat.

We make frequent visits to the islands and mainland communities and interact with the people. The Guna work hard to feed their families. The men fish in their ulus on both sides of the reef, sometimes in ocean waves that are daunting for the small size of their craft. Their ulus float just inches above the sea and appear unsteady. The men also free dive for lobsters, crabs measuring up to two feet across, conch, and octopus. When they are not fishing or diving, they paddle to the mainland and walk with women and children to their communal orchards, called fincas, where they gather bananas, coconuts, mangoes, papayas, yucca, avocados, and sugarcane. They cut and haul the heavy, non-sweet white cane that they use as supports for their thatched huts.

Guna Yala is a matrilineal society, where the young men move into their bride's homes when they marry and take on the bride's last name. Women control finance and commerce, and hold equal power. They hold many of the highest-ranking positions: judges and council-leadership representatives.

Girls and women spend time in sewing groups making molas, colorful reverse appliqued fabric art that they create for clothing, artistic display, and to preserve the community's history and sacred beliefs. The bright geometric mola patterns create vibrations that radiate energy. It is said that as a woman focuses on each stitch, she is in contact with her inner world and can communicate with nature's sacred spirits, bringing peace to herself and her community.

We get a lift to the island on a passing ulu. Thatched huts sit just above the water. Laundry dries in the gentle breeze. Dirt paths wind through a maze of homes and palm trees. A man walks by, a long bamboo poll balanced on his shoulder; a basket of ripe mangoes hangs off each end.

Under the palm trees, women sit in groups wearing bright mola shirts, fabric skirts, and artful scarves with animal patterns of frogs, turtles, and crocodiles. Red, orange, and yellow beads, wound into intricate patterns, cover much of their arms and legs. Several women have gold rings in their noses, red vegetable dye on their cheeks, and thin black lines on the bridges of their noses. They chat and laugh, smile, and wave as I pass.

The Guna are wise. Their contentment with a life without much material wealth is a welcome reminder of what is truly important. They live in harmony with their surroundings, rising with the dawn, paddling currents, and harvesting the sea. They appear present and aware of the moment at hand. If I mention tomorrow or next week they often stare. They rarely pay attention to schedules except for the daily rhythms of night and day, dawn and dusk.

While it is hard work gathering food and raising a family, the people are healthy, generous, and exceptionally happy. Children laugh and play, adults smile and wave. Often children hold my hand or do cartwheels and handstands. This is the closest to paradise I have ever been, a long way from the streets of my childhood Philadelphia and my fear of storms.

The next day, Eileen and Mark on *Wavelength* sail in and drop their hook next to us. Eileen smiles and waves. They have traveled a long passage from Grenada past Colombia to prepare for their journey to the South Pacific. I'm grateful for their company.

We spend several days together, the only two foreign boats in this peaceful anchorage. Dennis and I work on *Centime* in the mornings, relax, swim, or meet the Guna in the afternoons, and often join Mark and Eileen on one of our boats for dinner in the evenings.

One hot morning, as I sand *Centime*'s teak, I hear a commotion on *Wavelength*.

"Snake!" Mark says, jumping up, holding a seat cushion.

"What kind?" I say, rushing to *Centime*'s beam, closer to Mark.

"How big is it?" Dennis asks, coming up from below.

"I don't know what kind," Mark yells. "It's three or four feet long and it's pissed!"

"Be careful, it could be deadly," I say, remembering Marina's snake tale.

"Yeah, Eileen's in the cabin closing ports and hatches." he says. "She says if it bites me that she'll suck out all the poisonous venom." He prods the snake with a boat hook, and it rises up and hisses at him. He grabs an oar from his dinghy and pushes the snake toward the edge of his boat. He struggles back and forth, prodding the snake away with the boathook while blocking an escape route with his oar. Then, splash, the snake is overboard. It struggles to right itself and disappears. I scan the water's surface, hoping it doesn't climb back aboard or come to our boat. The snake reappears, hissing, just above the water's surface.

"It's climbing up your dolphin striker!" I shout, watching as the agile snake makes its way toward *Wavelength*'s bowsprit.

Mark runs to the bow and jabs the snake with his oar until it once again falls into the water and disappears. For a moment all is quiet. Eileen enters the cockpit. We search for signs of the snake.

"There it is!" Dennis yells, pointing to *Wavelength*'s stern. "At your rudder."

Mark rushes to the back of his boat and hurls the snake hard off the rudder with the boat hook. It swims away in a wave pattern. I climb into our dinghy, row toward it and take photos. If similar snakes climb on our boat, I want to know whether they are deadly.

A few weeks later, a Panamanian snake expert identifies the snake in my photo as a boa constrictor, common in the rainforest, rare at sea, this far from land. Although they kill prey by stopping blood flow, and bite when threatened, they aren't venomous. Deaths to humans are rare.

Leaving *Wavelength* for a few days, we sail to Esnasdup, an uninhabited island to the west. A mother dolphin and her baby swim by the anchorage and she gently guides the baby away from our boat, their bodies touching. Gunas believe dolphins embody the spirit of birth and rebirth. This bay is quiet, ideal for young dolphins to swim and grow. A magical place for rebirth. We glide past them and set the anchor.

As the boat settles, I pull out our blue Grand Trunk travel hammock. Made from light parachute nylon, it is a compact delight. Lying suspended in part over water, in part over the stern is dreamy. Cooling breezes rock the hammock as the boat swings on her anchor.

The clear water reflects every shade of azure and blue. To my left, the water is deep with rich hues of midnight blue. Under me is clear turquoise. The sea glistens. Anchored in twenty-five feet of water, I can see clean, white sand below, dotted with bright orange starfish bigger than my hand.

Vivid bands of aquamarine define the shallows between two islands. Waves crash high in the gap as they hit the outer reef, sparkling in the sun with champagne brightness. A sleek egret, with its S-shaped neck and dangling feet, flies across the bay, its alabaster feathers in contrast with the blue sea.

Writing in my journal, I lie peacefully in the hammock. Descriptions of night terrors and words of childhood torment clash with the harmony and beauty around me. Setting my writing aside, I focus on the present moment and watch the sea's blues pass by.

No other boats are in this remote anchorage. My sleeveless pink T-shirt and purple bathing suit bottom are quick to remove. Tossing them aside, I dive naked into the clear water, feeling its refreshing coolness.

A Guna man had once told me that I needed a Guna nickname. When I asked him to give me one, he laughed and called me "Ansu," meaning mermaid.

The clear aquamarine water is silky on my skin. I swim like a mermaid letting my arms stream behind me as I twist and turn, my breath underwater forming channels of bubbles that dance across my ample breasts and curvy hips. The muscles in my extremities are strong from cranking winches and raising sails. I feel blessings: a body made to birth and nurture, feminine power and beauty, connection to Mother Earth and her creations. I am humbled to have birthed Nico and honored to be his mother—not a perfect mother but a good mother.

For the first time in my life, perhaps, I embrace my femininity. If I am to be reborn on this sacred journey, let me be female.

CHAPTER 15

A Women's Place

I have all I need — Paradiso!

Guna man, Banedup Island, Guna Yala

Lemmon Cays, Guna Yala, Panama, February 2014

I am alone on *Centime*.

The quiet dawn awakens my senses. Distant waves rumble in Zen-like rhythm. The boat rocks in the gentle breeze. Dennis has left for a visit home, yet I feel he is holding me safe in his arms. Through the day, I am grateful for this calm Guna Yala anchorage, the reef blocking the wilds of the open Caribbean Sea, *Centime* secure with her anchor buried deep in the sand. Later, the evening sky appears endless, with more stars and bright planets than I have ever noticed in Maine. A white meteor streaks across the sky. Nature surrounds me. The sea, wind, and boat are still.

This week, I alone am the skipper, reliant only on myself.

A friend, Lucinda, arrives in a bright pink sleeveless dress with a medallion around her neck. She grabs *Centime*'s hull as she stands unsteady, bracing her tall body with both hands. She catches her hat just as a puff of wind blows it off her face, tipping the boat farther, and laughs. "Well, this is quite the start!"

"It's just the beginning. Are you ready for adventure?" I ask.

"Always!"

In the thousands of miles I have sailed, I have never skippered *Centime* without Dennis somewhere on the boat. I'm excited to try. Though Lucinda has sailed before, she is not an experienced cruiser. I have spent the past few weeks perfecting my anchoring, handling sails alone, creating and uploading routes on the electronic charts, reviewing my notes from Marina. I've learned unique ways to start our old defiant generator, which I swear was made by a man because of the strength needed to pull its starter cord.

The next day, I wake early. Lucinda is already up. I check the oil, close the ports, upload the route, and prepare the anchor. Lucinda is a natural when I give her a quick lesson on steering *Centime*, which she will do for the brief time I handle the anchor.

Soon, the anchor is up and we're free. I take the helm and weave through a busy anchorage with sailboats, swimmers, and coral reefs. We head to the open sea. I slow the boat, raise the mainsail, unfurl the genoa and turn off the engine. A dozen dolphins surround us—a good omen. We ghost along with them for several minutes. Holding my hand on my chest I smile, whispering words of thanks.

Pulling in the sheets to fill the sails, we fly. Lucinda looks at me, her eyes wide, smiling, as she grips her seat. Soon, she's singing Helen Reddy's song, "I Am Woman." I laugh and join in. Sailing fast, we pass pristine islands and half-naked men in ulus. After four and a half hours, we reach magical Esnasdup, my favorite hammock-lying place. *Wavelength*, Eileen's boat, is framed in the gap between the two small, green islands.

Picking a spot, I head into the wind, drop the sails, and drift to a sandy, twenty-foot spot. The anchor falls through the clear, aqua water and holds. I dive overboard, donning a mask, to find it resting solid in the golden sand below.

Through the week, I skipper the boat to three islands. Each anchorage brings new challenges: reefs to navigate, a variety of sea floor conditions for anchoring, and varying configurations of boats, wind, and protection.

I contemplate the power of Guna women to nurture their young, respect nature, and bring creativity, wisdom, leadership, and vision to their communities and beyond. I breathe in Guna strength and feel emboldened to sail beyond my previous experiences. I shed weight and gain courage.

After a week, Lucinda leaves. Dennis returns. We're like young lovers, just the two of us in this tropical paradise. We swim naked in clear, aquamarine waters, snorkel through remote abundant reefs, and read and write in nooks on the boat, postponing work and luxuriating in shared moments.

I'm glowing from skippering *Centime* without Dennis and, after five months in Guna Yala, I carry a new appreciation for feminine strength. The Guna way—with deep respect for women and for Mother Earth—has altered my perceptions. I've dismissed the harsh judgments and false beliefs I had held as a teen and young adult, that females were weak. I bathe in cultural norms where communities thrive when they value and encourage all people.

Unnerving whistles sound when I activate our single sideband radio system. The computer screen flashes subject lines through a slow download of emails. Fidgeting and glancing back and forth to our brass clock, my eyes catch on a headline from Annie's husband. "So sorry, Heidi."

I drum my fingers on the navigation station waiting for the full email to download. The turtle sisters are due to fly to Panama City this morning and take the long trip by jeep and boat to Guna Yala for our annual visit. Layne is unable to come however Bonita, Judy, and Annie are soon to arrive.

"Annie has a bad flu and can't get out of bed. She canceled her flight. She says to tell you and the others she'll be okay but can't come. She sends her love." I slump down in my seat.

Grabbing an iced tea from our small fridge, my comfort drink, I climb to the cockpit. Annie's friendship has been close to my heart since we met in Europe thirty years earlier. It is a loss to not see her and to know she will miss the female energy of the turtle sisters in this matrilineal society. I imagine her flowing auburn hair and how she glows on the boat in the early evening light. I remember deep conversations trying to convince each other that what we experienced as children wasn't our fault. I think of Bonita and Judy, breathe deep, and find renewed excitement for their arrival.

The sun is full and high in the sky. A green and yellow wooden boat with a large green, yellow, and red flag arrives in the bay. It is packed to the gunnels with produce, barking dogs, and people of all ages. Guna women dressed in molas and covered in beads hold baskets overflowing with fruit. Waving frantically at *Centime*'s bow I catch the eyes of the driver. Judy and Bonita squeal when they see me. Dogs bark louder, jump, and wag their tails. The small boat rocks.

"Over there," Bonita says as she points.

"Nuedi, welcome," I say to the driver, with a large wave of my hand, as Dennis joins me in the cockpit. This week, I will joyfully think of Marina, and call this space our clitpit.

The driver turns his boat, throws a line, and rafts on our port side.

"This must be the most beautiful place I've ever seen," Judy says.

"Colorful too, and the people are amazing, full of smiles," Bonita says.

"We missed you," they say in unison and laugh.

Soon *Centime*'s anchor is up, the sail is full. We fly past tiny island after island sailing smoothly toward a favorite anchorage. Like most of the hundreds of island groups here, the Holandes Cays are lush with green vegetation and rimmed with white sand beaches. We anchor in a large oval bay among a cluster of islands scattered around the turquoise bay.

A nearby island has two huts structured with bamboo cane and thatched roofs. On our third day, we sisters don bright-colored swimsuits and swim to shore. The tropical air is fresh with sweet hints of ripe fruit. The sand is smooth under our feet. The sun warms our bodies.

A fit, shirtless Guna man, perhaps in his forties, is opening a coconut near one of the thatched huts. He wears brown shorts that blend with his deep tanned skin.

"Nuedi," I say smiling. "An nuga, Heidi, Bonita, Judy." I greet him and ask his name. "Igui ben nuga?"

"Jose," he says with a broad smile and sparkling teeth, handing us fresh coconut.

"Your island is so beautiful, bonita," says Bonita, blushing and laughing at herself. "We are grateful to walk here. We are from the US, Estados Unidos. I will go back to the US soon. What can I bring to you from America as our gift, regalo?"

"I have ua (fish), dulub (lobsters), suga (crabs), quiquir (octopus), masi (bananas), ogop (coconuts), yauk (turtles)" the Guna man replies, smiling and pointing at his surroundings. "I have all I need—Paradiso!"

We spend the week together in Paradiso, savoring each moment. I pull out the hammock and a worn Buddhist text. The Dalai Lama graces the cover in his plum and gold robe. I read that we are most fully alive when we are in the present moment, absorbing every detail with all of our senses. Tilting my head back, I feel the sun on my face. The boat gently rocks. The sea laps against *Centime*'s hull. A faint warm tropical breeze kisses my face, and I smile.

It is early morning. The turtle sisters have left. The sun is rising, and the sea and wind are calm in our quiet anchorage near the dense green island of Nuinidup. A small boat approaches. A striking Guna with dark penetrating eyes, Lisa, brings her small boat next to ours and grabs *Centime*'s gunnel. She has bright white teeth, and mid-length, wavy jet-black hair. Holding a plastic bag with a cell phone inside, she drops it off for a battery charge. Some families use cell phones to call relatives on different islands. Most don't have any electricity to charge them. They put them in plastic Ziploc bags, row their ulu to a visiting sailboat, and leave the phones overnight or for several nights. Lisa will find us in one of our favorite anchorages later in the week.

A few days pass and she returns waving and shouting, "Nuedi."

"How are you, my friend?" she asks. She visits often and tells us of Guna folklore and traditions. Lisa's chiseled, artistic face is framed with dangling silver earrings, each in the shape of a leaf, blowing in the light breeze. Her purple slacks and blue embroidered blouse flatter her fit body.

"I am happy because of your smile," I say. Lisa is a superb artist, master mola maker, leader, and a keeper of Guna Yalan cultural wisdom and tradition. Because she calls herself Mola Lisa, I lovingly tease her about her beautiful smile.

"I bought you a regalo, a gift." She stands up in her boat and holds out a five-inch piece of wood carved into the shape of a thin doll. It is a sacred talisman meant to bring healing to our friend who is battling cancer. The Guna are a generous and thoughtful people and Lisa has come a long distance to bring us this gift. As I receive it, she wraps her hand around mine, and stares deeply into my eyes while hers glow. "It is a nuchu, a spirit to bring light to your sister's sick friend. It holds the spirit of the forest," she says.

I place my other hand over hers and feel energy in her warm touch. "We accept your gift with deep gratitude. Please, come have breakfast with us. We would love to hear another story," I say.

Lisa is one of several generations of gifted mola makers. Her mother had seven sons and no girls to pass on her important artistic heritage. Sensing the existence of feminine energy in her grandson, Lisa's grandmother asked him if he would like to dress and grow up with gender fluidity and learn her master craft. He became Lisa.

In Guna Yala, women are powerful and revered. To be selected by an elder to have the chance to live as a girl is a privilege. It is common to decide if a child has a sense of belonging to a female world, thinking with the heart of a woman. Those who do can grow up as "third gender' or "omeggid." Like all beings here, they are treated with honor. Lisa loved growing up as "third gender," and now identifies as a happy, proud woman, and a master mola maker.

She climbs into *Centime*'s cockpit, brushes back her rich silky hair with her hand and accepts a cup of steaming hot coffee from Dennis. She stirs in a half-dozen heaping spoons of sugar and takes a few small pieces of pineapple, banana, and mango.

"I will tell you the first story of our four sisters, Ina." She begins:

"A long time ago, there were four sisters who shined as bright as planets in the sky. One day God sent them to Guna Yala. Ina was a medicine woman; Igua represented the trees in the forest and the wood for ulus; Olo and Mani were gold and silver. The women came as spirits to visit four Guna brothers who lived as humans in the mountains.

"None of the older brothers believed they were true spirits, although the youngest did believe, and he fell in love with Ina. He asked her to stay when the other sisters went back to the sky. Soon, the two were married, and after a long happy life, Ina died. The villagers dressed her in a white mola with geometric patterns vibrating with sacred energy. After two days they put her body in an ulu and sent her down the river. She met many jungle animals on the way. Each one loved her and said, 'Take me with you on your journey to

Paradiso,' but Ina said, 'No, you must finish your time in Guna Yala. It too is Paradiso.'

"Ina taught our people to live in harmony and respect all plants, animals, and each other—women and omeggid, third gender, equal to men—and only take what we need. Our children too come from the heart. They can be whatever they want to be: boy, girl, or omeggid. They know inside who they are. Ina reminds us to appreciate each moment, every day we live on Earth, because we already live in Paradiso."

Lisa's energy is tangible. Her dark eyes penetrate mine. She places her hand on mine and stares as she speaks, "Ansu, you and I are part of Paradiso. We must know who we are and embrace the energy and power each moment brings."

s/v Centime, South African Shearwater, Dudley Dix design (Photo/Dennis Jud)

My risk-taking, bungee-jumping partner Dennis (Photo/Heidi Love)

Peter Island, BVI looking toward Salt Island (Photo/Dennis Jud)

Turtle Sisters at Spanny Falls, Dominica (Photo/Dennis Jud)

Lisa, master mola artist, Guna leader (Photo/Heidi Love)

Guna ulu paddler, Playon Chico (Photo/Dennis Jud)

Heidi manages *Centime's* Panama Canal lines (Photo/Eileen Morgan)

Puente Centenario, Panama Canal (Photo/Dennis Jud)

PANAMA CANAL TO FRENCH POLYNESIA

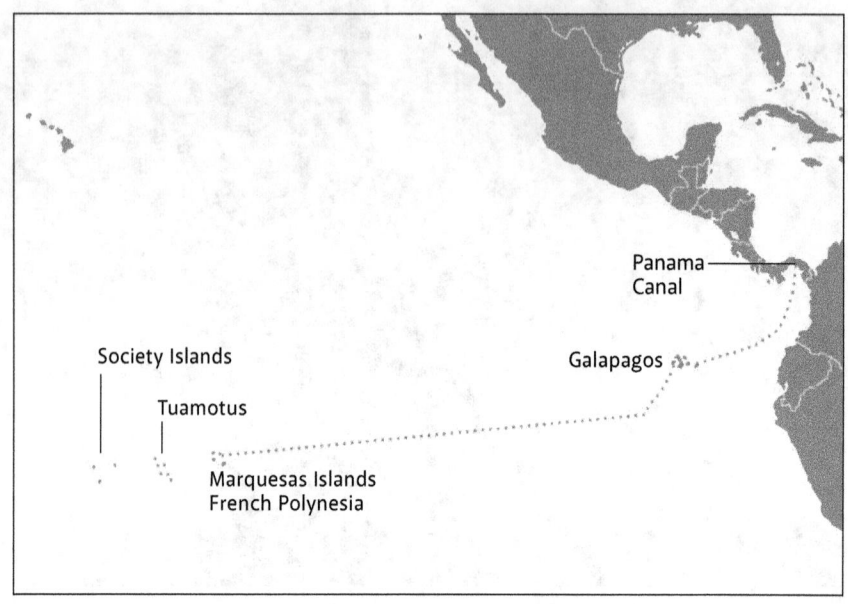

MARQUESAS ISLANDS

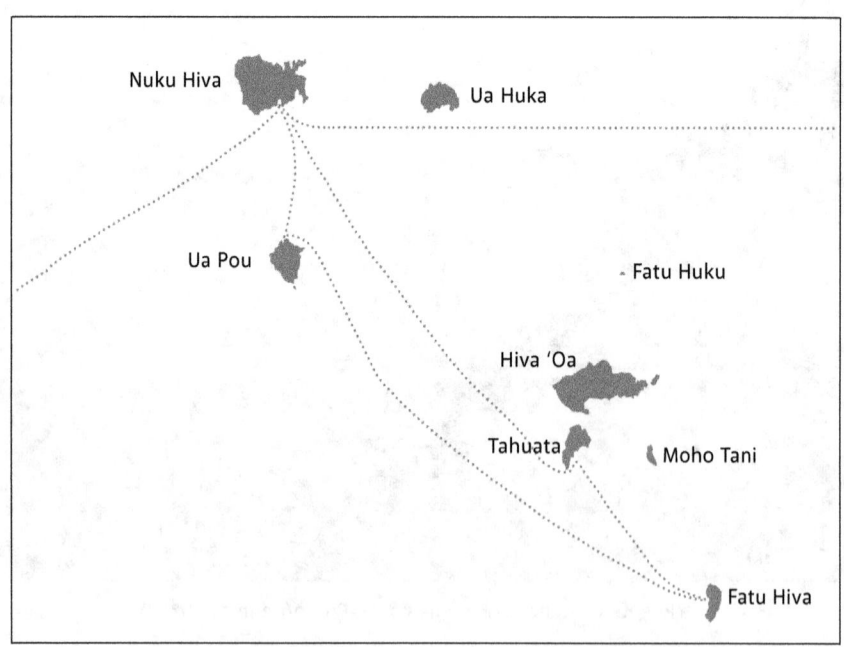

PART TWO

Crossing the Divide

*Turn your face to the sun and
your shadows will fall behind you.*

Maori Proverb

CHAPTER 16

If Life Is a Dream

The journey is the reward.

Taoist Proverb

Colón, Panama, January 2015

    Magnificent royal palms, eighty feet high, stand in tight rows along an abandoned road that stretches beyond the horizon. The road's surface is cracked and rippled where tree roots have expanded under the compacted coral surface. A littering of giant palm fronds, measuring twenty to thirty feet, block the way. These lofty trees shed what they no longer need.

    Dennis and I have sailed near the northern entrance of the Panama Canal. One hundred years after the building of the canal, nature is repossessing the rainforest and coastline. With American personnel gone from the west side of the Caribbean entrance, Panamanians operate the canal from the east, allowing the old Kennedy Loop Road to decay. Jungle vegetation invades ghostly abandoned edifices. The sea erodes the land where waves, traveling unimpeded for over a thousand miles, pummel the shore. Nature reclaims her territory.

    Shelter Bay Marina, where *Centime* rests, is carved out of jungle rainforest. Here nature flourishes. Dozens of howler monkeys scamper across the coral road and swing in the high canopy. A four-foot-long northern tamandua, cousin to the giant anteater, with black-and-white fur and a thick long tail, grazes at the edge of the jungle. Two-toed sloth babies hang upside down, puppy-dog smiles across their faces. Hundreds of tropical birds—yellow and black bananaquits, red-legged honeycreepers, multicolored macaws, and golden-collared manakins—fly through the palm trees with melodious voices. Large migratory hawks and harpy eagles search for prey, while great white herons parade close to the sea.

Monkeys roar like fearsome lions and swing away as I jog under their perches. Their sudden movements create a cacophony of bird screeches above. Running is often meditative for me, quieting my mind, and helping me to relax. Today it's hard to find stillness knowing that we will soon transit the canal from the Atlantic into the Pacific. Once through there is no turning back for us.

A cluster of turkey buzzards takes flight as I run past. Indigenous cultures believe that turkeys symbolize release, giving away what is no longer needed. What do I need to release? What needs to be shed before we take *Centime* through the canal and cross the Continental Divide?

Ignoring nature's signs of shedding trees and give-away birds, I slip back into Western culture and adjust my headphones. Anna Nalick's calming voice sings, "Breathe." With no soul around, I sing aloud and questions spiral through my brain.

What mistakes am I making? Why do I relive past horrors? How do I release these habits?

An iridescent blue butterfly flies down to greet me and follows as if I'm in a Disney animation. Butterfly is the Native American symbol of transformation…blue symbolizes the throat chakra. It seems life is giving me an abundance of hints. It's all surreal.

The song on my iPod changes. I'm transported to a Looney Tunes scene from the movie Space Jam. "I Believe I Can Fly."

Growing up, Nico loved this song. When he was almost five, we found ourselves exposed at the top of a ski mountain in a sudden ice storm. We were stranded after the lift shut down due to high winds. We headed down, skiing close, me worried about losing sight of him in poor visibility. I was close enough to hear him sing. He bellowed out the tune, as strong as his young voice could carry.

"Nico, I'm proud of you," I said when we reached the lodge. You made it by yourself through sleet and ice."

"At first, the ice stung my eyes and I tried not to cry," he said. "I started to sing, Mom. Then, I believed in myself, and it was easy. I'm not going to let a little ice get me down."

I miss Nico in Panama. I look across the jungle. How can I be courageous like him? What must I do to believe in my own worth? I've worked hard with therapists and I'm exhausted. I let the crush of fear weigh me down.

My playlist progresses. The first notes of the *Rocky* theme song play, chasing away defeat. I run hard. The jungle is hot and steamy, the air fragrant. Sweat runs down my face. The sun blinds me. I wipe off the salt and run harder, harder.

The next song by Pink increases the beat as she belts out, "Fuckin' Perfect."

The words surge through me. I spew anger as I sing the words aloud.

I am not worthless. I am not damaged goods. I am not ... ruined. My legs hammer against the coral road. I swing my arms. I run as hard as I can, stomping out the words.

Without warning I'm startled by the loud flapping of wings. I tear the headphones out of my ears. A large bird of prey with a three-foot wingspan and sharp orange talons dives toward my head. I stop abruptly and duck as she swoops over me. Her feathers blur past, inches above my head. Her talons curl with pointed claws, close to my eyes. My breathing is fast and heavy; my heart pounds. Salt stings my eyes.

She lands on a tree branch ten feet away. I absorb her absolute magnificence. I gasp at her stunning black-and-white feathers and powerful presence. Her head and sides are solid black. The very top of her chest is bright white. Her body is a tapestry of black-and-white spots. Her shiny beak is sharp and pointed with an orange spot that matches her claws. Her black eyes glare. I have never been this close to such a remarkable or powerful bird of prey.

I slowly straighten, take a cautious, slow step backward to heed her warning, and stand still. I feel a rush of adrenaline, a transformation: fear shifting to courage, to power. My senses are heightened. Her energy and strength surround me with unexplainable force. I stand tall and squeeze my hands into fists. She is my omen, a talisman I will carry through squalls, darkness, waves, and lightning.

Back at the marina, I find a photo on my computer that matches my bird—a peregrine falcon. In many birds of prey, the females are larger, stronger, and have greater wingspans. She and her sisters can fly at over two hundred miles per hour. I vow to soar with her and carry her force and her courage across the divide.

Today is the day. I wake with the sun, nervous and excited about transiting the Panama Canal. By afternoon, Eileen climbs aboard *Centime* with a huge smile. Her joy is contagious, and we laugh and hug. She and Mark will sail on our boat to help us get *Centime* through the canal, leaving *Wavelength* for a few days at the marina before they travel through again.

Dennis motors *Centime* slowly to the flats, a staging area in front of the canal. We anchor in darkness. A tugboat speeds toward us, her lights are bright. Her powerful wake sends *Centime* into a roll. Roy, a Panamanian advisor, throws me his backpack from the tug and jumps on the deck, timing his movements with *Centime*'s roll. His arms are strong as he lands at the edge of our boat and pulls himself on board. He will take us up through the first three locks to Gatun Lake where we will spend the night.

I have dreamed of this journey for years. My dream is to transit the canal and sail 1,000 nautical miles, over the equator, to the Galapagos. If we succeed, we will continue for another 3,000 nautical miles to Nuku Hiva and finally Fatu Hiva, French Polynesia. The journey will take several months if all goes well. I take a deep breath and vow to take one nautical mile at a time.

The canal has a sordid history. From landslides to diseases of yellow fever and malaria, it claimed tens of thousands of lives in its construction. Today, one hundred years after the first ship transited, we sit on the Caribbean side, ready to rise eighty-five feet through three locks to Gatun, a manmade lake at the halfway point, its sinuous arms encompassing the Continental Divide.

The sun has long set. The wind howls in the dark sea of the flats. Blackness surrounds us: black sea, black sky, black voids blending into one another. Eileen is forward, her voice muffled, lost in the wind. Dennis, Roy, and Mark are forward too, pulling up our anchor. I am alone at the wheel driving *Centime*.

Simultaneously, our compass and instrument lights blow out. Darkness floods the cockpit. I jiggle a switch and bite my lips. The rain, wind, and darkness obscure Dennis's hand and voice signals. Disoriented without instruments, and unable to leave the wheel, I steer *Centime* to where I hope the anchor lies.

Roy rushes midship and relays information to me at the wheel. He orders a quick move to starboard. I obey, blindly driving the boat, my heart pounding. I hate sailing without instruments. I hate the dark. It feels like a metaphor of this journey—driving blindly forward. Anchor up, I follow Roy's command to steer toward the lights of the canal as Dennis fixes the loose electric connection.

Giant gates of black steel dwarf *Centime* as she floats in front of them; her small, white hull appears insignificant and vulnerable. Like a scene from a futuristic Steven Spielberg movie, the gates present an aura of pending doom, opening to unknown worlds. Their massive structures appear endless, stretching from below sea level to high into the sky, blending and becoming one with the darkness.

On the far side of the gate is a wall of water, thirty feet above us, a massive force against the huge panels of thick steel. Eddies of water leak though gaps in turbulent curls. Soon, the first lock will be at sea level and the gates will open to receive us.

We raft together in the dark with two other sailboats, acting as one vessel. Though each boat has a canal advisor on board, Roy is the leader for all three. Dennis takes over the helm while Mark, Eileen, and I tie *Centime* to the catamaran *Free Spirit*, catching their lines and securing them to our boat, and adjusting large black truck-tire fenders between us. *Tuvalu*, a forty-foot sailboat owned by a Swiss and Spanish couple, is to our far right. *Free Spirit*, in the center between us, has German owners. The advisors are Panamanian. Like hundreds of thousands of boats that have gone before us, we are a diversity of nations crossing from sea to sea.

The gates open slowly, regally, before us. Golden light floods through the opening, illuminating our path as we enter. In an instant, the scene is transformed from one of dark ominous gloom to the bright promise of a hundred lamps. Together our three boats enter the first lock.

Seasoned canal workers high above us carry monkey fists, hard rope balls the size of small softballs, attached to strong lightweight twine. Eileen and Mark are at the bow, waiting to catch the first monkey fist and secure the twine to our thick, heavy lines. I'm at the stern waiting for the second pitch. Dennis steers *Centime* in harmony with the other boats according to Roy's instructions. My monkey fist comes in hard like a major-league baseball pitch. I grab the twine and tie it with a bowline knot to one of our heavy lines. The workers on the canal wall pull in the twine and secure our heavy lines to their strong metal bollards. We stand ready to pull in the excess line as the canal water, and our boats, rise.

The gates close, locking us in. Loud screeches of machinery, moving rusting metal, echo off the wall. The vast sea and the route from where we came are now blocked. We are imprisoned in a huge metal trap as we rise—beyond the point of no return.

A giant cargo ship is in the opposite lane. The forty feet of exposed black canal sidewall merges with the black hull of this massive ship. It is hard to discern where the wall ends and the boat's hull begins. We are at the bottom of a lock that is flooding, while the giant ship across from us is at the top heading down in a separate lane. The ship, like an Imperial Star Destroyer from a Star Wars movie, is a massive futuristic monstrosity that dwarfs everything in its path. We sit directly across from her, three toy boats tied together.

Over the next few hours, lines change hands and *Centime* repeats the process, rising through two more chambers, to travel to the canal's highest point, eighty-five feet above the Caribbean Sea. By 10:00 p.m., we enter Gatun Lake. It is still and black. We throw off the lines from *Free Spirit* and float free.

Large crocodiles live in this lake. A nine-footer weighing roughly eight hundred pounds was caught a few days ago after terrorizing canal workers. His photo became a centerfold in the local tabloid before he was safely anesthetized, captured, and released. I've read that the largest can weigh over two thousand pounds. Man-eaters have ended dreams in Gatun. They wait in the dark for unsuspecting sailors who like to swim in the lake unaware or are just reckless.

A six-foot, rusted metal donut floats a foot above the water next to *Centime*. Jumping from the boat onto the donut's wobbly surface sets me on an unexpected, dizzying spin like an amusement park ride. Water rushes over my boat shoes. I think of how fast an eight-hundred-pound crocodile could eat me. Slipping on the tipsy float, I grab *Centime*'s teak rail. As I hang on the rail with most of my weight, the donut moves out from under me. Screaming, I reach down fast with one hand and thread the line. Mark pulls me up like a Raggedy Ann doll and grabs the line. Relief floods through me. We will spend the night here.

Mark sleeps in the forward berth after the long, exhausting day. Dennis sleeps aft. Eileen sits with me in the cockpit. Filled with renewed energy, I open a special bottle of red wine from Patagonia, called Fin du Monde—end of the world—and we raise our glasses.

The Continental Divide feels metaphorical; I am at a crossroads. My sense of adventure, inherited from my dad, clashes with the insecurities I learned from Mother. My Alaskan wildness of spirit battles with fear born on the streets of Philadelphia. At this moment, I remember my falcon and her power. I am strong. I am here. The wine and Eileen's euphoria lift my spirits. I have risen with *Centime*, soared to this height, halfway through my journey.

"You made it, girl," Eileen says. "You're at the Continental Divide!"

"We made it together! I'm so relieved you're sailing *Wavelength* to the Galapagos with us," I say.

"I wouldn't go if you weren't. You give me courage."

"Really? I thought it was the other way around."

"Are you crazy? You and that *Rocky* shirt you're wearing propel us all forward. You're my Rocky."

"Ha, Nico wrote to me about Rocky before we left. I'm wearing the shirt for him. Do you want to hear what he wrote?"

Grabbing my iPhone, I read, "I'm really proud of you and wish I could be with you on this next step. Remember I'm there in spirit! Listen to *Rocky* when you cross the canal and know that in this world anything is possible. From the streets of Philadelphia to cruising through the canal—if life is a dream, you have made yours beautiful." Tears cloud my eyes. Eileen pulls me into an embrace.

Later in my berth, I reread Nico's words while humming the *Rocky* theme song. *Centime* gently sways me to sleep.

I awake in darkness. The boat is quiet, the lake calm. I tiptoe out to the cockpit with my blue wool blanket. Stillness washes over me, and I gaze at the sky filled with stars. I love being awake while the world is asleep, a part of the wind, water, and sky.

The varnished teak in the cockpit is wet with large round beads of rain. I wipe a bench with a quick-drying cloth. As I wring the excess water overboard, I notice the coolness of the fresh water and pat it on my face.

As dawn creeps in, the jungle awakens. Sounds rise: howler monkeys roar, birds whistle, there's a repetitive *reep reep reep* and a low, slow *whooompp whooompp*—animals I can't identify. I look across the bay and see the misty shape of a great blue heron feeding near shore. The land beyond is infinite and lush with jungle vegetation: mangroves reaching up to palms, below a canopy of large deciduous trees, prolific with white and yellow blossoms.

The sky fills with the red, orange, and yellow of the rising sun of a new day. The aroma of fresh-brewed coffee nudges me away from dawn's beauty back to life on *Centime*. I head below and sort through breakfast. The frying pan sizzles with onions, garlic, and peppers as Eileen and I cook and assemble breakfast burritos and douse them with hot sauce, guacamole, and salsa.

The water is muddy and brown as we motor for hours across the lake. Birds soar above us and land in the thick jungle. Searching for crocodiles and monkeys, I laugh about memories of the Jungleland amusement ride I loved during summers at my grandparents' New Jersey cottage. This is Jungleland on steroids, with real and lethal crocodiles.

At the southeast end of Gatun Lake, we raft again with our neighbor sailboats for three down-locks. By late afternoon, we finish our descent in the last lock, and the giant gates open in slow motion. All eyes are on the massive black structures as they slowly reveal the vast, blue Pacific. Again, I feel transported to a futuristic movie where new worlds await. Nervous excitement fills the air. *Centime* inches forward. It is a new season, a new chance to sail beyond fear. We are committing to a 4,000-nautical-mile journey to the center of the South Pacific, embarking on an adventure to find Fatu Hiva's hidden waterfall.

Horns blast. Champagne pops. Sailors on *Free Spirit* cheer, and the couple on *Tuvalu* hug. I release our lines from *Free Spirit* and *Centime* floats free.

"Can you take the helm?" Dennis says. I look up, ready to grab the wheel, and realize he's asking Eileen.

A streak of jealousy flashes through me and my cheeks burn. Why is Eileen driving our boat on this momentous occasion? I want to drive her. I feel like a snubbed, sixth-grade girl. Dennis disappears below as Eileen steers us toward the gates.

"I'll take her," I say to Eileen.

"No, I'm good," she replies, shaking her head, refusing to let go of the wheel.

Music fills the air. The *Rocky* theme blares on a portable speaker. Dennis pops up with a giant smile. He grabs both of my hands pulls me into an embrace and leads me into a dance.

Swirling around and around in the cramped cockpit we laugh as we sway and boogie. The festive mood is contagious. People with tanned faces and Panama hats lining the land side of the canal cheer us on and clap to the beat, as if we're swing-dancing stars on a ballroom floor. Mark and our advisor are clapping too, along with the crews on *Free Spirit* and *Tuvalu*, while Eileen wears a large smile at the helm.

Centime's American flag and Panama's red, white, and blue flag fly free in the wind under a bright blue sky. Her white hull glistens while her decks are littered with lines and extra-large canal ropes.

As the song nears its end, I jump up onto a cockpit seat, waving to onlookers, as tears of joy stream down my cheeks. We both mimic Rocky's voice as he says, "Yo, Adrian, I did it!" I thrust a fist into the air. My voice is strong.

CHAPTER 17

A Patch of Clarity

*Escape from the black cloud that surrounds you.
Then you will see the light as radiant as the full moon.*

Rumi

Las Perlas Islands, Panama, January 2015

It's Friday the thirteenth and "blowing stink," the mariner's phrase for poor weather. The winds howl at thirty knots. The wind generator screams an unnerving, high-pitched warning, like a whistle on an out-of-control train. My body tenses with each sound burst.

We have arrived in Las Perlas, a Panamanian archipelago on the Pacific side, a day's sail south from Panama City. Anchored off the island of Espiritu Santo, we have protection from all directions, except north. Today's winds come from the north.

A gale is approaching. We let out an extra fifty feet of anchor chain to strengthen our hold. We wrap heavy fire hose around the lines at the chocks to act as chafing gear. The boat pitches up and down, back and forth at the end of her chain and rope snubber, like an excited guard dog on a short leash. The boat appears secure; we have done all we can to prepare.

A line of flying birds stretches for miles in long formation. Black cormorants stream in a large arc around the top of the island, passing *Centime* eight feet away. *Wavelength* is anchored a few boat lengths ahead of us and the birds funnel between our two boats. Dennis and I stand on the bow, watching in silent awe. The collective flap of wings stirs something deep and powerful. I listen, spellbound. It is the second time, after the peregrine falcon that I've heard the close flapping of wings. I read once in *National Geographic* that a bird flying in formation can trace the same wing pattern as the one in front of her, like walking behind someone in deep snow who has broken the trail.

One by one in rapid succession, the birds take refuge on the beach two hundred feet away. Soon the white strip of sand turns black as hundreds land. The line of birds still in flight continues toward the crowded beach, until a second formation veers off to land at another small cay. It too is soon overcrowded. The line appears endless. There must be two or three thousand birds. They look exhausted, flying against and across the wind. How far have they come? How far must they still travel? What drives them and why?

I think of my own journey, what has brought me to this place far from home and what compels me to continue. At times, I feel like I'm in a *National Geographic* journal embraced by nature and adventure. Other times, I feel more like I'm in an Alfred Hitchcock drama, trying to outrun fear.

Darkness falls, the wind continues to build. My stomach growls from skipping dinner. Hoping to fall asleep early, I toss about in the rolling berth, jumping up periodically to look through the dark porthole to try to determine where we are in the cove. Blackness is all that is visible. I wonder what might happen when we're halfway to the Galapagos if the wind is this strong. By 3:00 a.m., the wind is relentless. Sleep has proven elusive.

Giving up on rest, I climb over Dennis to recheck our anchor on the GPS screen. Dozens of black pinpricks appear in a circular pattern around our original boat mark, indicating that the anchor is holding. I look at a second screen on an iPad application. The two instruments confirm our position.

I don my rain jacket. As I step into the dark cockpit, a mix of fresh rain and salt spray saturate my face and rain gear. My hair whirls around my eyes. Wet strands stick to my face. Gripping the lifeline, I walk uneasily in bare feet across our shifting, jerking boat. The deck is wet and slick, and I curse myself for not wearing my lifejacket. My feet grip the rough nonskid. From the bow I see a dark obscure shape ahead, *Wavelength*. She appears secure and well positioned; both of our anchors are holding.

The only light is in Eileen's cabin.

Returning to the cockpit, I huddle under the dodger and listen to the wind, waves, and rain. The wind generator continues its high-pitched squeals. Darkness too remains.

By dawn, the squalls have passed, the sea is calm.

After pulling up the anchor, we hoist the sails and head southwest toward the Galapagos, starting our 1,000-nautical-mile journey across open ocean. *Centime* is majestic with full sails under a steady fourteen-knot northwest breeze. *Wavelength* follows a mile behind.

Glimpses of Panama's outer islands recede and then disappear into endless blue. Large white birds with black-tipped wings dive for fish. A pod of dolphins crosses our bow, diving through *Centime*'s bow wave as she skims across steady winds and strong favorable currents. The day is warm and the sky cloudless. I take off my shoes and bra, and leave behind expectations and social constraints of land.

The bright day turns into a dazzling night. The sky is alight with hundreds of stars and familiar constellations: Orion, Pleiades, the Big Dipper, and Cassiopeia. An orange-gold crescent moon waxes overhead. My first night watch of this passage starts at 8:00 p.m. while Dennis sleeps below. By midnight, the moon sets, the sea turns black, and the stars appear brighter. A familiar river of sparkling white phosphorescence flows behind *Centime* as she sails with grace, creating patterns of radiant white foam.

On night watch I feel small, at times helpless, in a vast, powerful, and borderless sea. The horizon has no clear boundaries; shades of gray blend into more gray shades in all directions. It's me and the boat versus the wind and sea.

Tonight however, *Centime* dances with the sea as the wind fills her mainsail and genoa. Her hull, her body, glides and dips, propelled through crests and troughs as if she's a tango dancer arching her back and rebounding under a tent of twinkling lights. Magic and enchantment overwhelm as mystical energy surrounds me.

The sky overflows with stars and suddenly I feel larger than a moment earlier. A hard-to-explain expansion encompasses me as if I'm an enraptured dervish connected to immense power beyond my control. Tears run down my cheeks as gratefulness for spirit, power, and love, completes me, unfolding into euphoria. The sea, the boat, and I—are one.

It's not me versus nature fighting for control that I can never achieve, but rather being connected and aligned with forces more powerful than I can imagine. It's not a conquering of fear, it's living through the fear and finding courage beyond what I thought I had. It's not being alone but instead being a part of something far greater than myself. For one brief night, the sailor in me steps outside of everyday life and feels the profound.

At 1:00 a.m., Dennis takes over. I crawl into the bunk with *Centime* heeling to port and then starboard. Mother ocean rocks me to sleep in my cradled berth.

Days and nights pass as we travel farther from land. *Wavelength* has disappeared behind us. No boats are visible. *Centime* is a tiny speck alone in the midst of an endless sea.

After a few days at sea, I adjust to her rhythm. During my night watch, the genoa flaps in the wind; I jump to reset it. Hypervigilant, I adjust the sails to go as fast as we can, to arrive as soon as possible and shorten our time at sea. *Centime* catches the wind with her sails well-balanced, and my body relaxes. The sailing is perfect; the night is perfect. With so many miles to go, I wonder why I am rushing. My continuous vigilance won't make much of a difference. I try to let go of my perceived control.

Moving forward in the cockpit, I stare at the vast universe. Cool fresh breezes touch my face and blow my hair away from my eyes. The sky is filled with stars with the fascinating Southern Cross to port, and a stunning, golden quarter moon to starboard.

Who else might be eyeing the same moon or any of these stars? Eileen and Mark, a dozen miles away, are seeing them. Nico in Montreal might notice the sky tonight. All whom I love, and those who have come here before me, are here with me. I am not alone. This night, I am not afraid.

I remember a song, "I'll Be Seeing You", released during World War Two. In the song, love transcends time and distance as war separates a woman and her lover. She imagines him in places that they had been together. At the end of the song she sings about looking at the moon and seeing him.

The air is warm, yet I have goose bumps on my arms. I begin to sway to my own song, of wind and sea, performing a light, half dance on a sloping deck. We have traveled 400 nautical miles with 600 left before arriving at the Galapagos. There is nowhere else I would rather be.

I notice movement forward, another trick of shadow and light. A large, sleek bird appears, flying above the bow, and is gone. She fades in and out of vision like an apparition. As the boat rocks to the left, she is illuminated. Her orange beak and bright white body are brilliant. Contrasting black feathers trail at the edge of her massive wings.

She soars with the wind, aligned with the boat, without flapping her wings. She must be four feet across. She glides effortlessly, hundreds of miles from land, three feet from me. As the boat rocks to the right, she appears smaller and fades to a point of invisibility before the light illuminates her again.

A second bird appears, her mate. They fly together at the bow, drop back to the stern, circle the boat and repeat their motions. As they get close, I watch them dive, and surface with small fish. They use the light of the boat to lure and find prey. They fly with me for hours, through my entire watch, offering a dazzling display. I later read they are Nazca boobies, cousins to the famous blue-footed boobies, endemic to the Galapagos. They appear every night and accompany us toward their home.

When we are halfway to the Galapagos, Dennis makes a celebratory dinner with potatoes, chickpeas, carrots, onions, peppers, and aromatic spices. We sit together in the cockpit, savoring the food as *Centime* sails with the wind vane, steering a smooth and steady rhythm.

"The food is spicy, fitting for a midway celebration. This sail is one of the best I can remember," I say.

"Did you notice the white sparkles on the sea last night?" Dennis says.

"Yes, so beautiful: the sea, the sky, the stars, and the moon."

"I wrote about it in my journal."

"Will you read it?"

He pulls out a small leather journal. "Thousands of stars in the sky, millions more unseen, a milky way of phosphorescence trailing behind *Centime*. Curious how *Centime*'s trailing universe and my own universe exist through agitation, alive by being jostled … ephemeral, eternal."

"Wow. Beautiful. Do you really mean that your universe exists through agitation?"

"I'm not wired for normal. I feel most alive when I'm at the edge of risk."

"That's true, yet you had this soulful, awe-inspiring experience just sitting still and being present under a star-filled sky. Your writing about those micro ecosystems being their own milky way, that's profound."

He smiles, and we both giggle. We're tired and giddy. Soon the giggle becomes a full laugh at the absurdity of this moment in the middle of the sea.

A couple nights later, I'm on watch as Dennis sleeps below. The sky is bright with stars. The golden waxing moon illuminates a path forward on the sea. The breeze is steady, and I have three sails up and full.

Suddenly, the light dims. The moon disappears. I can still see very bright white ahead. I turn to find dramatic, black clouds roiling behind. The wind is light and warm. I feel a chill.

Dark clouds move fast to overtake *Centime*. I memorize the position of the most ominous one. Heading into the cabin, I grab my rain jacket, close the ports, turn on the radar, and rush back to the cockpit. As the darkest clouds race toward us, my heart beats fast; my mind spins. I take off my life jacket, put on the raincoat with the life jacket over it, and hook my tether to the boat.

Pulling in the staysail by hand, I turn the winch around and around, sweating under the jacket. Clouds surround *Centime*, everywhere except directly overhead. The stacked clouds form an odd sight: forward, aft, left and right, with an unusual point of clarity directly above. I am sailing under the only open patch of cloudless sky.

I repeat a sailor's rhyme … "Rain before wind, bring the sails in. Wind before rain, maintain." Am I remembering it correctly? The wind has diminished, and it is raining. I consider waking Dennis and decide to wait. I use the hand winch to reef the genoa into a small triangle. The boat slows. My heart pounds. My throat is dry, and I take a large gulp of water from a nearby travel mug.

The darkest sky is to the right, moving toward us. The clouds appear ready to release the anger of the universe. The patch of clarity in the clouds remains overhead, moving with *Centime*. I release the wind vane, start the motor and turn on the autopilot for more control in shifting winds. I can adjust our course, but I can't outrun a squall.

I need to reef the mainsail to make it smaller. My hands are clammy as I rub them together. To reef, I have to go forward on deck to release the preventer, a line that keeps the boom from jibing. I clench my teeth, envisioning myself on the low side of the angled deck as the squall hits, without a preventer, in shifting winds. I hyperventilate, remembering the mantra Annie told me to use when I'm afraid: "Breathe in strength … breathe out calm."

I hook the tether of my life jacket on a safety jackline and slowly creep out on the low side of the deck. The boat heels close to the water. Sitting on top of the sloping cabin, gripping the lifeline, I slide one inch forward at a time. It's dark ahead. My flashlight jiggles on my wrist. Placing it in my mouth to hold it steady, silently cursing for forgetting my headlamp, I continue slowly, hand over hand, toward the preventer. A gust of wind batters my face and *Centime* heels at an acute angle to the sea, racing ahead, faster and faster. Waves splash on deck. I blink to remove the salt sting and clear my vision.

The clearing overhead is gone. Bracing my body, hunched low under the boom, I release the preventer. Next I secure the newly released preventer line to the hull. The boom springs free with a strong force against my hands. Holding my breath, I inch further forward to secure the preventer. *Centime* pitches in the waves. I grip the mast through fresh seas while Dennis sleeps below.

Sitting on the low side, the water and waves are close. I gasp for breath. We're whirling ahead fast like a sick amusement park ride. My head spins. "Rain before wind … wind before rain … Rain, rain, go away, come again another day … breathe in strength, breathe out calm … breathe … just breathe… just breathe."

I am near helpless with vertigo.

The sea churns. *Centime* moves like she's sick too.

Breathe … breathe … Remembering my falcon helps my head to clear. I inch back to the cockpit and finish reefing the main.

The loud grinding electric winch and flapping mainsail wake Dennis.

He yells from his porthole. "Need help?"

"I'm okay." The smaller, properly-set sails make a sharp improvement in our sailing. The boat is now under control. The clouds are moving fast with a shifting clear spot ahead to starboard. Turning, I scan the horizon aft to search for *Wavelength*. It's black where *Wavelength* should be. My watch shows 12:18 a.m. I wonder if Eileen is on watch; she often has the midnight shift. I hope all is well.

The squall passes, and the wind drops. I unfurl the jib and put out the staysail. *Centime* moves ahead at a steady speed.

I grab the last chocolate bar and savor slow bites of luscious flavor. It is my reward. Closing my eyes, I lick the melting sweetness from my lips. Eileen loves chocolate too; we both deserve rewards for sailing alone tonight in the middle of the sea while our spouses sleep. I don't know how she's fared, but I'm proud of us getting this far. I let the chocolate linger.

Dennis emerges at 1:00 a.m. for his watch. *Centime* sails smoothly without a hint of the night's turmoil, the sea's anger, or my deck acrobatics. All that remains is my secret pride in handling the squall alone.

CHAPTER 18

A Journey of a Thousand Miles

An awake heart is like a sky that pours light.

Hafiz

The North Pacific Ocean, February 2015

    Three days later, the wind is steady. The sky is bright blue, with low, puffy fair-weather clouds. The clear horizon stretches far into the distance. *Wavelength* passed us several days earlier. Not a single boat, buoy, bird, or dolphin disturb this vast expanse. *Centime*'s sleek white hull slices through the blue monotone, creating a white froth of wake lapping against her sides in a natural rhythm of sea against hull.

    The wind whips around my face. Untamed hair swirls in the breeze, tickling my salt-encrusted eyelids. I dip my hand into the sea, creating my own plume of spray, and laugh. We have traveled for 727 miles since Panama and have ten miles to go until we reach the latitude of zero degrees, zero point zero minutes—the equator. I watch the numbers on the GPS diminish, and smile.

    We sail southwest in the trade winds. Like hundreds of thousands of seafarers before us, we will soon cross from the Northern to Southern Hemisphere. A naval tradition celebrates the first time a sailor crosses the equator. Before the crossing, the sailor is a "pollywog." To become an official "shellback," or experienced sailor, one needs either to swim around the boat or be doused with salt water as she crosses. Part of this tradition is to give thanks to

Neptune by spilling a bit of alcohol overboard.

A wake filled with bubbles trails behind *Centime*, reminding me of the champagne that I'm chilling below. As a safety precaution, we usually don't drink when our anchor is raised. Today we plan to break tradition and open a bottle of Moët et Chandon that we've saved for over a year. We bought it as a symbol of hope and inspiration to encourage this crossing.

Straining my eyes, I look toward where we will cross the equator. In the far distance a faint white shape fades in and out of vision. I wonder if it could be *Wavelength*. I haven't seen them for days. I rush below and turn on the AIS, an instrument that identifies boats nearby. *Wavelength* is seven miles ahead. I hope she waits and doesn't cross without us.

I put my face into the wind to feel the breeze on both ears. Once, when I was twenty, I sailed with a wise old racer who said my ears were my most precise instruments. I face the wind and adjust the angle of my head to feel the wind pressure equally on both ears. I whisper words of thanks to my old racer friend and his boat *Feather*.

As I adjust the sails, the boat picks up speed. I disengage our wind vane, which we've nicknamed Grace, and hand steer. *Centime*'s creamy white sails are full and bright, reflecting light from the late afternoon sun. Three sails propel us forward, each in balance with the next. *Centime* catches my excitement and performs perfectly as she races ahead. I smile and hold the wheel tighter, bracing my leg against the cockpit seat, as she heels.

I hear Dennis stirring below as he wakes from a nap. I've been on watch for four hours and it is time for him to take the helm.

"Nine miles to the equator," I shout, and he lifts himself halfway out of the cabin.

"Where's *Wavelength*?" he replies.

"Six or seven miles dead ahead. She must be waiting for us because we're catching up."

"You're sailing fast! Perhaps we're gaining on her."

He goes below and I hear water pouring. The rich aroma of coffee mixes with the fresh, salty breeze. I breathe in the welcome fragrances and imagine sipping coffee at a sidewalk café.

Wavelength gets clearer, faster than I expect. My eyes jump from her to our speed indicator and back.

The wind builds and my heart races. *Centime* is heeled over at a sharp angle close to the wind and sea. Pressure on the wheel mounts as I wait for Dennis to emerge from below.

"Dennis, can you come up in ten minutes?" I ask. "We'll be on top of *Wavelength* in twenty. I'd like you to take over."

"Twenty minutes? Six miles? Honey, even if they're sitting still, we won't catch up for another hour," he replies.

Dennis's response is logical. It will take us an hour to travel six or seven miles, more to catch up if *Wavelength* is still moving forward. His logic doesn't match the view before me. We're closing in at a rapid pace. Ten minutes later the shape of their hull is clear. I hold the wheel tight to keep her steady.

"She'll be here much sooner than you think, matey!" I say, smiling broadly.

Dennis cocks his head back and rolls his eyes as he looks at me, reminding me of Marina's dismissal when I told her about the flashing green navigation light. I point forward, laughing. *Wavelength* is racing toward us, less than two miles away. Bright white waves break off her hull. She has a full cache of sails hoisted and looks brilliant, glistening in the sun.

"Woah! I'll be right up," he says, grabbing his coffee mug.

Dennis arrives in the cockpit as *Centime* heels at top speed. *Wavelength* approaches on our starboard side.

"Mind if I take the helm?" he asks.

"Mind if I go forward?" I reply.

"Go right ahead. Hold tight."

Grabbing the camera and securing it in a pocket, I hook my life vest tether onto the safety line. Inching forward as I sit on the high side, I hold the lifelines with both hands. *Centime* pitches with the waves like a crazy horse. Reaching the bow seat, I wedge my body into a secure position. We fly past each other in opposite directions and I yell a joyful "Ahoy!" and Eileen waves excitedly from their cockpit.

The bright sun is descending in the sky ahead. The moon, nearly full, is rising behind. Our two boats are perfectly aligned between the setting sun and rising moon.

In less than a minute, Mark has passed us and turned *Wavelength* around, racing to catch up. *Wavelength* is a long, fast ketch with two masts, greater sail area, and a longer waterline. *Centime* puts up a good race. I watch the expression on Dennis's face as he concentrates on taking advantage of every bit of wind, smiling from the excitement of the game. Mark and Dennis are competitive helmsmen who enjoy jockeying for position. Each has an intimate knowledge of how to push his craft to her limits.

The sun is low in the sky, creating a gorgeous golden path directly ahead. The scene is magical; the path mystical.

"This is sweet," Dennis says. "Less than half an hour to the equator. We're really doing this, honey."

"*Wavelength* is beautiful," I say.

"So are you," he replies, smiling.

Across from us on our port, Mark sits on the low side of his cockpit, twenty feet away. I watch Eileen hand something to him. He puts on a red pirate's bandanna, with long, black hair.

"Arrggg!" he yells, reminding me of the Pirates of the Caribbean. We laugh as he lets go of his wheel with one hand and swings a fake sword in our direction.

"*Wavelength*, this is *Centime*," I call on the radio.

"Go ahead, *Centime*," Eileen replies.

"Looks like Johnny Depp has captured his beautiful damsel. Don't fight him off too hard. He's kinda cute in a rogue way. And that boat he's stolen is a handsome ship," I say.

She laughs. "I surrendered long ago. He can sail me into the sunset and beyond."

I slip below to get ready to cross the equator, putting on my favorite blue swimsuit. Remembering Nico's request when I crossed the canal, I don my red *Rocky* shirt in his honor. I put on a gray leather ring that Eileen's sister made and a lucky seed necklace from Belize that Bonita gave me. Annie's stone turtle is in my pocket. Many friends and family members have supported this dream; I will carry them with me across the line.

Grabbing a plastic tub, I fill it with two wine glasses, saltine crackers, a wedge of Spanish Manchego cheese, and a handful of Judy's homegrown, preserved dilly beans. With the boat heeling, it is tricky to open the refrigerator and balance the food. The refrigerator containers are stacked like a game of Jenga, threatening to crash to the floor. I wedge my body against the counter and use both hands and an arm to try to keep a semblance of order as the boat flies through the waves. With minutes to go, I force the door on the fridge closed, grab the champagne and take my seat next to Dennis.

"*Centime*, who is going to do the countdown? Johnny here has his hands full ravishing me; it's up to you," Eileen says.

"You've got it … Zero degrees, zero minutes and point zero … two … zero to go … and the excitement builds."

Dennis races *Wavelength* toward the equator. His eyes dart from sails, to instruments, to *Wavelength*, to me.

"This is unbelievable!" he shouts.

"Zero sixteen, zero fourteen, the crowd is going wild."

The sun is close to setting and the entire horizon is aglow. We couldn't have timed it better. Two booby birds soar and glide in circles around *Centime* and *Wavelength*.

"Zero ten, nine, eight, two birds join to escort the pollywogs across."

"This is fucking awesome!" Dennis says as he grabs the camera, steering with one hand, muscles bulging in his forearm. He aims the camera at the GPS to record a screen filled with zeros.

"Zero four, zero three." My voice cracks. I have no more words.

The sun is at its lowest angle. The sky is a mix of gold, pink, and crimson. The dial on the GPS reads 00.00.00.

"We're across! We're shellbacks!" Dennis says, laughing. Mark heads off to port and Dennis puts *Centime* on autopilot.

"Come here," he says, reaching out. We embrace as the boat rocks. Falling over, he braces his body against the pedestal that holds the wheel and presses me tight against him.

"Thank you! Thank you!" I say and linger in his arms.

I click a button on the iPod and the *Rocky* theme song plays while we hum and dance. My breathing is quick. I'm charged with energy. I look across at Eileen, jump onto the upper side of the boat and try to click up my heels in a modified jig, while the boat sails at a steep pitch. It's a clumsy attempt.

The sky is streaked with color.

"Neptune says we gotta either swim or get doused," Dennis says, his eyes sparkling. "What's your preference, matey?"

I stare at him, my mouth open. If the wind and sea were calm, it might be an option; they are not.

"Don't you DARE go overboard in these winds. If you do, I WILL NEVER EVER sail with you again." Dennis loves risks and might really do it.

He laughs and grabs the bucket, throws it overboard and fills it with seawater. He pulls off his T-shirt and hands the full bucket to me. "Do me the honors, princess." He grins.

He has never looked so happy. I grab the bucket and douse him, full force, with cold seawater.

"Ohhh," he shrieks. "Now it's your turn, pollywog."

He fills the bucket faster than I can remove my red *Rocky* shirt and throws the water at me, laughing. I grab a handhold to steady myself, soaking wet, water dripping from my hair into my eyes as the wind whips it into a frenzy.

"You better pop that champagne, boy, or I may throw you to the sharks myself, just for spite."

Dennis pops the cork into the sea and the champagne flows over the top. The crimson colors fade from the sky.

A day later, the sky is clear, dotted with dim stars, the moon, full and bright. The sea is alive, sparkling with reflected moonlight. *Centime* sails slowly in light winds.

We are near the Galapagos. I yawn, exhausted, ready for a calm anchorage and a full night's sleep. We have 23 nautical miles to go and should arrive by early morning. This is our last night at sea on this leg of the journey.

Dennis takes over the watch, and I fall into a deep sleep. I wake in the gray of dawn with a hope that we are outside the harbor. Like a child on Christmas morning, I scurry up to the cockpit, stumbling on the steps as the boat rocks in an erratic motion. I scan 360 degrees of the horizon. No land, no harbor, are in sight. My heart sinks. *Centime* is dead in the water without a puff of wind, moving from side to side in the waves like a ghost ship.

"How far to go?" I ask Dennis quietly, unable to disguise my sadness.

"Twenty nautical miles," he says.

"What?!" I cross my arms over my chest. "You've only sailed THREE miles in FOUR hours? Why aren't we motoring? What's going on?"

"We're waiting for *Wavelength*. They're having a coolant issue. The wind has died, and they don't want to run their engine for long. I want to be close if they need a tow."

Disappointment floods through me. I am desperate to be on land.

"I want to be there. I want to sleep. I am so tired." I become a whiny five-year-old.

"Honey, I'll stay on watch. Why don't you get more sleep? The wind will pick up as the sun rises. We'll be in soon," he says. I head below, pouting. We spend the day and evening adrift in an uncomfortable pattern of seasick motion. I take a sleeping pill.

Waves splash against the hull. The boat heels, forcing me awake. After a full night of aimless drifting, *Centime* is sailing again. Light streams through the porthole. I poke my head into the cockpit. Jagged, burnt-umber mountains pierce a golden sky, a silhouette of splendor. The sun rises above the mountains through layers of clouds of all shapes and sizes, illuminating edges. I close my eyes and clench my fists with excitement. This is the first land I have seen for nine days. "Yes," I whisper, and bound into the cockpit.

Centime sails herself with the wind vane as Dennis takes pictures. Every instant, the morning light changes, from a vibrant gold, to pink, and crimson. I bathe in beauty. The land is close, the details clear. As the sun rises, the ocean changes from indigo to luminescent teal. Every feature and color are an artist's delight.

Round, dark shapes dot the sea ahead. Dozens of turtles lie sleeping on the surface. They float slowly at our side. As the boat's wake gives them a small nudge, some poke their heads out of the water and then dive. Others float undisturbed, with their dome shells high above the waterline. The clear water offers a distinct view of dome tops, flapping feet, tails, and diving heads.

Splash. Splash. Splash. Dozens of sea lions arrive, jumping and frolicking around the boat. A few lift their necks and strain to look left and right, making eye contact as I hang over the lifeline. They swim on their backs next to *Centime* as she sails forward. Several do somersaults and twist over each other as they play. They grunt and blow air from their lungs. We laugh at this entourage of noisy sea lions and sleepy turtles as they escort us toward the harbor.

Dramatic black volcanic outcrops contrast with the pure aqua sea, white clouds, and blue sky. Hundreds of birds glide above the rocks. Most of the outcrops are covered with sea lions, black iguanas, boobies, and storm petrels.

Nearing the harbor, tears of joy stream down my cheeks: forty-three years, nine thousand miles, and the first of two childhood dreams realized.

CHAPTER 19

The Galapagos

It is not the strongest of the species that survives, not the most intelligent that survives. It is the one that is the most adaptable to change.

Charles Darwin

Philadelphia, Pennsylvania, June 1967

    It's a sunny day, the first of June. I'm eleven years old when a large moving van parks in front of our home on Wayne Avenue, Philadelphia. Mother and I sit, numb, on the porch and watch souvenirs of our lives disappear into the back of the large truck. Did they pack the box under my bed, the one with my poems and my skate key? It doesn't matter—nothing matters—yet I still want to linger with what once was.

    I ask Dad if I can ride in the back of the moving van alone with my stuff; he won't allow it. He starts up the silver Chevy with Mother sitting next to him. I sit behind Mother and stare at the home I grew up in: the three-story, narrow, brick twin house, with the porch where we fed homeless beggars, the sidewalk where I played hopscotch and double-Dutch jump rope, and the alley that separated my home from Terry's. No one is home at Terry's. My best friend is gone. I can't say goodbye. I haven't seen her since before the assault. I will never see her again. I feel a thickness in my throat.

    A part of me, my best part, has been torn away. For seven years, Terry was my twin and my hero. I was her shadow. I looked up to her and envied her wildness. I can never replace her. Something inside me aches, and the pain won't go away, will never go away. I believe I have ruined her life, and I can't tell her I am sorry. I hold back buckets of suppressed tears. Terry, I am so very sorry.

Vern sits across from me in the back seat. His eyes cold, he frowns, turns his back to me, and moves closer to the window. He's just finishing eleventh grade and won't be able to graduate from Northeast high school in Germantown or be close to his girlfriend. It's my fault. On our hour drive to the suburbs no one says a word. Vern no longer looks at me.

The drive to our new home takes me away from much of what I love. My fear and shame travel with me.

Our new suburban home and neighborhood are pretty, yet I don't belong. My well-worn rummage-sale clothes are visible reminders that I am an outsider from a different class with a different history. With only two weeks left in the school year, Dad insists I finish sixth grade in our posh neighborhood. He hopes I will make new friends before summer vacation. He wants me out of the house, separated from Mother as he starts his new job.

One of our neighbors has a daughter, Nancy, who is my age. Dad asks her if she will walk with me to school on my first day. Mother isn't well enough to take me; she has her own trials. I hear her crying after Dad leaves for work.

Nancy arrives on Monday morning, and we walk toward school. The street is lined with large homes and big, green maple trees. It is greener and quieter than my school route in the city. Nancy, who is tall, thin and has carrot-red hair, swings a bright red book bag as she walks, chatting.

"You got a boyfriend?" she asks.

"Nope," I say. Our move happened fast, and I never had the chance to give my friends our new address or ask for theirs. I wonder if I'll ever see any of them again.

We stop at an intersection. A boy our age, wearing a yellow chest strap and a silver badge, smiles at Nancy and me. She giggles. He spreads his arms wide, his back to us, blocking our way as a car passes.

"That's Robbie," she whispers, her hand cupping my ear. "Would you go out with him?"

"No." I shake my head as the word catches in my throat.

"Why not? He's so cute. Anybody would die to go out with him."

"I … I just don't want to," I say, looking down at the ground, holding my black-and-white notebook close to my chest.

"C'mon, don't you like him?" Her voice gets louder.

"Leave me alone," I whisper. A flash of orange-brown eyeglasses invades my thoughts, and I begin to burp.

"Hey, Robbie," she says. "She thinks you're cute."

The guard turns and smiles as he looks at me. "Yeah? You think I'm cute?" he asks.

"I … I …"

"Tell him," she says as she gives me a not-so-gentle nudge.

"I … I can't." The glasses aren't going away.

"I guess she thinks you're ugly." She shrugs and laughs.

"Tell her she has fat lips. No one would want to kiss those fat lips anyway," he says.

I turn and run back toward my house with tears streaming down my cheeks. The orange glasses follow.

An old weeping willow tree stands bowed in the far corner of our yard. The tree has two large trunks: one that stands erect, the other bent for dozens of years, like a hunched-over old crone. Low-hanging branches from the bent trunk touch the ground and provide a hidden curtain, a partially opaque screen from the world. Sitting under the willow, I cry until dinnertime. I miss school that day. No one notices or cares.

I'm different from the children who live here. My dad tries to help. He makes a tree swing on one of the willow's branches, using a single thick rope and a wooden planked seat; the neighbor children throw it up in the tree, beyond my reach. I set out drinks of iced tea on a picnic table for our neighbors; when I go inside for chips, they throw one bench and the tea into a small muddy creek behind our home and run away. They invite me to play a game where several hold hands and twist through each other. The person meant to untwist the human puzzle closes their eyes and counts. Before I finish my count to twenty-five, they are gone.

By the second week in June, a thick screen of new yellow-green leaves from the old willow totally obscures the view from our backyard. Underneath, the ground is damp from an earlier shower. An earthy petrichor fills the air. My dolls, Barbie and Midge, sit hidden with me under the tree dressed in their miniskirts and high heels. I am absorbed in their arguments as they hit one another with full body blows. I no longer remember the exact words, yet the content remains:

"Why are we under this tree?" Midge says.

"We're hiding, stupid," Barbie says.

"Why are we hiding?"

"Don't you know anything? Nobody loves you anymore. You're dirty and ugly."

"I wanna go home. I'm leaving."

"No you're not. You're going to live under this stupid tree forever."

I throw my once-cherished dolls into the creek. It's the last time I play with them or any of my childish playthings. Instead, I retreat further into dark thoughts.

In seventh grade, my classmates from my new suburban neighborhood are better prepared than I. The classes are labeled one to thirteen. The 7-1s are the brightest, the teacher's favorites. I am placed in the 7-13s. I attend special classes for children who can't read well. On my first reading test, taken with the lowest of the low scorers, I get my first of many big, red Fs. I don't like red. I was an A student in Philadelphia, but I've forgotten my lessons. I feel numb. When I am present, it doesn't feel good.

One day after school, Vern faints, falling on the sidewalk. He bruises his face and loses two front teeth. It is not the best of times for any of us. I make him milkshakes to drink through a straw; they sit untouched.

Mother walks around in a daze, avoiding me.

Grandma Katie, whom I adore, no longer visits; her daughter, my mother, no longer wants to see Grandpa Lloyd.

These are my forgotten years, the ones I try to forget. Plotting my escape, I decide that I will run away from my fear, my mother, and my unhappy life.

In tenth grade, life begins to change. While I continue to long for New

Jersey summers, away from Mother and toward life near the shore, my interest in sea life grows with *National Geographic* articles and TV specials on Jacques Cousteau. Through a curious assignment in a biology class and an observant teacher, Mrs. Drake, I discover Charles Darwin and his historic voyage on the HMS Beagle. I dare to imagine that I might follow in Darwin's path. I dream of living in the Galapagos and swimming with sea lions. These ideas give my life focus, taking me to an imaginary wonderland inside my head.

At fifteen, planning my escape, I write to the Ecuadorian government for information on how to become a resident of the Galapagos. Seven months later our front door rattles. I amble down the stairs to find an oversized, fully-stuffed package, in a paper-thin airmail envelope, wedged in the mail slot. I tug at it, pulling it through. The outer envelope rips as it falls out of the metal slot. More than a dozen brochures scatter across the floor.

Splayed out before me are bright-colored photos of ancient dinosaur-like land turtles, huge iguanas, and odd-looking Disneyesque fish. I sit down encircled by playful sea lions, green sea turtles, and swift-swimming penguins surrounded by their own air bubbles. The torn front of the envelope reveals exotic stamps: green mountains, red birds, and blue butterflies. I smile and tear it completely open. More tourist brochures and scientific papers spill onto the floor. A single white, tissue-thin letter with an official-looking stamp catches my attention in the middle of the pile.

Dear Miss Heidi Malin,

We, the people of Ecuador, thank you for your interest in Islas Galápagos. People who live in the archipelago must fulfill one of three requirements:
1. Be born as Ecuadorian
2. Marry an Ecuadorian citizen
3. Be a marine biologist

We hope this resolves your inquiry.

I decide at that moment to study marine biology. I will live in the Galapagos and spend my days swimming with turtles and sea lions.

I never lose this dream.

Forty-four years pass. I wake up confused. Someone is coughing. It sounds like an old man in a nursing home. I look across to Dennis and he looks back with a wrinkled brow. He isn't coughing. The barking, hacking, and wheezing continues. I pinpoint the sound directly below my porthole. A large sea lion is swimming next to *Centime*. My laughter explodes as I listen to a crusty, old sea lion clear his throat.

We're here! We sailed 1,000 nautical miles from Panama to the Galapagos, ourselves.

Wearing gym shorts and an old yellow skinny tee, I rush to the cockpit. The harbor is crowded with boats. Small local fishing boats sport red, blue, and yellow Ecuadorian flags. Sailboats ranging from twenty to fifty feet fly German, French, British, Canadian, and American flags. An empty barge, a gray Guardacostas ship, and a rusty brown tanker frame the deep end of the harbor. Fishermen next to us prepare their nets for a day at sea. Water taxis speed by from the town docks and maneuver through the lively harbor.

Colorful buildings line the harbor's edge, bordered by green palm trees and flowers of every color and shape. A small red and white lighthouse sits on a rock pile at the edge of the buildings. Beyond the lighthouse, a white sand beach expands in front of a school where dozens of children play. What must it be like to grow up here, swimming with sea lions in the crystalline aqua water?

It's what I longed for when I was fifteen.

Dozens of sea lions sun themselves on fishing boats. One slides off a nearby skiff into clear water. He stretches his large body partway out of the water to get a better look. His whiskers are long and they twitch as he wrinkles his nose and stares. His smaller companion does a double somersault underwater next to him, and I marvel at her grace. She surfaces next to him, and they swim on their sides, noses and heads touching, flippers flapping, in an energetic sea lion embrace. The sun is warm, while the gentle breeze is cool. The sea sparkles with the low morning sun. Black frigate birds glide overhead.

Today, March 10, would have been Mother's birthday. Her biggest joy in life was to watch her grandchildren. Whenever she saw Nico, Adam, or Amy, her whole being would light up. Before they arrived, she would nervously bite her fingernails. When one would appear and smile, she would match their smile and be at peace with the world.

She visited me in Maine the winter Nico was turning three. I had built a fire in the fireplace and the living room was warm and cozy. We had glasses of warm tea sitting on the end tables. She sat on my cobalt blue sofa and called out his name.

"Nico, come see Grammy," she said patting the sofa.

He ran into the living room and jumped up on her lap.

"Do you know how to sail like your mama?" she asked. He slowly nodded yes, and she bounced him on her lap.

"Nico sails to Boston, Nico sails to Lynn. Look out little Nico or you might … fall … in." She spread her knees apart and he fell playfully toward the ground.

"Again," he said.

He crawled back onto her lap and touched her cheeks and lips. She took his small hands in hers and kissed them numerous times, making him giggle. In those moments she was most beautiful.

She had once taught in a church preschool in Philadelphia, and learned numerous little ditties and childish games, yet I wondered if she had done these games with Vern or me when we were young. I remember Vern saying she couldn't take care of us in Alaska, that we overwhelmed her. Watching her with Nico, I'm curious how life had changed for her.

Today in the Galapagos, on her birthday, I make fresh iced tea in her honor. Writing an email to Nico, I remind him of his grandmother's love. I hope she has found true peace and is smiling down on him.

After a few weeks at the welcoming island of San Cristóbal, we sail to Isabela, the prettiest inhabited islands of the Galapagos. The wind is light and *Centime* is sluggish as we sail hour after hour. Nearing Isabela, the wind begins to fill her sails. Our speed increases: four, five, six, seven knots. I sail *Centime* toward the harbor, enjoying the rush of the wind as Dennis naps below.

A gust overtakes me. The rough movement wakes Dennis. Dark clouds gather above, darker ahead, and we have lost visibility. Storm clouds roil above. Dennis puts on foul-weather gear and his life vest, and enters the cockpit.

"We need to reef," I shout over the deafening sound of wind and waves.

"What do you want me to do?" he asks.

"Let's get in the genny first."

Dennis pulls in the sail with one line as I manage a second one to keep her in control. Squalls roll toward *Centime* as she pitches through the waves.

"I'll keep hand steering while you reef the main," I say, and he readies the lines.

She sails fast, even with reduced sails.

"Are the ports closed?" I ask.

"I'm not sure," he says.

Dennis takes the wheel. I rush below to close the portholes and don rain gear, seconds before the sky opens. As I return to the cockpit, rain falls in sheets, blurring my vision through wet glasses. The sea is whipped into a frenzy of large waves, white with breaking foam tops. *Centime*'s small sails are full, and she heels at a steep angle. As she slices through waves, the sea spray splashes against her as she races toward the harbor.

"We're not going to try to enter the harbor in this squall, are we?" I ask.

"Let's just get close while we have the wind and see what it looks like," he replies.

Waves crash to starboard. The chart shows miles of shallow reefs.

Then as fast as it came, the squall passes, darkness turns to light, and the sun sparkles again on the water. A bright, double rainbow stretches across the harbor's entrance. As we round the point, the sea flattens. The harbor is peaceful and welcoming with a natural wall of black, rugged, volcanic rock acting as a breakwater from the rough, open sea.

The wall defining the harbor entrance appears to be moving. I blink my eyes and wipe the rainwater from my glasses. Large, slow-moving iguanas, some over four feet long, cover every inch of the wall. Their skin is black, rough, and jagged, camouflaged by the black volcanic rocks. They look prehistoric. In contrast to this black-on-black landscape, a dozen white booby birds with bright blue feet adjust their positions as the iguanas move. It's a fairy-tale picture.

We anchor near the jetty. Between it and our boat is a pure aqua-blue channel, with water so clear that colorful fish are visible more than fifteen feet below. A brown stingray measuring seven feet across glides past. A sea lion raises her flipper as she floats by with the current, as if she's waving hello.

The following morning begins with a radiant sunrise, a splash of colors: persimmon red, tangerine orange, and starfruit gold. I get in the dinghy and clean *Centime*'s waterline stripe with a large sponge and metal scraper. As if arriving for breakfast, two unusual foot-long, black-and-white-spotted fish come over to munch on the dark green algae that I scrape off my boat. Next, a pair of penguins speed past.

An unexpected wave pushes the dinghy a foot from the boat. I hang, half-suspended with my hand in the water, lying on the dinghy's pontoon, facing the sky. A sea lion has swum under my arm inches away and is now circling me and the dingy within inches. He has a perfect backstroke, chin and head held high out of the water, slowly swimming past, stretching his neck to look up at me from his floating position. He raises his flipper as he floats by and then slaps it down on the water. He drenches me with a sizable wave. I imagine him laughing as he swims around the dinghy frolicking like a clown. We're both ready to play. I dive in. The sea lion cavorts in a sensuous dance.

Later dressed in a black, sea-lion-like wetsuit, I snorkel in a remote bay. A sea turtle two feet long is munching on seagrass. I float above her mesmerized, slowly gliding through the bay as the current pushes us in a Zen-like motion. With a flick of a flipper, a very large turtle, twice the size of the first, comes between us. I suspect it is her mama as female sea turtles are larger than males. Either way she clearly wants me to leave her offspring alone.

Surprised, I splash backward away from the mama turtle, which attracts a sea lion's attention. He circles my legs, swims from my calves up the front of my wetsuit pressing himself against me. Then he moves over my head knocking off my mask and snorkel. He continues down my back and around my legs again. As I pop my head out of the water he follows. In an instant our heads are both above the water less than a foot apart and we stare at one another. If sea lions can look surprised, this frisky male certainly does—so must I. It reminds me of the *Shrek* movie and Smash Mouth's rendition of an old Monkees' song, "I'm a Believer." It's when the beautiful princess turns into an ogre. I guess my face and snorkel weren't exactly what he had in mind.

By sunset, I'm ravenous. On the cockpit table a blue plastic plate is overflowing with grilled tuna. Another holds large slices of ripe tomatoes sprinkled with salt. An open bottle of Spanish wine and two full glasses rest in the wooden cup holders. Sea lions bellow. Their splashing and cacophony of marine sounds complement our pulsating dinner jazz.

I take a sip of wine. "You are such a good husband, father, brother. I've read that love is not only about what you see and feel for another person but also about how much love you feel for yourself. Coming through storms, facing challenges, arriving in the Galapagos, forgiving pieces of my past, I feel like my love for myself and for you is expanding. You bring out the best in me."

"Wow, honey," he says. "I'd never be here if it wasn't for you."

"Me neither. I got an email from Annie," I say. "She said she cried when she read that we made it to the Galapagos. She was afraid we might die, and she'd never see us again."

"I suspect there were quite a few people who thought we wouldn't make it this far, but I never guessed that some thought we might die."

"At times I thought we might die." I look up at Dennis. "Remember how Annie used to call the ocean 'the big bad ocean,' and later in Puerto Rico she changed it to 'the big, beautiful ocean'? She has fears like mine, and she works hard to reframe them. You know what happened to her as a teen. She said her fear of death reminds her of those times."

Dennis takes a sip of wine and clears his throat. "When you told me a few years ago about your friends who had been raped—women I know—it was crushing to hear each story. It was a revelation for me. Then when you read me the CDC statistics, that half of the women have experienced sexual violence and a quarter raped, I was shocked. I had no clue how pervasive it was or the magnitude of its lasting effects. I remember afterward being in a restaurant and having a beer with my friend Dave, who was astounded by your story. I told him, 'Look around this room,' and told him what you told me. He was as aghast. I suspect many men don't understand the enormity or the lasting impact. I sure didn't."

"Many of us, men and women, are silenced and afraid or ashamed to tell, and when some do tell they're often dismissed and not always believed," I say. "I felt silenced at eleven. My family and I never talked about my rape or even rape culture—not as a young adult, and certainly never as a child. I didn't tell Vern until I was in my late forties."

I reflect on my youth and how I learned secrets from my friends. By fourth grade I knew fathers and grandfathers who read *Playboy* and *Hustler* and had pinup calendars hanging in garages. Like me, many of my girlfriends had seen exhibitionists exposing themselves in the train station, in the park, and on the streets, without alerting our parents. Some boys, if they were aware, thought it was funny; the girls I knew found it repulsive—a violation.

By high school, after we had moved out of Philadelphia, I learned which friend got monthly internal exams from her father, a doctor, who explored her private parts with his own. I knew which friends' boyfriends or dates said they got "carried away." I knew about one who came back from her beach vacation different from when she left, and one who was forced at gunpoint by a man more than twice he age. Not daring to tell my own story, I started keeping a list in my head of which friends were raped and which weren't, or at least hadn't told. By college, my list 30 to 40 percent of close girlfriends.

I wondered how so many girls kept so many secrets, while I locked mine far away where no one could touch it. Though it saddened and revolted me that others experienced what I had, the list kept me from feeling isolated, offering a delusion of normalcy.

I had been called frigid in high school because of my fear of being kissed. On my sixteenth birthday, my uncle teased, "Sweet sixteen and never been kissed." Not kissed—fucked.

I did reveal part of my secret once, during college, after I started serious dating, and considered getting married. I believed then that I was soiled. I also believed that if my boyfriend, the man who was to become my husband and Nico's dad, were to drop me as damaged goods, it should happen before we got married. It seemed fair that he knew. After all, I reasoned at the time, don't men want virgins? He listened and responded with love and compassion, yet my sense of being damaged lingered for over three decades. Much of my silence remained: my full story, trapped in my throat.

The next day, Dennis and I board a fast, twenty-two-foot tour boat, *Isabela*, with Eileen and Mark. She is a sturdy wooden boat with two gray, 200 horsepower engines. Two-thirds of her deck is open with bench seats along the outer edges. Three Ecuadorian men arrive: a thirty-year-old captain, a naturalist a few years older than the captain, and a young mate, perhaps eighteen. All have golden-brown skin and are rugged and fit from years of hard work at sea.

We slam hard through erratic waves for an hour to arrive near the entrance of Los Tuneles, a maze of natural volcanic rock formations. It is part of a national park in the Galapagos, its fragile ecosystem protected.

Large breaking waves stretch across the path ahead, the full width of the entrance. The waves come from two directions, at a wide angle, colliding at a point between the boat and the entrance. As I look ahead, I grip the rail of the boat. Eileen braces her hands and feet. The water crests five to seven feet with the tops breaking and colliding in angry white foam. The power in these seas could easily break a woman's body. A strong current pushes the boat forward toward the chaotic sea. Crashing waves dull all other sounds, and I yell to Eileen to be heard.

"We can't be going through there, can we?" I ask.

"We are!" she replies, staring ahead, her eyes large.

The captain turns the boat around and I breathe a sigh of relief. After heading away for ten yards he turns the Isabela back toward the breaking waves and slowly edges forward again, trying to find the calmest path in the center of a vicious, whirling sea. His dark eyes stare forward in concentration. I study his body language and watch his head nod slightly. He counts the waves, timing his entrance. It seems near madness to enter.

No one on board says a word, not daring to break the captain's concentration. Tension builds. Everyone is braced in silent accord for possible impact.

The captain pushes the throttle full forward and we fly like a jet toward the area where the waves cross. There is no turning back. The bow of the boat lifts off the water between waves. We become partially airborne and splash down with force into the calmer, rolling sea on the other side. Large waves break over the bow and rain down hard on her deck. The captain's timing was perfect. We are drenched in sea spray, but the boat, crew and passengers are still intact. Only my nerves are shattered. The captain smiles like a reckless teen. I hope there is another way out.

We glide to a tranquil backwater, through an expansive maze of black volcanic walls, tunnels, small island mounds, and natural rock bridges. The landscape is stark and dry; the only vegetation is a scattering of tall, narrow cactus. Low, white clouds move fast across the scene, and sunlight streams through scattered holes of blue sky to create patterns on the water.

Seabirds crowd the jagged labyrinth of rocks: white boobies with bright blue feet; tan boobies with red feet; black frigates with red balloon-like pouches at their throats; squat, black guillemots; flowing white tropicbirds with long tails; and penguins with tuxedo-like chests.

The water is a rich, clear aquamarine, painted by gods. Large sea turtles swim through the calm, clear water. Their shells, four and five feet across, are speckled in brown and aqua, the tops glistening in the sun. White-tipped sharks crowd the shallows. A brown-and-black spotted eagle ray glides by; her powerful fins guide her like a true airborne eagle through currents in the narrow channel.

The captain navigates through the lava outcrops to a place where we can snorkel. Below the water is a plethora of sea life. Fish of every color, corals, invertebrates, and sea lions flourish, different from the creatures in the Caribbean. The naturalist points out a seahorse, camouflaged and still against a brown, vertical tower of seaweed. I swim behind a six-foot mama turtle. We drift through strong currents, holding our breath to duck under the water below a lava bridge. I surface to find a penguin on a rock a few feet above my head, looking down at me. Dennis snaps a shot, and the penguin looks like she's photobombing his picture.

The animals and landscapes appear to have come from someone's creative imagination. I remember my childhood dreams, the picturesque brochures scattered on the floor. Now the fauna surrounds me.

At the end of the day, we make our exit, snaking through the maze of canals to the open sea. As she heads out, the speeding boat pounds head on through wave after wave, each one larger than the last. The opening is still treacherous. The captain opens the throttle. The bow stands high in the water as she races ahead. One wave towers over the bow and crashes against the hull. We swerve to the right. As the wave recedes it exposes a large black rock only a few feet away on the port side. I gasp, point, and hear a man yell, "Rocks … rocks to starboard." He must be confused, and I scream, "No! To port!" soon realizing we have exposed rocks close on both sides. There is no margin of safety. I close my eyes, hold my breath, and brace for impact as the captain narrowly avoids disaster.

The next day, a woman is thrown from one of the tour boats and the tour is shut down until the waves subside. We were the last boat to enter and leave with everyone intact. Three days later we see the woman with a full leg cast, sharing a park bench with a sea lion.

We enjoy the islands and the national park for a month. On our last evening the harbor is calm, disturbed only by the occasional splash of a playful sea lion. The moon is almost full, the sky alight. Warm breezes flow through the cockpit as I sip red Ecuadorian wine. Savory fragrances of onions, cumin, and turmeric waft through the air as Dennis prepares green curry. We have lingered in these magical islands. Tomorrow, we leave. This is our last relaxing meal for three or four weeks, until we finish our 3,000-nautical-mile passage to French Polynesia.

Dennis longs for the sea. I cling to the land. In twelve to fifteen days, we will be 1,500 nautical miles away from land in every direction and only one way forward. I'm still afraid. Is it wise for me to attempt this? What draws me; what holds me back?

After dinner, the romance of the evening takes over and we head below. Dennis opens the hatch above our berth and a fresh sea breeze caresses our warm bodies. He knows I'm worried about our journey ahead, and holds me close, wrapping his arms around me until I feel his strength and determination melt into me.

CHAPTER 20

Rites of Passage

I shut my eyes in order to see.

Paul Gauguin

The South Pacific Ocean, March 2015

The golden light of early dawn seeps through the porthole of my berth. It is a still morning with soft sounds of brewing coffee, a light clink of the metal halyard against the mast, and the occasional splash of a sea lion foraging for breakfast.

I rise as the aroma of fresh coffee fills the air. The coffee beans are from the high mountains around Boquete, Panama, and produce a rich, dark roast with a hint of chocolate. Our lovely Boquete musician friends come to mind, and I smile.

The weather is calm. The water in Isabela's harbor is flat, a brilliant, clear aqua, sparkling in low light. The sky overhead is light blue with puffy, white, fair-weather clouds on the horizon. A dozen sailboats nearby look empty, their crews asleep. *Centime* rests at anchor, rocking gently in the light morning breeze. We have delighted in the Galapagos and experienced much of her natural beauty.

In less than an hour, we will start our 3,000-nautical-mile passage to the Marquesas Islands of French Polynesia. We calculate this to be a three- to four-week journey away from land, halfway across the South Pacific Ocean. If it weren't for my anxiety about leaving, this moment would be perfect. I try to be present with the morning stillness.

Eileen and Mark are up early on *Wavelength*, with Eileen driving her boat toward their anchor. I check our engine oil, turn on the instruments, secure the ports and finish last-minute preparations for a month at sea. *Centime*'s engine jumps to life with a low roar. Our friends on a nearby boat, *Talulah Ruby*, scramble on deck when they hear our engine, snap photos, and wave goodbye. They will leave in a couple of days too and be part of our ten boat-to-boat radio safety net during the passage.

In all our challenging passages, we find sailors who are traveling the same route who agree to report on a pre-designated radio frequency once a day. We've collectively named the net the Tangaroa after the Polynesian and Maori God of the wind and sea. While the boats will be spread across hundreds of miles, we can still offer some support to each other. We hope to see them all in the Marquesas.

Dennis leaves his coffee in the cockpit and heads to the bow to raise our anchor. I drive *Centime* slowly forward to ease the strain. Soon he gives me a thumbs-up; our anchor is free. I steer the boat toward the harbor entrance where red and green buoys mark a safe route around the extensive reef.

A large green supply ship with rust on her aging hull sits in the center of the channel. A dark-haired, sun-weathered man in black clothing is leaning over the deckrail, looking toward the open sea. I wave, but he doesn't respond. I wave harder. My brain registers that if I were to die at sea this may be the last human I see besides Dennis. The ridiculous thought rushes through my brain unwelcome, bringing instant darkness. I wave more frantically. The man smiles and waves back. I dismiss my negative thoughts and laugh at the absurdity. What you focus on expands. Focus on joy, love, and fair winds.

We leave the channel and raise two large white sails as the creatures of the Galapagos appear to bid us farewell. A dozen white boobies fly past. Twenty-five spinner dolphins jump high in the air, putting on a grand show. A brown turtle, measuring five feet long and weighing hundreds of pounds, floats in our path. She bobs up and down with our wake, sleeping undisturbed. These pelagic creatures are Neptune's gifts and good omens.

Packets of near-frozen strawberry, melon, mango, and coconut rest under my shoebox-sized freezer. The Galapagos has an abundance of ripe fruit.

Farmers process the fruit, removing skins, seeds, and husks, and freeze packages of pulp that weigh a half kilo each. I open the coconut package and scoop out two large servings. The thick, sweet, half-frozen concoction is a welcome treat in the warmth of the morning.

Rock cliffs line the desolate southern edge of the island. Large waves crash, filling the air with high plumes of spray. The distant roar of the sea mingles with the wind's nearby whispers. The land rises at a sharp incline to a jagged ridge on top of a high volcano. Isla Isabela is painted in four shades of green. Diverse plants smooth her contours, representing broad horizontal bands of unique ecological zones of varying altitudes and rainfall. Dramatic clouds hide the top of the Sierra Negra Volcano.

I sit, slumped in a corner of *Centime*'s cockpit, staring at the land we're leaving behind. Rubbing my chest, I memorize the details of these last Galapagos images before they disappear—postcards to remember. While Dennis is at the helm looking toward an endless sea, my gaze is fixated on what's left behind. We have been in the Galapagos for a month yet I'm not ready to leave.

Time passes quickly on land, slowly at sea. I hope to come back to Isabela. If not, perhaps Nico will bring my ashes to the island one day. I hold my necklace tight, close to my heart; it's a piece of shell carved into a turtle, hanging on a leather string.

Dennis wears a blue and green sarong with a swirling pattern, knotted at his waist. He has no shirt, shoes, or hat, just one light piece of fabric wrapped around his fit body. The light cloth flutters in the cool gentle breeze. I watch him as he trims the genoa, his muscles strong and well defined, his body toned, and his skin golden brown from the sun. He is in his element at sea.

At noon he starts the first of a multiweek radio net, calling boats nearby. Dennis was formerly a radioman for the Coast Guard and enjoys this safety ritual.

The only boat on the net today is *Wavelength*. Our two boats are leading the ten-boat fleet. Bigger, faster boats will leave in the next several days and pass us en route. All is well on *Wavelength*. Dennis marks their position on our chart.

"Hey, girl!" I say to Eileen. "I want to wish you fair winds and a safe trip."

"You too," she replies. "I wanted to give you a hug last night. It's hard to imagine I won't be able to hug you for a month."

"We can send virtual hugs every day. I will think of you when I see the moon, just like in that song."

"Fair winds. See you on the other side."

It's hard to dismiss the risks involved in making this passage or the churning in the bottom of my stomach. Eileen and I know there may be boats that won't make it. We both hope we won't be among them.

By evening I'm on watch alone. A red moon close to full sits on the horizon. No land is in sight, nor boats, nor manmade lights. Bright, shining planets, Venus the brightest, make a path of light on the sea. I smile thinking of the anthropomorphic qualities the moon and Venus symbolize, feminine energy lighting a path through darkness. I am in love with the moon. The clear sky is filled with twinkling stars forming many constellations: Orion, Scorpius, and the Southern Cross. At home I could watch the Big Dipper point to the North Star, circling around it in all positions. Here in the Southern Hemisphere, the North Star is below the horizon, and the Dipper's cup is upside down, pouring its contents into the sea.

As a child in Seward, Alaska, I knew mountains faced north, and Santa was at the North Pole. I thought anything above me—mountains, stars, sky, and heaven—were north. Traveling this far south has shifted my perspective.

I stand with my face to the wind. Is it a test of courage, or the fulfillment of a lifelong dream? Are travel and adventure in my genes—are they my destiny? Or am I escaping demons and searching for wholeness? The sea is vast, stretching in every direction, and the star-filled sky is endless. My questions no longer matter.

Afterward, in my berth, I feel safe and at peace.

I wake up shivering.

My body is feverish, an infection raging. I rush to the head. It burns to urinate. I moan in pain. Dennis can't hear me over the sounds of wind and waves.

Centime pitches up and down in an erratic motion. I open the medicine cabinet and the door bangs with each roll. Vials of medicine spill out and roll across the floor. Without my glasses it's hard to read the prescriptions. My hand shakes as I open the child-proof caps and find the right size pill indicating an antibiotic and painkiller. Slamming the cabinet door shut, I push against loose duct tape to reseal it. Filling my hand with foul-tasting water I gulp down the pills. The large one sticks in my throat, and I choke down more water and immediately need the head again.

Centime sails at a steep angle, water rushing past. Stumbling through the cabin like a toddler learning to walk, I slip on books and papers that have fallen to the floor. I force open the hatch and glance outside. The cockpit is wet and Dennis is hand steering in his yellow foul-weather gear.

Grabbing my rain jacket, pants, and boots, I stumble back to the head. In spite of my sickness, Dennis needs sleep. It is dangerous to be sleep-deprived on a passage. Sick or not, I will stand watch.

The boat rocks like an amusement ride. Struggling to get my feet and legs into slick Gore-Tex overalls, I fall onto a cabin bench. The gray multilayered pants are bulky, and the inner fabric sticks to my sweaty, bare legs. Holding a wooden handrail, I stand to pull them up, securing the Velcro straps, and slump back onto the bench. The blue and white horizontal stripes on my boots blur as the cabin heaves back and forth. Sweat drips down my forehead stinging my eyes.

Breathe … breathe in calm. I put on my life jacket, holding up the elastic tether so that I don't trip. Staggering up to the cockpit, I attach my tether to a wet metal hook.

Horizontal rain whips through the cockpit. The wind howls. The cool air at first soothes my sweating body, and then I shiver. As my head spins, I try to focus on the sails to determine the wind direction and what needs to be done. I slump down onto the low corner seat.

"I'm sick," I say.

"What's wrong?!" Dennis replies, eyes wide.

"Bladder infection."

"Oh nooo, I'm so sorry. Go back below. I'll stay longer."

"No, it could be worse later. You need sleep."

"Can I get you anything?"

"No. I took meds. I'll be all right."

"I'll put on the autopilot to make it easier. Call me if you need anything. And stay hooked in. Promise me, Heidi! You need to hook in."

After he leaves, I pull myself up from the bench to look forward. The horizon is solid black. I collapse back onto the seat. Within minutes I run below to use the head. The burning continues. This cycle lasts for hours. Whenever I head below, I must first check the horizon for lights and possible boats, remove layers of rain gear, and then put my wet clothes and life jacket back on. Each time the pain is more pronounced. I'm too exhausted to finish my five-hour watch. I wake Dennis.

My berth pitches from side to side as I fall into a fitful sleep. Dennis wrestles with the weather through the night. Winches grind over my head as he adjusts and readjusts the sails. His boat shoes squeal against the wet deck.

My sheets are damp with sweat. My arms shake as I pull myself out of the berth. Holding tight to the rails, I stumble to the head.

The burning continues.

CHAPTER 21

The Farthest Point

*When you come out of the storm,
you won't be the same person who walked in.
That's what this storm's all about.*

Haruki Murakami, *Kafka on the Shore*

The South Pacific Ocean, April 2015

    I choke on the bitterness.
    The large antibiotic sticks in my throat like the pearl from my night terrors. Exhausted, I rub my throat and stomach. Should we turn around? Would it be crazy to turn back against these trade winds and strong ocean currents? Like boxers in a ring, emotions want to turn back, fighting the rationality of knowing we can't buck these currents, winds, or waves.
    My stomach growls. The cupboard near the companionway stairs has an old, damp box of saltines with an unbroken wax seal. The cracker feels thick in my throat. I grab a bottle of cold sweet tea to help my swallowing.
    Struggling to relieve Dennis, I head to the cockpit and settle into my watch.
    There are no stars to follow, no clear path ahead. An ebony ocean blends into a leaden sky, broken only by gray seafoam.
    Slumped in the corner of the cockpit, I fight to stay awake. Cushioned by bulky rain-slicked foul-weather attire, I slide lower on my bench seat. My eyes close, and my breathing deepens. An errant wave hits the hull. My body

stiffens. I reach over the side and splash bracing seawater on my face, and then stand to recheck the autopilot, and make a circular scan of the horizon.

Foreboding clouds close in, dark gray over light gray, nearing *Centime*'s stern. I unhook my tether, attached to the boat, and scurry below. Squalls pop up as large inkblots across the radar screen, like a daunting video game. Scanning a cloud identifier, I find cumulonimbus: dark, ominous, associated with strong winds and frequent lightning. A damp fear grabs hold.

I rush to the cockpit, hook in, and put a double reef in the mainsail, making it the size of a small tablecloth. Meter after meter of reefing lines pile around my ankles. I pull in more of the genoa, balancing the wind on two pieces of shrunken canvass. *Centime* slows. An unsettling calm descends, as I begin to gather the excess lines heaped on the bench seat and cockpit floor.

Without additional warning, hard rain strikes the dodger. Large droplets hit my glasses, blurring my view, running down my face and neck like cold tears.

A thirty-eight-knot gust of wind forces *Centime* onto her side. Slipping on the deck, I drop the half-coiled lines to grab a handhold, and let out the tiny mainsail to spill wind. An alarm shrieks as the wind and waves overpower the autopilot. With no one steering, *Centime* heads off course, accelerating upwind.

Adrenaline surges through my body as I rapidly unhook one side of my tether to reach the wheel. The shrill alarm continues to wail. The half-coiled reefing lines wrap around my ankles tightening as I pull away like a child's Chinese finger trap. I trip, landing hard against my right knee. As I fall across the bench, constricting rope coils are tangled around my legs. I grab the edge of the wheel with outstretched hands and try to drive *Centime* downwind. Steering my small boat backward, in the middle of a dark sea—I face a gale.

Dennis, exhausted from covering my earlier watch, is in a dead sleep below, unable to hear the alarm over the heavy wind and groaning motor that reverberates in his berth. I bang as hard as I can on his window and yell for help.

Freeing lines from my ankles, I careen around the wheel and grab the proper side of the wheel, trying to head her away from the source of the wind to a place where she might be more stable.

Dennis rushes out in his boxers. "What's wrong?" he yells, shoving his body against the companionway door.

"I tripped on the reefing lines and couldn't reach the wheel. We blew a fuse and she headed into the wind."

"What do you need first?" he says, turning his head back and forth to assess our position.

"Let out the main and staysail to spill more wind," I shout over the wind's roar. "I can hardly hold the wheel."

Using the full force of my body angled against the wheel, I bring *Centime* back on course as Dennis lets out the tiny sails. Waves splash over the hull. Cold water hits my face. The compass and wind gauge blur beyond my sea-streaked glasses, and I can't let go of the wheel to clear them. Salt stings my eyes. I blink hard and angle my head down to look over the top of my opaque glasses.

"Can you change the fuse for the autopilot?" I strain to hold the wheel. My mouth is dry as I lick the salt off my lips. I grip the wheel tight as he heads below. The sky is black.

We slowly gain control through the fury of the squall. With the autopilot working again and the squall past, we organize the lines. Dennis scans the horizon.

"Why don't you get some sleep?" he asks. "I can take over."

Looking across a field of waves, I take a deep breath. "I can do this," I say, and Dennis heads below to sleep.

Before the end of my watch, I fight three squalls. At the end of my watch, I collapse in my berth.

The aroma of coffee fills the air. *Centime* rolls in uneven waves. The blackout curtains keep the sleeping area dark, day and night.

"What time is it?" I ask, opening the blue curtain.

"It's 9:00 a.m.," he replies. "How are you feeling?"

"Better. How's the weather?"

"The squalls are gone, and the wind's died. The waves are huge: close to three meters, but at least when they combine they hit us off the port quarter, not broadside."

"Can you make some hot tea for me while I dress? I can take over."

I look out across fields of waves. It's a strange phenomenon. When on land with feet firmly on solid ground, I experience large waves as they crest and crash against or over a sea wall or a rocky beach. The impact can be quite strong and powerful against a wall or felt as a slap against a swimmer.

On a seaworthy boat like *Centime* however a large wave, three or four meters high, advances quickly toward the boat. As the waves build my mind brings a land perspective expecting them to crash over the stern of our boat, filling the cockpit. Instead, each one hovers momentarily behind yet above me. Then, the boat becomes one with the sea. It rises and falls as the wave flows smoothly underneath with the grace of a dancer. I wonder at the symbolism. Life maintains balance as powerful forces move through and around her, present in each moment in harmony with nature.

Dennis makes my tea, and downloads weather information. An email comes through on our high-frequency radio.

"There's a note from Dawn," Dennis says.

Randy and Dawn, owners of a forty-two-foot sailboat *Nirvana Now* are friends we made in Panama. When we first arrived in Shelter Bay, Dennis had a mishap and fell into the water. Dawn, a nurse, rushed over with antiseptics and bandages. They are crossing from Panama to French Polynesia, ahead of us by several days.

"It's a bit odd," Dennis says. "She's addressed the email to her kids with a cc to us. They are having a problem with their rigging at the bow but she says not to worry, they're okay. She thought she saw the island of Nuku Hiva, but at over a thousand miles away, it was only an apparition. She's taking it as a good omen and she hopes they will make it."

"Hopes they will make it? Shit, rigging problems in the middle of the ocean." Why is she copying us on a message to her kids? What isn't she saying?

The afternoon air is warm in the cockpit. Waves jostle *Centime*. Stretching from side to side at the end of my tether, I see an endless field of large waves. The crests are lined up in rows, like two battalions of marching soldiers. One battalion hits *Centime* forward of her beam on her port side, and the other forty degrees behind.

The next few hours of my watch we pitch and roll in an uncomfortable rhythm. It's a repulsive cycle: I drink large quantities of puke-yellow, lemon-lime Gatorade to fully flush out the infection, struggle back and forth to the bathroom in our tipsy boat, and fight nausea. Heated through the day by the tropical sun, the cabin below is warm and claustrophobic. Above, the air is cooler, yet the horizon is dizzying.

My pink iPod has more than a dozen podcasts on managing fear. I pick TED radio hour's "What We Fear." It features Colonel Chris Hadfield, an astronaut who has been "launched off the planet three times ... at five miles a second ... with the chance of survival as one in thirty-five." He's the model astronaut for David Bowie's Major Tom. He talks about fear being good to help a person plan, react, and survive. He also speaks of the evolution of one's response to perceived danger, how to shift perspectives. I look at the endless seas, wave after wave, and wonder how to shift and evolve.

Nearing the third hour I crouch in the corner of the cockpit and stare at the wave trains. Focusing beyond the boat helps my unsettled stomach. Bright white foam catches my eyes. Two eight-foot waves head toward a collision point a few feet away from the port side. My heartbeat quickens.

I grip a metal bar as I watch the waves collide in what appears to be slow motion. Eight-foot wave against eight-foot wave, they smack together, rearing up twelve feet. The sea spray towers above me a few feet from the port hull. Their combined forces surge as a single, large breaking wave. This powerful force, leading with white foam, rages toward *Centime*. I close my eyes and suck in air before it hits.

The super wave forces the boat "hard over" on its side. My body falls against the edge of the cockpit, my head over the rails. Water rushes below my head and waves hit my eyes. Slamming doors and jarring sounds of tumbling cans fill the air. *Centime* immediately jerks back and I brace my feet on the wet floor as my body is flung to the opposite side. The sounds and motions repeat. Like a child's punching bag, she rolls back and forth before settling back on course. I blow air out of my cheeks in relief as Dennis rushes into the cockpit.

"What the hell was that?" he yells, his face pale, his eyes wide.

"We're okay. Two waves from different angles combined into a massive wave that broke short of the boat. It shocked us but *Centime* bounced right back. We're fine now … unless another one hits."

He looks out to sea. His black boxers are wet, clinging to his muscular legs. "Holy shit, we've gotta get the hell outta here," he says. He shakes his head and teases, "Why do these things always happen on your shift? You must have done something to anger Neptune."

"You can go back to sleep any time now."

"Yeah, right, the berth is flooded."

"What?"

"I was sound asleep, and felt this bump. Then the water shot in through the open port window like a fucking fire hose." As I look closer, I can see Dennis is drenched. "It was cold water, shocked the hell out of me. I thought we were taking on water, that we hit a container, and got a hole in the boat."

"You … had the port open?" I stammer.

"Yeah I know, it was stupid. I was boiling hot so I opened it. I thought it would be safe on the leeward side. Guess not. Everything in the bed is soaked: sheets, pillows, clothes."

"It's never going to dry with the salt. How's the mattress?"

"Soaked through. It's a mess. It felt like a tidal wave."

"Do you want to take the watch for a bit and I'll try to clean up?"

"No, I'll take care of it."

"Dennis, how big does a wave need to be for a knockdown, for *Centime* to get pushed so far over that her mast hits the water? Theoretically, I mean."

"One-third the boat length, so roughly thirteen feet in our case. It has to be breaking and we don't want them to hit us broadside, perpendicular to the hull."

I wait for reassurance. He stares at me in silence.

"Will you please send an email to Ken now for the best route out? I don't want to be in the wrong place if these waves collide and break again."

We have sailed over 1,500 miles and have reached the halfway point between the Galapagos and Nuku Hiva. We have only seen two boats in over a week, both from our fleet; one was *Wavelength*. We are close to a point on Earth that is close to the farthest away from land in every direction.

The wave trains continue.

CHAPTER 22

Conviction

I am terrified by this dark thing that sleeps in me.

Silvia Plath, *Elm*

Philadelphia, Pennsylvania, May 1967

It hurts to move, even to walk at a slow pace.

Dad's silver 1965 Chevy Impala is parked in the front row of the hospital parking lot. He has returned to fetch me. Though at the time I didn't know why he had left, I now suspect he went home to ensure my brother was safe with my mother, and to see what care she needed.

Although I had stopped holding his hand years ago, today I cling to it, determined to never let go. Reaching the car, I drop his hand for a second, scramble inside, secure the seatbelt, and reach over to touch his arm inside the car. If I hold his hand he won't disappear. I move as close to him as the seatbelt and bucket seats will allow.

We ride from the hospital in silence. If I speak will this dream go away? I had thought I would never see him again. My eyes start to close, but I force them to stay open, and stare at him.

Normally when we ride in the car, he tells me jokes from Reader's Digest; today he is silent. He looks ahead at the road, his face serious. I suppose he didn't know what to say. Perhaps he was afraid, too, and angry.

Decades later, I ask Dennis about this. "Dennis, if it were you, riding away from the hospital with your daughter, why wouldn't you talk to her, reassure her?" I ask.

"I would be so furious, trying to contain my rage, and wondering how I could find Mr. Hart and kill him."

I start to cry. "Knowing that you would have stood up for me means so much. My dad was probably doing his best. Trying to protect me and others, trying to control his anger. When I was eleven, I couldn't grasp what was happening. I thought I was abandoned. I wouldn't have wanted my dad or anyone to kill Mr. Hart, yet I have this sense that I wanted someone to defend me. I felt alone. We never talked. After all these years, I still feel that hurt."

Once, a couple of years ago, Vern told me he had overheard Dad on the phone with a lawyer friend. The friend had recommended that Dad not press charges against Mr. Hart because it would harm and expose me. I don't know why, in the end, Dad took me to court in spite of the lawyer's advice—for revenge, or to protect me or future victims—yet he did. He was the kind of man who tried to do the right thing.

I also don't know how much time elapsed between the hospital, the arraignment, and the court. They blur together as one unending day of my life.

Dad weaves through heavy city traffic and stops the car in front of a large building, the Philadelphia City Courthouse. The historic white marble and granite edifice covers a full city block with an overarching tower rising from the center. I wait in the car, uncertain. I've never seen such an imposing structure. I want to go far away with Dad. I imagine returning to Alaska and living alone with him in a snowy mountain village.

He opens my door, grabs my hand in silence, and leads me through a grand marble entrance that opens into an enormous white hall. Curved stone structures arch high above. A massive white statue of a seated man dressed in a robe sits in the center of the hall towering over me.

The place buzzes with activity; sounds echo from wall to wall. Policemen walk past us with shiny black shoes that click, like tap shoes, on the white marble, tiled floor. They wear blue uniforms and black hats with bright silver badges. Large, strong men talk with other large, strong men. Black men, white men, big men, all men. I am very small, the only kid, the only female.

Dad checks his watch. Room 104 appears ahead in our path, with its small wooden door closed. Dad knocks. A tall heavy-set policeman opens the door, revealing the edge of a small room with beige walls and a wooden desk. The cop has a black handgun in a holster at his waist. I feel sick. We don't have guns like this at my house—only Dad's Alaskan hunting rifle in a glass case on a wall. The police in my neighborhood carry guns, which scare me. The gun handle is below my eyes and I stare at it. Dad drops my hand and gently pushes me in front of him into the small room. I turn and try to grab his hand again, but it is balled into a tight fist.

(Trigger Warning) I spot a man sitting across the room on the edge of a wooden chair. Terry's father, with silver handcuffs, glares at me behind orange-brown glasses. I can't breathe. I'm still for a second, my heart pounds, and then I turn to run.

"Nooo!" I scream, crashing into Dad, who blocks the door. I pound my fist into his chest.

Dad turns me around, holding my shoulders. I cross my arms and peek up at Mr. Hart's face; it's red and he is clenching the muscles in his jaw. His eyes pierce through his orange-brown glasses. I shut my eyes tight, whimpering, "Please let me out. Please … please … please!"

"Tell me who this man is," the policeman says.

I open my eyes. The policeman is crouched down before me, his eyes directly in front of mine. I can't speak. I look up at Dad. Why doesn't Dad answer him and let me out of here? Hurry, Dad. Hurry!

"Tell the policeman the name of the man, Heidi," Dad says in a stern voice.

My heart races. I try to speak but no words come out. I can't remember the last time I spoke. "Heidi," Dad insists, squeezing my shoulders hard and giving me a nudge.

"Mr. Hart," I whisper and cough. I cover my mouth with one hand and hold my throat with the other. There are bruises on my neck.

"Is this the man who hurt you?" the policeman asked.

I nod my head yes, hold my breath, and look down at the floor.

Dad pulls me in tight, my back against his torso, his arms crossed in front of me. I look up again. Dad's face is red, his eyes wide. He stares at Mr. Hart. I've never seen Dad this angry.

I'm sorry, Dad … I'm so sorry.

We leave the small room. Silent tears stream down my face. We hold tight to each other's hands.

Dad leads me back through the giant hall of the courthouse and we stop in front of two very large closed wooden doors. A white policeman stands in front, blocking the way. A black woman, with bright red lipstick, a tight olive-colored dress, and wet cheeks, stands next to the policeman. She stares at me with dark, angry eyes. Dad talks to the policeman and the man opens the doors for us. The black woman tries to push past us into the room, and the policeman grabs her by the arm. She screams and hits him; the policeman shoves her away from the door as Dad guides me past.

"Whore," she screams at me.

The doors shut behind us. Inside, a large courtroom is packed with people.

Looking back, I don't know if there were multiple cases that day or why the courtroom was packed. I'm uncertain if the distraught woman was related to Mr. Hart, a mistress perhaps, or there for a completely different case. I can't remember having a lawyer represent me, if there was one. I don't even know how I came to be at the front of the court that day, yet there I was in the front—standing alone—that much is clear. I don't want to know more.

High above me sits a judge in a black robe. His robe reminds me of one Dad wears at church. Next to him stands a different policeman, a large man with dark skin. They look down at me. I close my eyes and want to disappear.

It hurts to stand. Pain throbs between my legs.

The judge speaks in a loud voice. "Tell me what happened to you."

I want to run, but my feet won't move. I want to scream, but I have no voice. Silence sits heavy on my shoulders.

A rumble flows through the court. I turn and see Dad sitting in the first row, far away. A loud bang, like a gunshot, echoes through the courtroom above my head, and I flinch.

"Silence!" the judge says. "Tell me what happened, young lady."

"… He has this ugly thing like … like … a hot dog …" I whisper.

The large policeman writes in a book. He turns to the judge and they converse. Then the policeman turns to the crowd and clears his voice. The large room is quiet. I can hear myself breathe.

The policeman's deep bass voice fills the court as he projects all my whispered words. "He has this ugly thing like, like, a hot dog, without skin, and it's covered with blood …"

To my eleven-year-old mind, the policeman mimics my baby talk. He tells everyone the secrets I had whispered only to the judge. He mocks me. I feel naked, exposed, with a hundred people staring at me. My body shakes. My cheeks burn. Everyone sees. Everyone knows.

For decades I dream of that courtroom and the large policeman. In my nightmares the room is packed; long aisles, and narrow spaces between the rows, are filled with people. Oversized windows fill one wall and every window is crowded with distorted faces, pressing against the panes from outside, staring in at me—laughing.

I am shamed.

CHAPTER 23

Mayday

We should not judge people by their peak of excellence; but by the distance they have traveled from the point where they started.

Henry Ward Beecher

The South Pacific Ocean, April 2015

"MAYDAY!" Dennis says. He is bent forward on the seat at the navigation station, eyes wide, staring at the computer, running his fingers through his hair. It is the most dreaded word for a sailor, only to be used in a life-threatening emergency.

"What?!" I drop my dishtowel and rush to his side.

A series of eerie tones bleep through the high-frequency, single sideband radio as it works to download the email content. Craning my neck to look over his head, I read the word in capital letters across the title window: MAYDAY! I squeeze his shoulder hard, and he turns to look up at me.

"It's from Randy and Dawn," he says. "It hasn't finished downloading."

Centime is sailing on the windvane through confused seas. Sounds of pounding waves mingle with the radio's static and its disharmonic tones. Placing my hand on my throat, I feel my pulse race. One window on the computer screen shows mostly red where green, yellow, and red blocks indicate our chances of radio connection. Another window shows the email headlines as their contents slowly download.

Clothes are strewn across the cabin seats. A fishing rod hangs from the ceiling with damp clothes draped over it. I hastily collect them, right the inside-out shirts and pants, and sort them into two piles: his and hers. The beeps and static continue as I glance again at the computer screen and wait. Dennis drums his fingers on the wooden navigation table.

Climbing quickly to the cockpit, I do a safety check. The sky is uniform gray. *Centime* is sailing well on her own with Grace, our wind vane steering. There is no boat traffic so far out at sea; I only need to check every ten minutes. The wind is steady. Endless miles of tall waves stretch in two directions. I t has been eighteen hours since the last double wave hit.

"Has her email come through yet?" I ask, yelling down to the cabin.

"Yeah, *Nirvana Now* is taking on water and they need to abandon ship. First a metal plate that holds up their rigging broke and punched a small hole where the hull meets the deck. Last night a large wave hit their stern and knocked out their steering. They installed an emergency rudder and tiller but it was broken by another wave. Now the emergency rudder is banging against their hull."

"Oh my God. Where are they?"

He pulls up the navigation software and plots their position.

"Six hundred miles ahead, west-southwest."

"How far from land?"

"Hiva Oa in the Marquesas is the closest land, about 1,000 nautical miles." A shushing sound indicates another email is coming through. The sender is "Safety Net," a group that monitors passages across the South Pacific.

We stare at the screen. The email heading reads "Mayday Relay." My heart races. "The Net says we're the closest boat," Dennis says. "They want to know if we can change course and try to reach them."

"Six hundred miles and we're closest! That's ... four days away," I say. "There have to be closer boats. Can they last four days? Are they gonna be okay?" My words rush together. I have an empty feeling in my stomach. Wedging my feet against the edges of the corridor and leaning on the galley counter, I hold my neck with both hands and stare at Dennis.

"I don't know, honey," he says, placing his hand on my arm. "Their bilge pumps should be working. I just don't know how fast the water is coming in. I'll email Randy and let him know we're on our way, and I'll email the other boats in our fleet to see if anyone is closer. I don't think the boats in our fleet are in contact with Randy or the safety net, so they might not be aware."

"Let's look at yesterday's position report. There has to be someone closer. Maybe *Talulah Ruby*? They're the fastest."

"They may be too far past. It would be hard to turn back into these winds. I'll check *Ruby*'s position, and in the meantime why don't you plug in *Nirvana*'s position on the cockpit chart plotter, change our course, and head directly toward them. We'll find out who is closest at the noon radio net. I don't know what else we can do. We're too far away to get through to anyone on the VHF radio. We must try to sail toward them."

Grabbing a Xanax my doctor had prescribed for anxiety, I swallow it without water. I feel a lump in my throat as it goes down. My stomach growls as I open an angled cabinet door. Bags of potato chips and boxes of cookies and crackers fall out of the closet hitting my face, head, and chest like a small avalanche. Picking up the mess, and putting a few saltine packets in my pockets, I shove the bags and boxes back inside the closet and slam the door.

The electronic chart in the cockpit shows over 1,000 miles of open sea around *Centime*, no buoys or navigation aids, no boats on the AIS, no land. I find *Nirvana*'s latitude and longitude, place a black X on the chart, plot a course toward her, and adjust our steering. Angling *Centime* on her new course, I trim her sails. Her speed increases and her ride becomes wild and reckless as she heads closer to the wind.

Centime pitches fore and aft, up and down. With this altered course, breaking waves will now hit her on her beam—the worst of directions.

I envision *Nirvana* being battered about in unsettled seas. She's sitting helpless without steering or forward movement to ease the blows. Waves must be pummeling her side, rolling her hard over until she rocks back to be hit again the way a boxer takes down a weakened opponent. On *Centime* it's uncomfortable moving through the waves. On *Nirvana Now* it must be worse.

I realize that although we received the email this morning we can't tell when it was sent. It could be brand new, or twenty-four hours old. My breathing is rapid. I put my hand on my chest.

They're still all right. They must be all right. Please still be alive.

The electronic chart shows an area that stretches from the Galapagos to French Polynesia. I zoom in to *Nirvana*'s mark and back out to make it look like we're close. Not too far, I try to fool myself, knowing it's a fabrication. I set the mark as our destination. The ETA reads eighty-six hours to their mark. *Centime is* flying at seven knots, close to her top speed. Making careful, small adjustments in her sails I'm able to increase our speed by a tenth of a knot. Checking the ETA once more it now reads eighty-five hours. At this speed we'll arrive at night.

Dennis starts the fleet's noon radio net: "Tangaroa net, Tangaroa net, this is sailing vessel *Centime* with emergency traffic. *Nirvana Now*, a forty-foot sloop has sent out a mayday, requesting immediate assistance." Dennis states *Nirvana Now*'s position and our position. "She's taking on water. *Centime* is 600 nautical miles away. We're heading toward them. When you state your position please determine if you are closer than we are and advise."

Voices respond with a sobering tone. One boat, *Continuum*, is 190 nautical miles away and has already changed course. We will continue to follow, second in line, in case *Nirvana Now* or *Continuum* need additional assistance or a search party.

The gray day stretches into a dreary night. I strain my eyes through the darkness to discern which waves near *Centime* may collide. My eyes dart from the sails to the instruments, to the waves, and back as I concentrate on sailing as fast as we can while keeping the boat at a reasonable angle to the waves and searching for the possibility of breakers. "Breathe. Breathe," I say, unsure if I'm hyperventilating.

By midnight, clouds have blocked fleeting glints of the moon. Every slap of a wave brings a disturbing image of *Nirvana Now* at the mercy of unseen waves. I shiver in the warm breeze. The sea and sky are now uniform black.

Ever since I was eleven, I've been afraid of darkness.

CHAPTER 24

The Butcher's Knife

You have to learn to get up from the table when love is no longer being served.

Nina Simone

Cape Neddick, Maine, February 1996

Nico is three and I've separated from his father. His dad is a good man and a loving father. He has always taken care of me, yet I can't find the strength and courage to shed my demons within the confines of the life we have built together. I need to learn how to care for myself, yet it frightens me to be alone. The nights are hard with flashbacks and night terrors.

My newly rented space is sparse. The separation from Nico's dad was quick, without furniture, plants, art, books, dishes, or photos, the historical artifacts of my life. The emptiness seems to echo in the empty house. When my phone rings the sound is jarring. Mother is on the line and she is screaming.

Standing before a full-length bedroom mirror I see my reflection, an aging fortysomething. My hand shakes as I hold tight to the blue telephone. The cord spirals far from its base. The dull blue carpet begins to spin. My breathing is rapid. Lightheaded, I sit on the floor and put my head below my heart, resting the phone on the rug to continue listening. All I can hear is her high-pitched shriek, "What have you done to me?"

Mother has two voice tones: loving and shrill. Her shrill voice paralyzes me. I had been afraid to tell her of my separation, afraid to hear her screams.

Now she has found out. What have I "done" to her? I have separated from my husband.

Tensions in my marriage began two years earlier when I went to graduate school for an MBA and took a class on leadership. I was a pushover in the program, easily manipulated by male students and professors. Having always had trouble with men and boundaries, I allowed others to cross important lines. I lost my confidence and my voice after age eleven; the voice I developed over three decades seemed as though it was still fragile.

During my second year of graduate school, I had a career-boosting internship opportunity that conflicted with a loosely scheduled economics class. Hoping for more clarity on class dates and times, I went to visit my economics professor during his office hours. I knocked on the side of his open door. "Professor," I said. "Do you have a minute?"

The professor was in his sixties, white, clean-shaven with thinning hair. His office was small, crammed with books, a large desk, and framed diplomas. He sat in an oversized leather desk chair. He turned his head and scowled as I knocked, staring at me over the top of thick black glasses. I looked down. My throat started to close as I waited for his answer. Finally, I continued without his response.

"Professor, can you confirm the days for our upcoming Econ 601 classes for the next two weeks? I have an opportunity for an amazing internship and the supervisor would like to know when I might be free to begin working."

The professor stood up next to me, moving quite close. He wasn't a big man but he seemed larger than I had remembered. I backed away.

"Come in and sit down there, young lady," he said, pointing to a small armless plastic chair. I sat where he pointed. He closed his door and stood over me. My head felt hot and I could feel myself sweat.

"You want me to tell you which days over the next two weeks we will meet?" he said.

"Yes, Professor, I don't want to miss any of your classes. They're important."

He placed his hands on his hips and raised his voice. "Why would they be important to you—a woman? Don't you have a husband?"

I squirmed in my chair. He leaned closer.

"Yes, Professor."

"What does your husband think of you being in school? Shouldn't you be home supporting him? You have to decide what you want. You can't have it both ways."

"He's supportive of me. I want this degree."

"Do you know how to drive a car?"

"Yes, I can drive." My cheeks burned.

"It sounds to me like an MBA is too hard for you, too challenging."

"It's not too hard, Professor. I'm in the top 10 percent of our class. I've earned a full academic fellowship …"

"Don't interrupt me! This Master's program is too hard for you. I can tell. I saw you sitting in the front of my class in your white T-shirt. You should have been home caring for your husband. You don't belong here. You don't belong in my class. And you certainly don't belong in the business world. Is that clear?"

"Yes, sir." I hung my head as I slinked out of his office.

Ashamed of my response to my professor, and to Mother's phone call, I seek help. A friend recommends a therapist from Wellesley College. During an introductory phone call my words feel stuck in my throat and then they rush out.

"Look I'm totally over being raped at eleven, I mean he was convicted a long time ago, the cuts and scars are healed, and I don't want to waste your time if you have more important people you're trying to see, like anyone who might really need you, someone suicidal, or thinking of hurting someone, and I know you're a specialist in trauma, and this really isn't a big deal, it's not trauma, but…" I don't tell her I have a young son I love deeply and am worried about his father taking him from me if I might be crazy, or about the PTSD episodes or the night terrors, instead I simply ask, "Might you have a minute?"

My therapist's office is arranged like a small sitting room. There is an overstuffed flowered love seat, two cozy chairs with pillows, a coffee table, and, in the corner, a tall plant. A painting on the wall captures a seascape with children playing. The room is meant to look comfortable and friendly, not clinical. There is a glass of water on the end table, and a box of tissues. We both know that the work is hard.

We meet every week, months on end. I recall minute details of my childhood assault: a particular orange-brown shade of eyeglasses, a pungent smell in the room, the rough feel of a woolen blanket scratching my naked skin when Dad carried me into the hospital, and wrinkles of blood on Mr. Hart's sheets. These details illuminated scattered parts of an incomplete picture. They are the first images that come when I panic. I'd seen them thousands of times in everyday thoughts, night terrors, and full-blown flashbacks.

I also saw a broader picture: I was hurt not just by Mr. Hart, but by medical staff, policemen, a judge, and the system behind them. My recall of these traumatic childhood events was clear and detailed, as if they had just happened.

Yet there was one memory that, for decades, I couldn't access. It was repressed, locked away where no one, not even I, could find it.

When I tried to recall the sequence of events of that day in May 1967, I had a ferocity of cues, leading up to a touch of amnesia: clear memories of sights, smells, and tactile details, and then everything goes black. The reaction was volatile. I could feel the intensity of fear but not see the cause. I knew something horrific was there, but I didn't know what it was or how to access it. I called it my "black place."

Memory is strange.

A paradox exists where large chunks of important information can lie dormant, like sleeping giants, invisible to the conscious mind, while the memories around them are dotted with vibrant intensity.

"Tell me about your 'black place,'" my therapist says.

My body stiffens. I squirm in my chair. My hand wraps around my throat. The pulse in my neck indicates my heart is pounding. I look across the room for an escape route; her door is closed. The windowless office feels warm. I move toward the edge of my seat, gripping the arms of my chair.

The room is quiet. I grab the glass and take long gulps. Lukewarm water travels down my throat.

She waits.

I have no memory of the black place—no voice.

"I … I … can't … remember that part. Only before and after," I whisper, my voice shaking, my eyes staring at the beige carpet. "I slammed the door in his face. I thought he was gonna kill me. When I was outside and I turned away from his door, the sun blinded me. I ran hard, being careful not to stumble. I didn't want him to catch up. I skipped steps racing up to my porch. I looked at every step. There was a drop of blood on one of my toes. My mind was racing, planning … and I just kept praying, 'Please God, please God, please God, let me get to my room.'"

"You wanted to go to your room?"

"Yes." I bite my lips, hard. "I had an intense urge to run to my bedroom, before Mother caught me naked. I thought if I could make it to my room and close the door, maybe I'd be safe."

"Interesting that you didn't want to run to your mother. Children in healthy relationships typically run to their primary caregiver after a trauma."

"I did NOT want to run to mine!" I say louder than I expect. I clench my fists. "As I ran across my porch, I plotted the route in my mind. I wanted to run across the living room diagonally to the stairs at the opposite corner. It's all very clear. I remember every detail up to that point.

"When I reached the front door, I forced it open with all my strength. It slammed against the wall. Then everything turns black. It feels so scary. It sucks me in like a black hole in space." Holding my breath, I puff out my cheeks as I try to remember.

"It's hell. I'm in hell." I break down and sob.

Months pass and I continue therapy through my separation. I open my personal journal and find Mother's recent letter. I bring it with me to my counseling session. The therapist sits up straight. Her eyes open wide. Her body stiffens as she begins to read the note Mother had sent a month earlier.

Dear Heidi,

YOU PUT A BUTCHER KNIFE THROUGH MY HEART!!!

HOW DARE YOU DO THIS TO YOUR MOTHER!!!!
Aunt Betsy stopped by last night for dinner ...

"Oh, my. This is a classic textbook case of ..." She stares at me, her mouth open.

"Of what?" I ask.

"Oh, I'm sorry. I shouldn't have said that. It's not appropriate, it just slipped out, by mistake."

"What were you going to say?"

"A therapist shouldn't diagnose someone they've never seen."

"You have to tell me. What is this a textbook case of?" I lean forward in my chair.

She sighs. "Well, the way this is written with two distinct types of handwriting and two very different messages, one flowing right into the other, and her hyperbolic language: 'putting a butcher knife through my heart.' Her letters flow back and forth shifting from kind and loving to mean and self-centered. It's a textbook example of borderline personality disorder. It explains so much."

"What does it explain?" I shift forward to the edge of my seat.

"People with BPD can exhibit extreme mood swings. They can alternate between being really positive about their son or daughter and then really disappointed. They often show intense narcissism. Help me to understand more. Your mother's response about your separation is that you put a butcher knife through her heart. That's a powerful image. How did that make you feel?"

"Guilty, ashamed, ruined." I take a deep breath and close my eyes, blowing the air out of my cheeks. She begins to write in her notebook. "I ... I ... caused her so much pain. I still feel terrible about going to the Harts' porch. I hold everything inside. Other than you, I can't tell anyone the whole truth. No one even uses the 'r' word—at least I can't. And I've always been afraid to talk about my trauma because I thought the reality, my memory of it, would kill Mother." Tears run down my cheek.

"What do you mean?"

"Whenever she's upset, she loses control. I'm afraid one day her heart will stop beating and it will be my fault." I stare at the painting of the children at the seashore on her wall. It reminds me of being a child at the New Jersey shore. "A few days after I got her note, my feelings started to change. I felt less guilty, but sad that she didn't care about what was happening with Nico, my husband, or me. It's been hard on us, and yet she seems to care only about herself.

"She called me on the phone and screamed at me a second time. At first, I felt overpowered and went to the floor. It's what I do when I'm upset: I either run or I fall to the floor, become smaller, and try to disappear." I wipe my eyes and sit up. "I told her that if she didn't stop screaming, I'd hang up. She kept screaming and berating me, so I hung up. She called back, started to scream again, and I hung up again. It actually felt powerful to hang up on her. It was the first time in my life I realized I didn't have to listen."

"How do you feel now?"

"Better." I smile. "Her letter and response were absurd, so different from how I would react to Nico if he were having a difficult time. It confirmed that my experiences from childhood were as crazy and unpredictable as I remembered."

"Like what?" the therapist asks.

"When I was eleven, after the trauma, Mother said that I wet my bed because I ate too many mashed potatoes. Isn't that absurd to say mashed potatoes were the cause?"

"It sounds like she was in denial of what was really happening."

"Yeah, but was she forgetting, or did she remember and hide it? She would often lose control, go from my loving mother who treated me like I was the most important person in the world, to a screaming woman who didn't like me. I thought it was my fault, something I did to make her lose control. I worked … so … hard … to not make her scream."

"Listen," she says. "Her loss of control was not your fault. It doesn't matter how hard you work, you can't control how she feels. You can let go of that right now."

"I wish I could change things and help her feel better. There were times when she was loving, too."

"You can stand beside her and offer support when she is in pain, if you choose to; you didn't cause her pain, and you can't carry it for her."

"It's out of my control?"

"Yes, you can't control her feelings, just as she can't control yours. She can only make you feel guilty or worthless if you let her."

Twenty years later, my friend Susan is sitting on an adjacent sofa in a living room where I'm house-sitting. She is a professor of psychology at the University of New Hampshire. We're drinking my homemade mint iced tea. The living room has golden-brown walls and a large oriental rug. Low winter light diffuses through large windows. Grand, built-in bookshelves stand on either side of a fireplace where a small fire burns. Mother's letters lie in a stack on an end table, next to a thick medical reference book. Susan looks up from Mother's letter.

"What can you surmise about my mother?" I say.

"You know I can't diagnose someone I haven't met, right?" Susan says.

"But you must have an opinion."

She brushes back her short-cropped, auburn hair. Her russet sweater looks new; her silver necklace, stylish. We have been friends for twenty-five years. She threw a baby shower for me when I was pregnant.

"The behaviors I'm reading in these letters show a strong indication of borderline personality disorder."

I take a sip of tea. "That's the same term my therapist used years ago. What does it mean?"

"It's a lack of ability to establish your own sense of self. People with BPD identify with other people. I tell my students it's like the movie Fatal Attraction."

"Really?" I say, eyes wide.

"Have you seen the movie?"

"Well yes, but doesn't Glenn Close try to kill her lover?"

"It is a Hollywood version of an extreme case, however, BPD is a disorder where people aggrandize someone and have trouble creating a boundary between themselves and that person. They're unpredictable and can have extreme mood shifts from one moment to the next. Often they become needy and exhaust the other person. Eventually, the other person does things they don't like, and they can turn against him or her in harsh ways. They're afraid of being abandoned because then they would lose that sense of self they've identified with."

"Mother's dad died at sea before she was born; it's possible she might have been afraid of being abandoned. I don't understand her reaction to my separation. If my son were to separate, I'd be concerned about him. I'd want to know how I might help, let him know I love him. She never showed any compassion. It was about her, not me. In this note, she wrote, 'You put a butcher knife through my heart,' … isn't that intense?"

Susan looks out of the window. Snow is piled on the porch; the trees are bare. "If she truly had a personality disorder, she may not have had the capacity to respond any differently. When she ranted about the butcher knife, she may have felt as if she had experienced her own divorce."

I set my iced tea on the table, put my hand over my chest, grabbing the edges of my sweater. "Wait, you mean instead of feeling like I was getting a divorce, it was as if my mother were getting her own divorce?"

"It was as if she felt the pain of her own divorce even though she had never been divorced. Perhaps your mother actually felt like she was struck with a butcher knife."

A log cracks and I flinch. Susan stares at the fire, rubs her chin, and leans in closer, staring at me.

"Heidi, you should know that it's not uncommon for people with BPD to have been abused themselves … repeatedly … as children."

"Wow!" I shift my hand from my chest to my throat. "Her being abused as a child would explain a lot. I've wondered about it. I suspect she struggled with her… stepdad, my grandpa. He was … inappropriate … with me and my cousin when we were children."

Memories flicker. Grandpa's rough farmer's hands, the light bulb that dangled by an orange extension cord over his workbench, his cold damp basement… Could he have taken her there? I shiver.

"Susan, I have an old photo of her when she was about five. She has the sweetest smile. She looks so innocent. I often wonder what happened to her smile… to that little girl … I can't even …." Tears form. Susan puts her hand over mine as I continue. "When I got divorced, I only thought of my own pain, and what my son and my ex were feeling. I knew Mother would be upset but I never imagined she actually felt the heartache as if it were happening to her, or ever felt any of my pain as her own."

I sink back in my chair. I bite my lip and take a deep breath. "Susan," I whisper. "When I was raped as a child … what would you guess Mother felt?"

That quiet afternoon by the fire was a turning point. For over forty years I had carried my story like a hidden wound. Every day I thought of my assailant's name, heard Mother's judgments, and held feelings of worthlessness. Susan left and I found the photo of Mother at age five. She stands by a porch rocker wearing an oversized coat. All but the tips of her fingers are hidden in the long sleeves. Her coat buttons are little flowers. She has tiny shoes, Mary Janes, with two straps. Her short hair has bangs; one unruly lock flies off to the side. I had never noticed the details before. All I remembered was her captivating smile.

I found a photo of me at age four or five too. I have Mother's smile.

CHAPTER 25

An Ant on a Toothpick

*The wound is the place where
The Light enters you.*

Rumi

The South Pacific Ocean, April 2015

"*Nirvana Now* has sunk."

Dennis reads an email title aloud from the boat *Continuum* and then stares at the computer under the blinking lights of our single sideband radio. We wait. *Centime*'s cabin is once again strewn with clothes, the deep sink filled with dirty dishes. I hold my breath, waiting for the rest of the message to download, hoping Dawn and Randy are alive.

Dennis reads: "A swirl of emotions overtakes me: relief and joy that we are safe aboard *Continuum*; gratefulness for Bob and Mona, who have saved our lives; and sadness that our beloved boat and home for fourteen years is at the bottom of the sea. Waking up this morning was very hard. Much love, Dawn."

Tears stream down my face. Dennis stands and wraps his arms around me.

"They're safe … and that's … all that matters. I was so afraid they would…" I pull away from Dennis, holding my stomach. "I … I don't feel good. I'm sick."

"What's wrong, honey? Is it your bladder infection or emotional upheavals?"

"No … I don't know. The infection should be over but my stomach is in pain. I've never felt this before, almost like I'm twelve months pregnant and bursting. Okay, this is a huge exaggeration but remember the horror movie *Alien* where the man is eating spaghetti?"

"Yeah?"

"His stomach hurts and then his abdomen explodes. It feels like there is a live object in my abdomen trying to push its way out. The pain is intense."

"Shit, honey! What is it: your bladder, your appendix? What's going on?"

"I don't know! I need to lie down."

"It's my watch. Lie down in the starboard berth. I'll open the porthole a crack so you can call if anything changes. We can reach Mark on the net in a few hours, and maybe he can diagnose your symptoms and tell us what to do."

"All right." I crawl into the berth and fall asleep.

Waking up with intermittent stabs of pain, I stumble to the head. Could my appendix be bursting? I pull out a book, Medical Emergencies at Sea, its paper brown and crinkled from seawater. Pages of possibilities loom before me. I start to sweat. Could I be constipated after eating saltine crackers and rice for days? I grab a handful of prunes and sit doubled over in the cabin, chewing. It's hard to swallow.

This is my worst sail, right up there with the Gulf Stream lightning and Providencia's northern reef. Should I just give up? Why am I torturing myself? After finishing a half-dozen stale prunes and a couple of dried apricots, I take a few sips of water. The pain has subsided for the moment and I head to the cockpit to relieve Dennis. He goes below and makes a quick dinner. Climbing back into the cockpit, he hands me a bowl half-filled with pasta carbonara.

"I'm not hungry," I say

"I'm taking over as medical officer. You need to eat. Eggs and noodles should be bland enough. Just try a few bites. How are you feeling?"

"My abdomen is sore, but the intense pain has subsided. I'll be okay. I'm just relieved that Randy and Dawn are safe." The pasta's warmth spreads through me. "I was scared for them. It must have been frightening to watch *Nirvana* take on water, and then wait hour after hour in these crazy seas, not knowing if *Continuum* would find them in time. I'm upset thinking about it.

Look at my hands—they're shaking."

"I can't imagine losing control of your boat out here and not knowing how far away a rescue is," he replies. "And when the rescue boat did arrive, it would have been no small feat to get Randy and Dawn on board without damaging *Continuum*."

"*Nirvana*'s mast must have been swinging with these waves. *Continuum* wouldn't have been able to get close, and they couldn't just swim over. I keep picturing them using *Nirvana*'s dinghy for the transfer. Imagine lowering a tiny, open boat into these seas and getting in, waves crashing over you. It was hard enough when we practiced getting into a life raft in a still pool."

"They had no choice."

"What a prophetic name for their dingy—*Purgatory*, the wait between heaven and hell."

"It is especially prophetic given that they lost *Nirvana Now*, their heaven. They put so much of themselves into that boat for so many years, and then to watch her sink."

"It would be devastating to lose *Centime*."

"Let's not talk about it. She's handling these seas well. When the waves hit, she rolls over and pops back up like a good cork. She's a sturdy boat and you're doing a fantastic job keeping her at the best angle to the waves."

"We both are. It's challenging when they come from two directions."

"Yes, but you're doing it, sweetheart, and you're managing your fear."

"It's strange … at times I feel very small, like an ant on a toothpick in the midst of a turbulent sea, and at other times I feel much bigger than myself, connected to something larger."

Once again, my abdomen is wracked with pains. I run to the head. The pain worsens. I sit in the head and cry. Later I stumble back to the cockpit.

"Dennis, I need to send an email to my doctor," I say, holding my abdomen. "I'm in huge pain and I … I … just passed a worm."

"What?!" he exclaims.

"I must have eaten bad food. The worm was ten inches long. There may be more balled up in my colon. It feels like it's distended."

"Oh, my God, what can I do? Of course, use the radio. Do you want me to send the message?"

"No, I'll do it, but there isn't any way we can send a photo, is there? I took a picture to identify it."

"No sorry, honey, you'll just have to describe how it looks."

A few hours later I hear the static and tones from the radio. Dennis is at the computer downloading emails. "Your doctor replied. He's sent the name of the medicine you need. He says it's important to get it immediately in case you have more parasites. There's a slight risk of obstructing and rupturing your intestine. Can you check our prescription list?" he asks.

I find the medicine bag and the list of our prescriptions. "It's not on the list. I'll have to wait it out. I feel a bit better at the moment."

My stomach growls; I've hardly eaten for forty-eight hours. Dennis makes tea and uses the boiling water to make a simple rice meal from a freeze-dried packet. He sits on the port corner of the cockpit shielded from the wind. I huddle opposite him, holding my warm bowl of flavored rice. I stop eating after a few bites; my stomach is bloated. I swallow a large antibiotic.

In an instant, my hands shake and I'm nauseous. "Dennis, I'm sick. Please… bucket … hurry …" He scrambles below.

Leaning slightly over the side I vomit, my head faces down above the water, the boat heeling at a steep angle. A wave hits from one angle, pushing me backward toward the cockpit immediately followed by another forcing me to slip, head down, to the sea. Cold waves splash high against the side of the boat as she races with the wind, and pitches through erratic waves. Damp hair clings to my face and salt stings my eyes. I clutch cold stainless-steel bars as I slide. My arms tremble as I hold my body rigid above the sea, like an amateur gymnast trying to hold an iron cross.

Water rushes by below me in a fast, dizzying stream. A blurred image of orange-brown glasses fades in and out of focus, reflected in a thousand droplets of water. I squeeze my eyes shut; the image expands and turns to black. I scream for Dennis but the sounds are lost in the wind.

As I slide toward the sea, my life jacket's tether catches. Using the tether and all my strength, I push myself back into the cockpit.

Dennis arrives with a pink dishpan. My dinner come out in a second round. I gag and cough. He places a hand on my back to help steady me, but I push him away. I can't stand the touch.

"Drink some water," he says, offering a bottle.

I wave away the water in a panicked frenzy. My head is feverish. Sweating under my foul-weather gear, I rip open the top to let in cool air. As the breeze flows across my hot chest, my body shakes. I try to re-zip my jacket but have no strength.

I'm too shaky to move. The boat, sea and sky are spinning. My abdomen has sharp pains. Closing my eyes, I vomit a third time.

The acid burns my throat. Grabbing the water bottle I had rejected earlier, I try to cool the burn. Not daring to swallow a single drop I spit it into the tub.

The sea churns. I stumble below, coughing, taking labored breaths between the coughs. Throbbing pains radiate through my abdomen.

I collapse in my berth.

CHAPTER 26

The Absence of Image

In a single glance our souls can be flooded with the most profound reflections.

Paul Gauguin

The South Pacific Ocean, April 2015

Memories surge through me as I lie in my quarter berth. The waves are relentless, forcing me side to side in the tiny bunk. My abdominal pain continues.

I drift to sleep deluged with heavy dreams. A slippery pearl sits at the edge of my tongue. This pearl has frightened me through decades of night terrors. In this dream on *Centime*, a peregrine falcon swoops over my head and lands on my shoulder. Feeling her power, I swallow the pearl. It lodges hard in my throat but doesn't choke me; instead, it turns to ash. Clearing the ash from my throat, I hear my true voice for the first time. I begin to sing.

As I wake from this dream, my face and left side of my body tingle. The hair on my upper arm is raised, but I'm not cold. I jot down the details in my journal and stumble to the head. The abdominal pain has dissipated. I slowly exhale.

Grabbing a lime Gatorade from the galley, I head toward the cockpit to relieve Dennis.

"I don't want to jinx anything, but I feel better. My head is clear. I actually feel … good."

Dennis's eyes widen. "That's a huge relief. What can I get you? Hot tea? Soup? Medicine?"

"No, I'm just gonna sip this. I can take over now. You need to sleep." I flop down on the cockpit seat and scan the horizon. Wave trains from two directions are smacking *Centime*'s hull in a stomach-turning pattern and I grip the back of the bench. "What's with these waves? When are they going to diminish?"

"I don't know. It feels like we're being whacked with a fucking sledgehammer. I can't wait until we get out of this bullshit. These waves are worse than last night. You must stay hooked in. Let me know if you need anything."

Craning my neck, I scan the full horizon. The sea is black. A fuzzy sliver of moon is waning, only bright enough to act as a warning beacon illuminating white foam on cresting waves. In a day or two all moonlight will be gone.

The waves continue for two more days. My thirst for land is almost unbearable, enduring through what a sailor once termed an endless sea of "undrinkable time."

When I imagined escaping to the South Pacific as an adolescent, I fantasized about what type of boat I would sail and what I would name her. I made lists of names and researched places in the Galapagos and French Polynesia. Early Polynesians were master navigators and believed their god, Ta'aroa, would protect them. Ta'aroa was the supreme creator of all and his tears created the sea. I wanted to call my dream boat Ta'aroa even though boats are usually referred to as female and often named after women. At fifteen, I naively believed women were weak. I wanted a man's name for my boat, to protect me across the sea.

Tonight on *Centime* the waves create a confused sea. The Polynesian gods Ta'aroa and Tangaroa seem enraged. The swells are the size of motor homes, seven, eight, nine feet high, stretching one after another. It looks like a mammoth trailer park with all the trailers aligned sideways against us. Waves from the east slap hard against our stern; waves from the southeast and south smack us on the port quarter, and occasionally broadside. These waves strike every six seconds like an unyielding boxer.

For several hours I clutch the rails as I move across the cockpit to check wind and wave angles. My red headlamp illuminates a small part of the sails in the dark. The wind generator makes an unnerving, high-pitched whirl.

There is beauty in this eerie scene of deep black night and occasional bright sparkling white, when I look beyond my fear. I envision my dream and falcon. *You are strong. You can do this.*

Sitting down, I watch the horizon rock at severe angles: up, down, back and forth, in an uneasy pattern. I feel dizzy watching *Centime* and the sea, yet my health has returned. I sip a lime Gatorade. Closing my eyes for a moment, I am overcome by exhaustion.

A powerful slap of a large wave sends a jolt through *Centime* and me.

My mind races: How high can breaking waves be before a knockdown? Dennis's voice echoes through me: thirteen … thirteen … thirteen feet. Lucky number thirteen. Crouching in the corner of the cockpit, I glimpse a sparkle of bright white foam. Two nine-foot waves head toward a collision point—a few meters away. Suddenly an image of orange-brown glasses appears. Holding tight to the rail, I fight the urge to fall to the cockpit floor and submit to the wave, to the vision, and to feelings of being ruined. My heart pounds hard in my chest. *I can do this. You and your horrid glasses will not take me down!*

I jump to *Centime*'s port side, straining at the edge of my tether. The waves crash together, sending a giant plume of sea spray before breaking. A white wall of angry water surges toward me. My hands tremble as I grasp a cold steel bar and brace my body.

I recall bodysurfing in New Jersey, as a preteen, standing before waves taller than me. I would take a huge breath and dive underneath. Instinctively, I take a deep breath and hold the air, staring ahead as I wait for impact.

The double wave hits *Centime* broadside. Like a sick amusement ride she rolls hard toward her side. I'm thrown across the cockpit to the end of my tether. The sea rushes past my face as my head dangles over the side. Salt water stings my eyes. Our boom and mainsail are close to the sea. "Please don't go under …" I say aloud as I gasp for breath. If the sail goes into the water and the sea weighs it down, we could lose the boom.

Instantly the boat springs back. If the preventer were to let go, the boom could break away from the mast.

Please hold … please hold.

The preventer holds. Energy surges through me. I hold tight to memories of Marina, my sister sailor. I grab the wheel to avoid blowing another fuse, settle *Centime* back on course, and move quickly back to the port side. My muscles tight, my jaw set, I glare at the sea, watching, waiting.

The horizon rocks at a severe angle. I strain my eyes, yet across the distance all I can see is black. Clouds obscure the stars. We have arrived at a phase of no moon. The blackness of the sea blends into the blackness of night without distinction. Fear surges through me.

I think of my so-called black place, the absence of image, this amnesia-based fragment I have tried to grasp since I was eleven.

Intrusive memories appear before me like landmines in a war-torn field, the landscape dotted with orange glasses, African violets, scratchy gray blankets, and one deep, black, obscure image which I can't make out.

Shit! What's with this blackness? I hate … black places. I start to shake. I don't want to think about it, yet I'm as powerless holding back the memory as I am to stopping the wave. I squeeze my eyes shut as hard as I can.

Philadelphia, Pennsylvania, May 1967

(Trigger Warning) I am eleven years old, aware of every second, every move. My mind and heart are racing yet the room is quiet and still. Mr. Hart lies spent on top of me like a sleeping giant. I believe with total certainty that he will wake up and kill me. I saw it, and felt it, in his eyes, framed in orange glasses.

I hold my breath, carefully squeezing from underneath him, his sweaty body stuck to mine. Uncoupled, I spring from the bed and rush through the living room past the brown sofa. My eyes target his front door. He lurches behind and reaches out to grab me.

"Nooo!" I scream. "Please, God, let me out. Please! Please! Please!"

I reach the door before him, tear it open, and close it hard in his face.

The sun glares off his porch. Squinting, I stumble toward home. I can feel warm air on my naked chest and rough cement below my bare feet.

Plans spin through my head racing like wildfire. I can't let my mother see my exposed body. I have an intense focus to escape Mr. Hart and hide in my bedroom.

When I reach the steps of my own home, I take them two at a time, and then sprint across our porch. Our front door is solid wood behind a screen door. At first the heavy inner door sticks in its frame, then I force it open and it slams against the living room wall with a bang.

Mother stands in the center of the room. She is wearing a green dress and a string of white pearls, a necklace that she typically wears when meeting friends.

Unable to stop racing across our living room, I nearly collide with her but hold back just in time. She towers over me. Her cheeks are flushed and her face is stern. Her lacy white handkerchief falls to the floor. Scanning my nakedness, her blue eyes widen. Her trembling hands clench and unclench. I cower before her.

A drop of blood trickles down my leg onto her plush beige carpet. I put my bloodied foot over the small blood stain on the rug and my unbloodied one on top of it, trying to hide what can't be hidden. Mother knows in an instant what has happened.

"You're ruined," she says in a low, deep whisper.

By eleven years old, I have withstood her outbursts before. "I'm sorry. Sorry. Sorry," I say. Shivering, I try to cover my exposed body with my arms and hands. Please, God don't let her hurt me. Please help me get away. My eyes dart across the living room. She is blocking the path to the stairs, the route to my bedroom. I glance at the door behind me. Where is Mr. Hart?

My mind moves in slow motion. A clock ticks on the side wall. We are frozen in place, frozen in time, she and I, alone in the middle of our living room. A breeze blows open the heavy golden drapes and sunlight pours through long windows. Harsh light reflects off the polished walnut coffee table where a small white pot holds African violets overflowing with purple blooms. There is no escape through our front door. I shrink farther toward the floor.

"You're ruined!" Mother repeats, louder this time.

Her nearness is suffocating as she bends toward me. Her white pearls accentuate the veins in her neck as she closes in. Reaching out with both hands, her outstretched fingers grasp my neck.

"No. No. No, Mommy, no!"

"No man will ever love you."

She clutches my throat and lifts me off the ground as if I am weightless. Struggling to free myself, I grab at her wrists. "You're … hurting …" I cry, tears streaming down my face, blurring my view of her hands and her pearls. Then my voice falters.

I breathe in shallow, intermittent gasps. She begins to shake me, or perhaps she herself is shaking. I'm dizzy and I can't take in enough air. The light fades. The room becomes as black as the place I couldn't recall for much of my life, yet I can still hear her screams.

"You're ruined. You're ruined."

A heartbeat's pause, and then, "You're ruined for life!"

It is the worst feeling, not being able to breathe.

I will never fully understand what happened that day or why. It is clear that Mr. Hart raped me, and then Mother, seeing me naked and bleeding, told me I was ruined for life. I know for certain that she put her hands on my throat and lifted me off the ground. I will always remember the sensation of lost breath. I suspect afterward I lost consciousness, went in and out of consciousness, or perhaps my body reacted in shock by feeling as if I were asleep. I only know that I woke up in Dad's arms, not in my home, but at the entrance to the hospital's emergency room, my naked body wrapped in a rough gray woolen blanket.

I don't know why Mother did what she did, or how she became the woman I knew. I will never know for certain if she had been abused as a child; if her stepfather, my grandpa, hurt her; if she truly had borderline personality disorder, as three therapists have speculated; or what my assault had triggered in her to cause her to lose control. I wonder if when she looked at me in all of my nakedness, she somehow saw herself, as a child who she believed was ruined. If at that moment, she saw and felt her own pain, her own shame, or rage. I do believe we both had lives tangled up in fear, shame, and rage.

I'd buried the memory of what Mother did for over four decades. Yet I carried my black-place fear and her scream—"You're ruined"—every day of my life. And now on *Centime*, along with obscure colliding waves, the memory is illuminated.

On *Centime*, cold sea spray hits me in the face. Although I am shaken, my focus is now clear, as clear as a photo of Mount Everest on my therapist's wall. Subtle glimmers of white are visible in the dark night and black sea. I stare hard and summon my courage. I take a deep breath, and then sing Rocky's theme song as loud as I can. Clenching the metal bars, I form two fists around them. Rocky Balboa versus Apollo Creed: I stand ready.

In the distance, white dots coalesce.

"Fuck. Fuck. Fuck," I shout to the waves.

Two more nine-foot waves crest toward one another in a faceoff. They slam together, rearing up fifteen feet, combining forces. The combatant wave breaks and rolls forward. The double wave towers above me. Images that were once debilitating flash before me, yet I stand strong and think of Rocky, my falcon, and swallowing the pearl. I hold my breath.

The wave slaps *Centime* with fury, forcing her to her side and catapulting me into the lifelines. Straining my eyes through sea spray, my head again below my body, I watch the boom and the full mainsail angle toward the sea. The farthest point of the boom touches the water. The image freezes in my brain. Air rushes out of my lungs. *Centime* immediately snaps back, her mast driving hard, to a place well beyond where she has ever been. As she rolls to the opposite side, I suck in air. The double wave reverberates through the hull and my body. The preventer holds.

Wave trains stretch as far as the horizon. My body shakes; my head pounds. He will not take me down. Making a fist, I rage at the sea.

"NEVER AGAIN, MR. HART. YOU WILL NOT TAKE ME DOWN. I AM BURYING YOU AT SEA!"

CHAPTER 27

Pouring Light

Only from the heart can you touch the sky.

Rumi

The South Pacific Ocean, April 2015

The sun is low in the sky to the east and endless sparkles fill the sea. In every direction, deep blue water touches a brilliant blue sky with a crisp, clear horizon. The wind is still. Not a single distraction is in sight: no planes, boats, birds, fish, or sea mammals. Long, smooth, rolling waves have replaced the wave trains, lifting *Centime*'s bow and then stern in an easy rhythm. Small waves lap her sides, adding depth and character to the light musical tones arising from water against hull. We have reached the latitude and longitude that Ken the weatherman recommended, to get out of the wave trains. Only the soft hum of the motor and the light flapping of a windless sail disturb the peace.

Hour after hour we rise and fall with gentle waves, progressing under a hot sun. I pull out my journal and flip to a page of my favorite quotes. On the top is one from Cheryl Strayed, a woman who hiked alone more than a thousand miles of the Pacific Crest Trail, from the Mojave Desert in California to Washington State. In her book, *Wild*, she wrote: "Fear, to a great extent, is born of a story we tell ourselves."

My old story was one of being ruined—I need a new story. What did Cheryl Strayed do to change her story?

I pull out my old dog-eared copy of *Wild*, with its scribbles in the margins, and find I had forgotten the full quote. It reads: "Fear, to a great extent, is born of a story we tell ourselves, and so I chose to tell myself a different story from the one women are told. I decided I was safe. I was strong. I was brave. Nothing could vanquish me."[1]

"I am strong. I am brave," I say.

A puff of wind touches my cheek. Placing the engine in neutral, I note that the instruments show six knots of wind, enough to keep us moving if I raise additional sail. I roll out the genoa and turn off the engine. For thirty minutes I make continuous, slight adjustments to sail at three and then four knots. I head farther southwest and pick up more speed. The gauge indicates four point eight knots.

Can I balance *Centime* on this angle to the wind to hold a third sail? I put on my lifejacket, clip in, and scamper around the dodger to change lines. *Centime* and I speed through the ocean, nothing visible but endless sea. My balance is steady, my body healthy. "Nothing will vanquish me." Grabbing the rails, I propel myself forward in a half-seated position. Moving with strength, I unhook and re-hook my tether in a steady pattern inching forward on the angled boat like a trapeze artist. Securing the lines on the boom, I take a deep breath and return to the cockpit.

The muscles in my arms respond as I heave out the staysail and she flies free. Five point one knots … five point seven. Her three sails are full and majestic, one balanced with the next. I adjust the traveler to change the angle of the mainsail closer to the wind. The gauge climbs: six-one, and six point eight knots as she heels at a steep angle. My joy soars. I am free, sailing in harmony with *Centime*. We sail at over seven knots, on our direct course toward Nuku Hiva, French Polynesia. A dozen flying fish jump out of the water in unison.

I grab my iPod and put on my new favorite song, "Return to Innocence." Produced by the German musical group Enigma, it features traditional chants by two Taiwanese farmers Difang and Igay Duana, members of an indige-

---

1 Excerpt(s) from WILD: FROM LOST TO FOUND ON THE PACIFIC CREST TRAIL by Cheryl Strayed, copyright © 2012 by Cheryl Strayed. Used by permission of Alfred A. Knopf, an imprint of the Knopf Doubleday Publishing Group, a division of Penguin Random House LLC. All rights reserved.

nous people the Falangaw Amis. Wind rushes past my face. My hair blows wild. *Centime* sails herself on the wind vane. I dance and sing out loud into the wind where no one can hear, words about believing in destiny and returning to yourself.

Is this my destiny? Can I return to innocence, to the girl of ten who was energetic, joyful, and strong? Is that small girl still inside, the one who bounced with glee? The hair on my forearm stands up, and my body shivers.

Five hundred miles left. The day is filled with sunshine, the sky cobalt blue. The only clouds are bright, welcoming fair-weather clouds. Moderate winds fill *Centime*'s sails without a strain. The sea is calm. We have made our peace with Ta'aroa and Tangaroa who rule the earth, the winds, the sea, and her creatures. I have made peace with my past.

A disturbance in the sea at our stern distracts me. I remember the ancient Maori belief that Tangaroa can appear as a whale. Suddenly, a pod of a dozen pilot whales play in the surf around us. Periodic glimpses of their slick black bodies, tall dorsal fins, and bulbous round heads as they breach and dive bring a sense of wonder and joy to my soul.

As the sun sets thousands of stars are on display, the brightest I have ever seen. The waning moon has disappeared, leaving behind the brilliant planets of Venus and Jupiter. Even the spaces between the stars and planets are luminous, reflecting the abundance of the universe.

As I look to the sky, memories of Dad fill me: churning homemade ice cream; making sure I licked the spoon; picking strawberries in a field, "one for the basket and one for your mouth"; putting Band-Aids on my skinned knees; introducing me to orphans, shut-ins, and homeless people, and trying to make a difference in their lives. Dad taught me to swim through rough ocean waves. He taught me to serve the less fortunate. He taught me to love the wilderness. There were many lessons; some were not easy, all were good.

I wish Dad hadn't died before Nico was born. Nico will graduate from his university in a couple of months and will choose his own destiny. Like his grandfather, he champions those who are marginalized. He talks of working internationally in places that are politically unsettled. I worry for his safety and for the safety of his future children.

At times I am lonely on night watch, but tonight, as I view the stars, I feel connected to something greater than myself. I stand forward and talk out loud to a sky filled with stars, hoping somewhere out there, Dad watches over us. I hope he will watch over my son, as he too meets his destiny.

"Dad, you would be proud of your grandson. He inherited your goodness and passion, and none of my fear. I'm afraid he might not choose an easy or safe path. How can I let him go? What if he lives somewhere violent like we did, or worse? Will you watch over him? Tell me how to protect him, Dad. How do I connect him to you?"

There is a vast stillness in the sky. Without warning, a giant fireball falls from the sky in front of *Centime* a dozen meters ahead. Flames of red, orange, yellow, and white are so close to the boat I wonder if sparks will hit us. Eyes wide, mouth falling open, I gasp. Dad's answer passes like an electric jolt. Vibrant thoughts flash before me: a message destined for Nico from his grandfather. Pressing my hand on my chest, I watch the air in front of me on fire for an instant, and then all is calm.

CHAPTER 28

Land Ho

*Gamble everything for love,
if you're a true human being. If not, leave this
gathering. Half-heartedness doesn't reach into
majesty. You set out to find God, but then you keep
stopping for long periods at mean-spirited roadhouses.
Don't wait any longer. Dive in the ocean, leave
and let the sea be you.*

Rumi

The South Pacific Ocean, April 2015

    Dawn breaks with golden light. A full hour before sunrise the sky brightens with a magnificent peach glow. The faintest of stars begin to disappear leaving behind the brightest planets, Venus and Jupiter. Dark cumulus clouds sit puffed up on the horizon.

    I change the settings on the chart plotter from night to day view and turn off our navigation lights. Often the wind and seas calm momentarily with the approaching sunrise. Today is no exception. This morning's eastern sky intensifies and becomes layered, an ink black sea grounds a bright yellow horizon, blending into oranges and fading to soft blues. I yawn and splash cold ocean water on my face.

My eyes widen as the faint silhouette of Ua Huka, French Polynesia appears in the distant mist like an apparition. I stand, one hand on my chest, immersed in feelings hard to describe: gratitude, relief, and deep joy. A gray and white shearwater with a wingspan of about twenty inches swoops in a large arc around the boat and is soon joined by a dozen more birds. As the sun rises, it reveals a second island in the background, Nuku Hiva, mystical and brilliant in the low sun. She rises 1,600 feet at a steep incline from the sea, lifting up a spine of dramatic peaks. Between *Centime* and land a brilliant rainbow pierces dark clouds.

"Land ho!" Dennis yells. "Look, honey, we're almost there!"

We laugh and embrace and then I go below to chill a bottle of French champagne we have saved for our long-awaited landfall. We play our favorite songs, "Rocky" and songs from Motown. We dance and sing, swagger, and swoon as Grace the wind vane steers us steadfastly to our goal.

Dennis, in bare feet and his blue-green sarong, has ditched shoes, shirt, underwear, and life vest. He scampers over the deck to set our drifter: a lightweight sail, forward of the other sails. The large, balloon-like drifter unfolds with full fanfare; her red and white stripes billow majestically in the trade winds. I adjust the sail's angle to the wind, rebalance the other sails, and then marvel as they power *Centime* toward French Polynesia with a great force.

Nuku Hiva rises from the sea, massive, wild, and ancient, with sheer cliffs. Large waves, hiding paddlers in outrigger canoes, crash ashore and send plumes of sea spray twelve to fifteen feet high. Hundreds of birds soar among the cliffs and pinnacles. I am humbled and grateful.

The southeast side of Nuku Hiva appears impenetrable until a hidden opening in this high island becomes visible. At the mouth of a steep-sided valley, we enter a fjord-like bay. Cliffs fringe the cloud-shrouded mountains, forming a large, circular, natural harbor protected from rough seas.

Five manta rays, eight feet across, circle the boat. Their black backs skim the surface of the water. Their mouths, oblong suctions, are iridescent blue. They dive for fish, turning at graceful angles and exposing their white underbellies. Fish with blue tails, twelve to sixteen inches long, feed in symmetry by their sides, taking advantage of the leftovers.

Above the water, dark cliffs rise at steep angles from the clear turquoise sea. A strip of pure white sand nestles between two cliffs. Green valleys with a profusion of palms trees rise to meet steep ridges. I fill my lungs with its earthy richness, scents I had forgotten.

Shafts of sunlight stream through windows in the clouds. A double rainbow, vibrant and glimmering, extends from one valley to the next. With a full spectrum of colors, the gray of the sky merges into an arc of purple, teal, green, yellow, and orange, a reminder of what lies at a journey's end.

The fickle sky beyond the rainbow offers a mix of intense whites and threatening grays. White birds soar across the highest jet-black peaks, the sunlight illuminating their wings.

I wonder at the contrast of light and dark.

I call Nico on the satellite phone. "It's me. We're pulling into Nuku Hiva!"

"I can't believe it, Mom. I'm proud of you."

"I'm proud of you too." He has grown far beyond that boy I dropped off first semester. "You're almost done with college."

"Yeah, school's hard but it's almost over. Tell me about your journey."

"Nuku Hiva is a South Pacific paradise, right out of a Gauguin painting. I can hardly believe my eyes.

"You'll think I'm crazy from being at sea, but I have to tell you something important. I was in the middle of the South Pacific asking the universe for guidance and I felt this overwhelming presence of your grandfather, my dad. Suddenly a fireball, like a flaming meteorite, fell in front of *Centime*. It wasn't high in the sky; it came right down, close to the sea." I describe the fireball, its powerful presence as it burned up before me. I later read that NASA estimates an average of forty fireballs fall to Earth every year, many landing in the sea, yet they are rarely seen. "Your grandfather sent a message from me to you; if you're ever in trouble, or searching for answers—your answer lies within—and it is love. I love you forever and all the evers."

"I love you too Mom, to the moon and back."

Sailboats *Wavelength* and *Talulah Ruby* are anchored in the still harbor. Eileen is on her boat's bow. She blasts an air horn, and Mark and other friends appear. Eileen shouts, "Ahoy! Hooray!" and Mark waves and blows the horn as we motor by.

After anchoring, we hop in the dinghy and motor to shore. Climbing up a metal ladder, my legs are wobbly. I want to stoop down and kiss the earth. I want to run, do somersaults, and bounce like Tigger. All my senses are heightened. Rich fragrances fill the air. Deep earth scents and the perfume of flowers: yellow ylang ylang, white frangipani, gardenia, and purple bougainvillea. Ripe fruits hang low and sensual: passion fruit, guava, green and red mangos, large bumpy breadfruit, and thick long stalks of bananas. The air is fresh and sweet. I feel a warmth radiate through my body.

We spend two weeks in the main harbor of Nuku Hiva, and then sail to Daniel's Bay, a spectacular natural harbor at the mouth of a secluded valley. Rising early, we hope to hike to the tallest waterfall in Nuku Hiva with Eileen, Mark and friends from *Talulah Ruby*. It's not my secret waterfall at the Bay of Virgins, yet I hope it will be enchanting.

The water is rough in Daniel's Bay, with two- and three-foot waves near shore. Dennis navigates our rubber dinghy like a daredevil, weaving through the wave troughs as I hold tight, bouncing and swerving past small rock outcrops. Waves crest in front of a small, fast-moving river that leads to a protected beach. I hold my breath as we pitch through the final waves. Half drenched, I jump over and wade through waist-deep water, leading the dinghy along a grassy inlet where palm trees angle over the river. We beach our dinghy and meet
our friends.

Adjacent to the beach is a Marquesan plantation, thick with fruit trees, flowering bushes, and a sturdy, rustic wooden home. We chance upon a man and woman standing in front of a dozen long rows of coconuts, split in two, glistening in the sun. The woman holds a metal bowl of white jasmine flowers, and the man is swinging an axe.

"Ia orana," I say, attempting the local greeting.

"Ia orana," the man replies, turning toward us and smiling. The entire right side of his face is covered with a startling tattoo that wraps around one dark eye, his nose, and mouth. He has a pointed, five-inch bone protruding through his left ear. His arms and naked chest are also tattooed in dark black ink.

The Marquesans have a three-hundred-year history of tattooing artistic symbols in intricate designs, each tattoo telling stories and signifying accomplishments unique to the wearer.

We speak in broken French. "My name is Heidi. What's yours?"

"Teiki," the man replies with force, and then points to his wife and says, "Hua."

"You have a handsome tattoo. May I look at it?" I ask.

He talks rapidly, excited to share the stories behind each symbol. His voice gets louder, his body animated, and he reminds me of the late Robin Williams doing a hyperactive stand-up comedy routine. He uses a mix of broken French, English, Marquesan, and hilarious charades. It is too funny to not laugh.

"Warrior!" he says pounding his chest. He sticks his tongue far out of his gaping mouth and makes a loud cry. I jump back startled, and he and his wife laugh and then give us hugs, French style.

His facial tattoo was made in an ancient way, using a shark's tooth to pierce his skin, instead of needles, and without alcohol, because he wanted to learn to endure pain. One of his designs represents the wild boar that he hunts; another is a "tiki" or spirit that guides him in the hunt.

We ask about the waterfall. He says he will guide us.

We spend the next three hours trekking through winding jungle paths. A fast-moving stream blocks our path and Teiki offers each of us a hand down into the water. We move across the river slowly, holding on to moss-covered boulders, and carefully watch our footing. Teiki runs as if he is on level ground or floating above it. One of our party of eight, a man weighing 180 pounds, has a bandaged leg he isn't supposed to get wet. Teiki picks him up, throws him over his shoulder, and bounces across the stream with him. He reminds me of the sorcerer in the Castaneda book, *Journey to Ixtlan*.

The layers of sounds are melodic. In the foreground are the caw-caw-caw-ruuu of a dove, the trill of a parrot, the sweet whistles of small yellow birds, and a soft chirp from tiny, jungle tree frogs. A loud swishing sound disturbs the sweet melodies, and Teiki points to the hidden path of a wild boar. Animated, he enacts a dramatic portrayal of a hunt.

A vast field stretches to the base of the falls. It is thick with green bushes and vibrant yellow flowers higher than my waist. As we wade through, the fragrances are intoxicating, like the poppy field in *The Wizard of Oz*.

At a pool in front of the falls, Teiki collects and distributes yellow grapefruits, juicy and sweet, larger and more juicy and succulent than any I've ever tasted.

A Spanish sailor, Pedro, from *Talulah Ruby* and I continue on, clambering over boulders, to get to the far end of the pool, where the waterfall ends. I dive first into the cold water and swim to where the last section of the thousand-foot-high falls pours over my head.

Arriving back at the plantation, Teiki sees a near-wild horse he has recently captured. He dances around it and then jumps wildly on its back. Riding it bareback through a stream, he yells victory chants.

Returning home, he twirls Hua in his arms. She laughs, dropping the half-dozen limes she was carrying. She roasts nuts for us on an open fire. They taste like rich, smoky chestnuts. Teiki grabs a long pole and plucks several green and orange papayas and passes them around.

After we say goodbye and thank them, Teiki makes a warrior stance. With one hand raised to the sky, his fingers outstretched, knees bent and feet planted solidly on the ground, he sticks his tongue all the way out and makes a fierce sound from deep in his abdomen. Then he collapses in laughter and wishes us a good travel.

Soon we will leave Nuku Hiva to finish the journey of my dreams. I vow to carry his warrior spirit and full-bodied laughter with me.

We have one final passage on *Centime* to reach our destination; *Wavelength* will sail with us as our buddy boat. Fatu Hiva is the southernmost island in the Marquesas and the most remote, with no airports or ferries. It is a difficult overnight sail directly into the wind. Our plan on *Centime* is to make this bay the journey's end of a lifelong dream.

CHAPTER 29

Laughing at the Sky

Nothing is worth more than laughter.
It is strength to laugh and to abandon oneself,
to be light.

Frida Kahlo

Nuku Hiva, French Polynesia, June 2015

After all these years, I have not lost the fear.

My hands grip the wheel as I drive *Centime* toward our anchor. Billowing clouds in varying shades of gray pour over high island peaks. Wind whips across the harbor. It's easy to imagine every possible catastrophe we might encounter en route to the Bay of Virgins.

A wall of waves appears at the mouth of the harbor. Bashing through them, windblown spray seeps through my clothes. Sails raised, we fly south close to the direction of the wind, the least comfortable point of sail and the longest distance to travel as we tack, or zigzag back and forth, across the wind.

Eileen and Mark's boat, *Wavelength*, sails by our side, struggling through headwinds. A feeling of unease settles on *Centime* like the low, moisture-laden clouds. Throughout the day, *Wavelength* falls farther behind and becomes a small white dot, before disappearing beyond the horizon. I call *Wavelength* on the radio. There is no response.

The moonless night and the uncanny howl of the wind generator offer little comfort. Dennis eats leftover curry in the cockpit while I nibble on a wheat cracker and drink cold sweet tea, my mother's recipe. He heads to his bunk to sleep as I take first watch.

Clouds obscure the stars. I scan the darkness for *Wavelength*; no lights are visible. "Where are you, Eileen?" I ask the wind. The wind generator squeals and I flinch. For five hours I sail *Centime* through darkness.

The next morning, I call Mark and Eileen again on the radio. *Wavelength*'s engine is overheating and they are heading to the closest island. They assure us they don't need our help. We continue toward Fatu Hiva at a slow pace. Crossing back and forth against the wind, we make minimal forward progress. The elusive peaks of Fatu Hiva remain in the far distance, appearing out of reach. Hour after hour we pound through confused seas. I wonder if the waves have formed at sea or have traveled with the southeast trade winds the entire distance from South America.

The light of day fades as we arrive at the entrance to Fatu Hiva's main bay. Steep mountains enclose a narrow cove shrouded in clouds. The wind funnels through the cove at an accelerated pace. There is little protection from gusts.

With the engine revving and whirling at high speed, Dennis weaves *Centime* through a small bevy of anchored boats like he's driving a race car. My heart pounds as I take the wheel. Driving the boat into the wind, I work to keep her straight as he drops the anchor. Suddenly a gust catches her bow and she pivots ninety degrees and heads fast toward a sailboat with a New Zealand flag. Pulling the wheel hard, I give her full throttle, losing control against the strong wind.

"Hard to port!" Dennis yells.

"The wheel is already all the way over at full power," I yell back trying to be heard. "I can't control her against this wind tunnel." Dennis clutches the metal bars of the bow pulpit.

"Fuck! Fuck! Fuck!" I yell, bracing for impact as the boat's owners look on in shock. We careen through a choppy sea directly toward their boat.

Centime narrowly misses sideswiping the sailboat. Holding my breath, I feel the anchor catch. She swings in a frenzied arc between three boats. The anchor holds but we're too close to the New Zealand boat. The owners peer nervously from their deck. Staying this close to the other boat is risky. Re-anchoring in this wind and at this proximity to the New Zealand boat seems like madness. I wonder how we'll get out of this clusterfuck and if we'll have to stay awake on watch until the wind dies—if the wind here ever dies.

Our neighbors yell, "We're leaving soon on an overnight passage. You can stay where you are."

The relief is visible on Dennis's face. I close my eyes and rub my temples, neck, and back. As our neighbors pick up their anchor, it appears caught on a rock or coral.

"I hope they aren't stuck on our anchor. They're close to where I dropped it," Dennis says, frowning as he looks back and forth from the compass, to the anchor mark I placed on the chart, to the New Zealand boat. I hurry to our bow and watch.

The boat owners struggle, trying to pull up their anchor from several directions as the wind pushes their boat around. I grip the lifeline at the bow. A heavy weight settles in my stomach, and I wonder for an instant if my parasite has returned. Suddenly their anchor pulls free; their motor whines at a high pitch, and they fly past our starboard side, waving.

Dennis joins me at the bow, his eyes shining. "We made it, honey, just you and me, all this way! We fuckin' did it! Want a drink? We should celebrate!"

"Yes, please. Something stiff," I reply, dizzy and uncertain, still staring toward our anchor, still gripping the bow pulpit. "A gin and tonic with extra lime… and extra gin." Dennis smiles and heads below.

My heart calms but my shock remains. I loosen my grip on the pulpit and force my eyes away from the anchor to scan the horizon. Silhouettes of sheer rock protrusions are barely visible in the fading light, yet I can picture them clearly, like an old photo in a high school library journal. The dreams of a fifteen-year-old girl come to life. I shake my head, smiling—we have arrived in Fatu Hiva.

A cool breeze blows through my hair, yet my body is warm. I want to dance, shout, and pop champagne. I am in the Bay of Virgins—my destiny!

A few faint stars appear in the sky as I head back to the cockpit. The pungent aroma of citrus wafts through the air. Pleasant sounds whirl in the wind: the pouring of gin, the opening *pop* from a can of tonic, and the distant cry of a seabird.

Dennis hands me a drink. "Here's to you and dreams come true," he toasts.

"And to the courageous captain and crazy cowboy who helped me realize them." The glass shakes in my hand. The salty taste of tears mingles with the bittersweet drink.

Grabbing my hand, he settles next to me. "Did you find what you were looking for?"

"We've made it to the Bay of Virgins. Is that what you mean?"

"Well yes, we're in the physical location, but I'm wondering if you've fully realized whatever you've been seeking all these years."

"I'm not sure. Something changed inside of me during the passage to French Polynesia. When that last wave train was about to hit, I stood strong … maybe I was looking for courage."

"Like the cowardly lion?" he teases. "You must have had courage from the very start or you would never have dreamed of this, never have started. We certainly wouldn't have gotten here, just the two of us, without it. What changed?"

I take a big gulp of the gin and tonic and feel warmth of the alcohol spread through my throat. "The first time that massive wave hit, I had a fleeting vision of Mr. Hart and wanted to fall down on the deck, get into a tiny ball, and disappear. The second and third time I stood up. I tried to believe I could do it, or at least I was gonna go down fighting. I raged at him like I've never raged before. I didn't even know I had rage inside of me. A storm of emotion exploded. It became a question of who was going to win—Mr. Hart or me. And I will fucking NEVER let him take me down again!"

"Then I'd say you found what you were searching for." His body starts to shake as he holds me tight in his arms.

"Are you crying?" I ask, pulling away to see his eyes.

"Yes." His body rocks with mine to the rhythm of the sea. "It's been … hard for me to watch you go through this, even to comprehend it. I never thought you wouldn't sail to Fatu Hiva—you always seemed strong. Whenever the shit hit the fan, you remained calm, or at least that's how it appeared. You did what had to be done. At first, I didn't fully appreciate what was really going on inside you … how hard you were fighting. Those times when we sat under the stars and you told me about your history and your fears, I started to understand. Then when you let me read your journal, the actual details of how he smelled, how you felt suffocated when he was on top of you ... I was so shocked ... so angry.

"I can't express how much emotion I feel ... how cranked up I get," he says. "What if it were my daughter when she was eleven, what would I do? I'd fucking want to kill him, and I'm not a rageful man. I just think anyone who does something like that should have his dick cut off. Whenever I envision what happened and your small body smothered under that asshole's ... I just break down. But honey, seeing where you are now and knowing where you came from ... it's huge. You're so courageous. You turned violence into power and that's fucking amazing!"

"Yes, I did!" I shout into the wind, grinning and thrusting my fist into the air. He stands up, grabs my hand, and we dance around the cockpit, humming to our own music.

The next day, a vibrant rainbow spreads across the harbor at dawn. It rises in a full arc across the bay, disappearing behind a steep black cliff. In the center is a small village with a red-roofed church. On both sides, precipitous rock ridges rise hundreds of feet to the heavens. Tall royal palms crowd their bases, and white mountain goats scamper around precipices. The tops of the dark towering spires are stark, windswept of vegetation except for a spattering of green moss. Two bright white birds soar between two of them. The tallest phallic rock protrudes in dark contrast to the white clouds behind it. Others are shrouded deeper in clouds, while the early morning sun backlights their sheer beauty.

The Bay of Virgins or Baie de Vierges in French, was originally known as the Baie de Verges or Bay of Penises. In the nineteenth century, missionaries, outraged by the name, added the letter "i" to change its meaning. Anchored in the harbor under these phallic pinnacles it's clear that the old name is more fitting, yet I like the newer name and being watched over by women.

I chuckle to think of this twist of fate. If *National Geographic's* waterfall caption had been "Bay of Penises" it might have saved me a five-year, 12,000-nautical- mile journey.

The bay is exposed to powerful elements. A gust of wind causes the boat to swing hard on her anchor. Columns of sunlight illuminate shafts of nine knife-edged pinnacles that plummet to the water. Large angry waves crash below them. Sea spray plumes shoot twelve feet high, pouring over the exposed rock as the wave recedes.

The bay's wildness stirs something ancient in my blood. It's hard not to think of King Kong looking down from a peak over this untamed mystical land. I imagine myself as my falcon, soaring through high peaks, embracing courage. I stand alone, stretched out on the top of the bow seat, my head high, my hair blowing wildly behind.

My voyage isn't finished until I search for the waterfall I discovered in the journal at age fifteen. Thinking back to that fateful day in the library, I'm no longer certain how the waterfall and writing about Gauguin and the Bay of Virgins relate. While I can clearly see the pinnacles of this bay I can't see a waterfall from the boat.

When I researched this part of the trip five years ago, I read sketchy information about an enchanting waterfall hidden in the steep mountains of this island. I couldn't find details on its location or any images. I didn't even know if it was a sailor's tale or real. I've since spoken to several cruisers who have tried to find it, and none that I know of have been successful.

Two sailboats rest on anchor in the bay with *Centime:* a second monohull from New Zealand and a catamaran with an American flag. I call over to the sailors to ask about the waterfall. Nobody has heard of it, yet all four sailors are eager for adventure. Dennis and I pick them up in our dingy. We set out on a hike together to try our luck, bringing bug spray, extra water, French brie, a baguette, and dark chocolate left over from Panama.

A narrow dirt road meanders beyond town. Both sides are thick with vegetation: royal palms and fruit trees with lemons, oranges, and guava. Colorful red and orange roosters scurry by, and an occasional cow and horse graze in the overgrown grass.

Two gorgeous Marquesan women with colorful flowing pink-patterned dresses walk toward us. They have bright red flowers in their long dark hair.

Their facial features are near-perfect reflections from a Gauguin painting.

"Ia orana," I say.

"Ia orana," they reply, smiling.

Gesturing with broken French, I try to tell them that the flowers in their hair are beautiful.

They laugh. One immediately pulls her flower out from behind her ear, gestures to my wedding ring, and then puts the flower behind my left ear. It is a custom to wear the flower behind your right ear if you are single.

As we continue down the road, two men approach pushing a wheelbarrow with a large brown sack. One of the men is in his twenties, the other perhaps in his fifties. They are handsome with golden-brown skin and slender, fit bodies. The older man has an engaging smile.

"Ka oh ha nui," I greet them, and switch to French. As the only French speaker of the sailors, I become our group's translator. "What do you carry in your sack?"

"We pick coconuts to dry for copra," the older man replies as he stops the wheelbarrow and opens the sack to show us. "Where do you come from?"

"We are from a boat in the harbor, sailing from Nuku Hiva. We started in the United States and our friends came from New Zealand," I say, introducing everyone.

We speak of our children. The younger man is the older man's son and they live nearby. The son has a large black tattoo on his left arm, with a Marquesan cross and several ancient symbols. He notices me staring at his tattoo and laughs as he flexes his muscles and makes his already large bicep bulge. He lets me feel his muscle and explains what the symbols mean on the intricate design. I squeeze his muscle and smile at him in a gesture that shows I know he is strong. I tell him he is handsome. He smiles and blushes while his father laughs. The Polynesian laughter is contagious.

A high rock formation stands as a backdrop to our conversation. The older man points to it and says it is a tiki, the spirit of a mother protecting her child. The symbolic child is this island. The face on the rock is recognizable and easy to find. He takes great care to make sure we see all the features, pointing out the part of the rock that resembles her head and breasts, and the baby. It seems important to him that we see the baby.

Fatu Hiva has an intriguing mix of ancient and spiritual ways, animism colliding with Christianity. Like the Guna Yalans, many believe the animals, plants, mountains, and sea have supernatural powers. Their land is sacred. Their mountains look down on them and protect those who honor the land.

"We're trying to find the sacred waterfall," I say. "Do you know the way?"

The older man becomes animated and talks too fast for me to understand. Bending down, he grabs a rock and draws a map on the dirt road. He shows a path veering to the left and the river it crosses. He speaks of a house, mango trees, and a cairn of three stacked rocks. I squat to study the confusing diagram and try to decipher his words and drawings.

"You will need nourishment for your long walk," he says.

Pulling out a knife he shows us the wooden handle carved in beautiful designs by his ancestors. The homemade blade is dented and sharp. He takes a large brown coconut from his sack and makes precise sweeping cuts, in swift progression, close to his fingers. His wrinkled hands are strong as he pulls the final coconut husks away from the nut, and offers the coconut for our journey.

The son takes a few steps away from the road, reaches up to a nearby tree and cuts a green coconut with his long machete. Opening the top, he reveals a vessel of milk. We share the delicious, thirst-quenching liquid. I offer them my chocolate bar, and they smile and eat it immediately. They don't get chocolate often on this island.

"You have a Christian cross on your tattoo," I say to the older man, remembering that most of the tattoos I've seen in French Polynesia have Marquesan crosses.

"When I die I want to go straight up to heaven, no confusion," he gestures, giving us a pantomime of an upward spiral. "I don't want to wait for a decision. I want it to be quick. This cross will make it clear which part of heaven I am to go to." His eyes sparkle and he laughs a full laugh, which spreads through our small group.

"You will go to heaven quickly because you are kind and generous," I say, and he smiles wider, laughs more.

"I hope you find what you are looking for," he calls as we leave.

"I hope you do too," I reply with a pause. "But not too soon. Your strong son needs you!" I hear them both laugh again as we walk away.

After great debate and much confusion, we start on a path along a river, comparing it to what we saw on the dirt map. The early morning temperature is cool under the shade of thick-leaved trees and a cloudy sky. On the side of the path there is a large field of five-foot-high grass. The delicate pink tops sway in the breeze in Zen-like rhythm. We use cameras and iPhones to try to capture the abundant beauty. The path divides again and again and we can't find the waterfall. We backtrack and try another rambling path and then a third. After several hours it is hot in the noon sun. We eat melted brie sandwiches in the shade of old trees and head back to town.

Passing a young man leading a sleek brown and white horse, I ask again for directions. We learn that in spite of the older man's earlier help, we started on the wrong path. Our friends are tired, unwilling to continue, and they want to return to their boats. One friend, David, is willing to try once more.

"I know this is important to you, yet I should probably take them back," Dennis whispers to me. "They're not going to be able to start our dingy motor. And, I have to say that I'm really exhausted and my back is sore. Just say the word, but will it be okay with you if I don't go?"

"It's okay." I say knowing this is my dream and my path. "Wish me luck."

"Bonne chance," he says with a big smile before handing me the radio and planting a large kiss on my mouth. "I hope you find what you're looking for. I'll be with you in spirit, waiting for your return."

David and I head off. The new path is steep, veering to the left past a vacant home. A dog with a fierce bark stands guard as we pass. I try to talk to him calmly but my voice shakes while he continues to threaten me. I stare at him, turning around and walking backward, hoping to not get bitten from behind.

David and I cross a branch of the river and then the path divides. On the left is a forty-foot row of hibiscus, towering above my head, exploding with hundreds of blossoms. The bushes appear to be moving. Bright yellow parakeets with clear-throated chirping flit through intense red flowers. The beauty is vibrant, and the red and yellow wall shimmers with the flutter of birds. A tingling in my chest makes it feel like a good omen.

We move forward with renewed energy, choosing the path along the bushes, and continue to reach the next crossroads. Both paths ahead are overgrown and uninviting. The sun is hot and my calves ache.

"This doesn't look right," David says. "Do you want to head back?"

"We've come so far and it's starting to remind me more of the dirt map," I say. "Let's just go a bit farther. Why don't I try this one on the right for ten or twenty yards to see if it opens up?"

"Okay, I'll do the same with one on the left."

After twenty yards my path peters away. I retrace my steps to follow David's path. It slopes up to the left where a bull and cow graze under a large tree. As I get close the bull looks up. He grunts and snorts and paws his forefeet. Suddenly he takes a few frisky steps, half falling, downward, to the middle of the path, and stops. He lowers his head and glares, daring me to cross, his large horns pointing at me. I back away slowly and then turn and scamper off the path into the jungle.

Palm fronds, coconuts, decaying fruit, logs, and jungle detritus cover the ground. I jog through it toward the river, watching my feet and glancing over my shoulder at the bull. A honeycomb covered with bees appears just below my right foot. Unable to stop my forward momentum, I stomp on the top of the honeycomb. A swarm of bees chases me back to the path near the bull. Stabs of pain sear through my ankle, hip, and back. Bees continue to swarm as I run in circles swatting at them while the bull stares.

I collapse on a log, half sitting on my side to try to avoid the pain in my buttocks. Six, eight, and then ten large, angry red welts erupt on my ankle and legs. Can a person be knocked unconscious from too many bee stings? At least I brought the water and radio ... David has a first aid kit ... but he's on the other side of the bull.

"David," I yell.

"Heidi, where are you?" he yells from afar. "Are you hurt?"

"I've been stung by a dozen bees. I need your first aid kit." Reason overtakes anxiety. I want to be near David if I pass out. I want him to know that I have a radio. I will run the gauntlet.

"David, I need to get past the bull in the path. You're from Texas, can you distract him?"

On the far side of the path, standing high on the incline above the bull, David faces him. "Go ... a ... way!" David yells, waving his hand in front of the bull. The bull turns his huge head toward David and snorts as I try to sneak by at the far edge of the path. My heart beats fast and the pain from the stings throbs. I hold my breath. As I near the closest point to the bull, he quickly rears his head, nostrils flaring, and makes a loud bellow. I freeze as he stares at me. Walking past the bull backward, my legs shaking, I escape up the path, not stopping until I pass David. I selfishly want to make sure David is between the bull and me.

My left foot is a uniform swollen red mass, dotted with a dozen black circles where the stingers entered. Trying to tease the first stinger out with my fingernail is pointless, worsening the pain. The first aid kit has a couple of packets of anti-sting remedy that I apply gingerly.

My throat is dry and my body is hot and sweaty. After I gulp down the last of the warm water from a plastic Nalgene bottle, my pulse starts to calm. My ankle and backside ache, my water bottle is empty, and the path ahead is overgrown.

"Good thing Cindy had me bring the first aid. She always seems to know these things," he says.

"Yes, you and your wife are my heroes today—Matador."

"Well, we've come this far, what's next? Do you want to turn around?"

"Are you crazy? I'm not taking another chance with that bull. We've already made him angry." After the bull, the bees, and sailing 12,000 miles, I want to find my waterfall. "Let's go." I test the strength of my ankle.

A few hundred yards ahead, a small indistinct path veers again to the left, and then branches left and right, like a maze. Uncertain of the route, David shakes his head. The heat of the day drains our last bits of energy. My shirt clings to my skin, wet with perspiration. My legs are dirty, swollen, and sore.

I slump down to the dirt and hang my head. A gecko catches my eye. It scampers under a small rock. Two more small rocks are stacked above it. I stare at the tiny pile and then lean closer. It's a three-rock cairn. After five and a half hours I have found my way. Forgetting my pain, I jump up and whoop with delight.

A narrow trail winds up the mountain along the edge of a fast-flowing river. Soothing sounds of cascading water ride on the breeze. Trees lush with green mangos, shade a path littered with over-ripened fruit and fallen brown leaves. A sweet, fertile fragrance wafts through the air.

Rock boulders protrude along the path. Many hold artistic cairns, each more elaborate than the first. One complex cairn consists of a dozen rocks situated with a careful balance of spaces and angles as if designed by an architect. Another ensemble holds six dark rocks aside a still-fresh, bright green mango, in a perfect composition for a still life. A third cairn with only three delicately angled rocks has Zen-like simplicity. They appear as surprising gifts to those who have traveled far.

Swift-moving clouds begin to gather, obscuring the view and the path forward. Ahead on the steep-edged path gray layers on gray, a pencil sketch in monochrome. Thick jungle leaves are etched across the few possible overlooks. As the foliage and dark clouds encroach, I stumble over obstacles.

Just then, in the midst of the gray afternoon, the sun glimmers fleetingly through the clouds, and the canopy is alight. A bright apparition appears in the distance between large green leaves. I rub my eyes and stare. Shafts of sunlight reveal a silver white waterfall surging over a dark rock cliff. Soon, as clouds once again block my vision, it disappears like a mirage.

Leaving David behind, I rush toward where I hope to find the base of the falls. Boulders block the cliff path and I scamper like a mountain goat up, around, and over every obstacle, as fast as my swollen ankles can manage.

Heading down a narrow winding offshoot of the main path I arrive at a deep reflecting pool. A smooth flat rock rests at the end, overhanging the basin's edge. The pool offers a palette of slate and unpolished emerald reminding me of Gauguin's writings: "Color … the language of dreams."

Heat radiates through my body. Throwing off hiking boots and clothes, I climb to the center of the high flat rock. I bathe in the present moment alert to every sensation: a light breeze on my chest; the coolness of shadowed rock on my bare feet; my rapid heartbeat, my labored breath, the expanding and contracting of my lungs; a myriad of bird whistles, chirps, and trills; the perfume of colorful flowers, the petrichor of moist fertile earth; the pool's inviting green hue, and the welcome sound of falling water. Having run ahead of David, I am alone on the rock surrounded by what feels like a universe of life and energy.

Rippled water under the angled sun has created wavy white streaks of light reflecting on the pool's surface, offering the illusion of a forward path. My gaze follows the light across the watery route. At the far end of the oblong pool, sheer cliff walls form a backdrop as if I'm standing at the edge of a natural amphitheater. The jungle unveils its life-affirming source. The once-hidden falls appears like a dream. The water rains hard on the pool's surface, sounding an applause for this magnificent scene.

Fate has brought me 12,000 nautical miles back to myself. The *National Geographic* image from long ago is before me—exactly as I remembered. I long to be immersed and cleansed by these falls. I move to the rock's edge and ready myself to dive in, four feet below my perch. My senses are focused, alert, and reverent. My eyes well up with tears and they flow down my cheek, dropping on my chest and into the water below.

At age fifteen I had imagined diving into this pool. I had slowly traced the falls in the journal to the source and then down again. Today powerful forces create the same urges, drawing my attention from the surface of the pool skyward as I savor all that surrounds me.

The stream drops 300 feet in one straight plunge. As my eyes reach the top, the dark clouds part. The light sifts through silver-tinged mist. My entire body shimmers, fully awash in sunlight. The darkness that had surrounded me has vanished. I am aglow.

Thousands of water droplets glitter like bright silver beads. Each one falls to become part of the pool I will soon enter, inseparable from my tears. My tears, flowing from my heart, are an infinitely small part of these pure restorative waters, to perhaps, one day, nourish new life in this verdant jungle.

Through a shift in optics, I can see into a wedge in the sky. Puffy white clouds move at what appears as an accelerated pace across a small opening in the cliff, revealing bright blue above them. A complete rainbow glistens below the high point of falling water. I feel gratitude. I feel love. I am love.

In a state of rapture, in the midst of this breathtaking South Pacific dream, euphoria washes over me. It starts as a soft giggle and soon I am bent over laughing hard. I straighten my body unable to stop convulsions of joy. I stand on my toes with outstretched arms, and plunge headfirst into cool, deep, silky water. Bubbles pour around me. The moments stretch in perfection as I swim across the pool and float under the stream, the waterfall raining hard above me, eyes closed. My head tilted to the sky.

I can't stop laughing.

At the end of this day, I will struggle to find the words to describe these feelings to Dennis. He will listen patiently as he smooths a healing salve on my bee stings. I will taste salt on my lips as once again tears flow. We will embrace for long sweet moments. Together we will watch the sun set over phallic pinnacles spreading red and gold across the Bay of Virgins.

Later in the month I will find myself sailing past dozens of remote islands and coral atolls. I will meet Nico, who will have graduated from college, and I will tell him how immensely proud I am of him, as I run my fingers through his unruly, curly hair. He will linger with Dennis and me for a month or more on *Centime*, through the Tuamotus and the Society Island groups. He has held my hand and heart close and from afar throughout my voyage. He has encouraged my dreams and at times been my sole reason to survive. He has taught me how to live and be love.

Afterward, girlfriends will gather in Moorea, French Polynesia to celebrate my sixtieth birthday and our voyage. Nico's friends will join with their beloved moms Joan and Lynn. Eileen, Mark, the Talulah Rubians, and more sailor friends will arrive. The turtle sisters will join in spirit. They know pieces of my torment, have guided and stood with me through challenges, and have supported this unfolding. I will honor each of them.

Over the years I will better understand the portent of those moments, how my odyssey offered resuscitation after losing my breath, my voice, and aspects of my wild Tigger spirit. I will ponder the distance I have traveled from a runaway child; to a lost adult who projected a future of never being unruined; to a peaceful more present woman who has found her home within.

At the falls that day, the past, present, and future found reconciliation. I felt the antithesis of the rage I released at sea, an upwelling of healing energy. Perhaps I needed to release the rage in order to have ample room for truth and grace to be present, and to "laugh at the sky." I will embrace those moments of transcendence at the waterfall, metaphorically diving in, again and again, to healing waters—to feel the pure infinite illumination of love.

THE END

EPILOGUE

Transcendence

Singular acts of compassion can have profound consequences across generations. You never know whom you might inspire or where the inspiration might lead.

Heidi Love

Eliot, Maine, January 2024

Ten years ago, I read a quote attributed to Vicki Corona from the book *Tahitian Choreographies*. I was sitting in *Centime*'s forward berth enjoying a cool tropical breeze, which funneled through the hatch. The boat was gently rocking. The tiny space was a nurturing, womb-like, familiar home, and I loved reading, especially anything about the South Pacific.

It was the second year of our five-year sailing odyssey, shortly after Mother forgot who I was. Vicki's quote seemed profound. She wrote, "Remember that life is not measured by the number of breaths we take, but by the moments that take our breath away." Tears streamed down my face as I realized the quote was meant to be happy. For me, it had a dual meaning. Would I ever shake the feeling of lost breath, of Mother's hands on my neck? Could I release the deep grief I carried in my throat and heart? Would I ever know the full truth of who Mother was, who I was to her, or feel—un-"ruined"?

The wind from the forward hatch dried the dampness on my cheeks and I began to reveal and better understand my story by writing and sharing. My friend Dr. Anne Hallward, formerly on the faculty at Harvard Medical School and Founder of Safe Space Radio says, "Silence after any devastating event is its own form of trauma because of the fear, isolation, shame, and hopelessness that result. Healing after trauma not only involves the compassionate witnessing of the unbearable experience of the trauma itself, but also the witnessing of the pain of the silences that define the experience of trauma."

How do we share our trauma and allow others to witness it? And how do we measure our lives? For forty years, I was unable to fully disclose my story. Filled with shame and fear, I measured myself as less. I had a wild, crazy belief that if I sailed to the Bay of Virgins, I would be whole again. Today, nearly a decade after that fateful day on *Centime*, after regaining my voice, I've experienced a paradigm shift. Now as I write the words, "moments that take my breath away," the phrase brings a different sort of tears to my eyes. My whole being is filled with gratitude.

When I returned home from French Polynesia, I shared lunch with a physician friend, Dr. Chuck. I wore a necklace with a single black pearl from the Polynesian island of Taha'a. It was a talisman and a reminder of my journey. We were having a pleasant chat. I was drinking a soothing cup of Earl Grey tea.

"Before we leave the restaurant, I'd like to look more closely at your neck," Chuck said.

"Do you like my pearl?" I asked, smiling as I touched its smoothness.

"It's beautiful, but as your physician I'd like to check something else."

He handed me a tall glass of water.

"Drink this slowly," he said.

I felt each swallow of cold clean water clear my throat as his hands gently massaged my neck. He then pulled out a pad from his pocket, scribbled a note, tore off the top sheet, and handed it to me.

"I'd like you to have a blood test to check the levels of your thyroid hormones," he said. "Your thyroid is enlarged."

Over the next several weeks I learned that my thyroid had cancerous cells that needed to be removed. I had never before, or since, had a serious illness. Though the operation was successful, and I was cancer free, it seemed an ironic truth to have diseased cells in my throat. I spoke to my endocrinologist about it.

"My mother attempted to strangle me when I was eleven," I said. "I've always felt like I've directed and stored negative energy in my throat, where she put her hands. For years I held on to words that were unspeakable. Can it be true that unprocessed trauma is stored not only in the brain but also in the body, perhaps in my throat?"

"There is no scientific evidence to prove or disprove this one way or the other, but there is a lot we do not know or understand." he replied.

While he is certainly correct that western medicine may not have full scientific evidence on how trauma is stored in the body, it is however central to holistic and traditional medicine, and to more recent studies in psychiatry. Psychiatrist Dr. Bessel van der Kolk, author of *The Body Keeps the Score*, states, "We have learned that trauma is not just an event that took place sometime in the past; it is also the imprint left by that experience on mind, brain, and body."

Scientifically proven or not, perhaps even fanciful, I prefer to imagine that I stored negative energy from my trauma in my throat, and that it was removed by the surgeon's scalpel. It makes me smile! Either way, my throat is now clear. My cancer is gone. My voice is strong.

A book of poems that Nico gave me rests on my nightstand. On its garnet-red cover an image of an ancient carpet with an intricate weave complements the beautiful binding. Its author, Rumi, was a thirteenth-century Sufi poet. A bookmark stands as a placeholder for one of my favorite lines: "The wound is the place where light enters you." How do we recognize the fullness of our wounds? How do we invite the light in, to illuminate our world? How do we put our voices back into our bodies? How do we transcend our silence, our shame, and our fear, to live our dreams?

The start for me was to break the silence and tell all of my story. When a survivor has the courage to tell her story, she often hears, "Get over it," or "Why did you wait so long to tell?" At times in the past, I often felt I "should" be over it, and tried to convince myself that my rape and Mother's reaction weren't a big deal. Of course, it never worked. My therapist says it is often easier to have compassion and understanding for others than for oneself.

My experience is proof that someone who has experienced trauma can spend decades trying to bury it; read dozens of self-help books; take antianxiety and antidepression pills; go to a hundred therapy sessions; and then sail 12,000 nautical miles through post-traumatic flashbacks and life-threatening squalls ... and still not "get over it." Maybe for me it's not "get-over-able."

What if the question isn't how to get over it but rather how to transform its gritty truth, in all its horror, into power and strength; to profoundly shift one's point of view; to transcend from ruined to strong and beautiful—to invite the light to enter and illuminate the wound and healthy scars?

At the beginning of my journey, I didn't understand the depth or complexity of my story or the part of me that held on to a false belief that I was "ruined." I had to pursue my dreams in spite of my fear, stumbling hard along the way, to understand how I had framed my thinking. I had to learn how I had participated in reliving the assault whenever I was afraid. Through the reliving, I unwittingly gave power to the perpetrator and the continuation of violence and assault on my mind and body. Though the rape was never, in any way, my fault, it was still a challenge to accept that in some ways, I became the perpetrator to myself. It was more challenging to know what to do about it.

In the middle of the South Pacific, when fifteen-foot waves crashed over *Centime*, something altered my perceptions. That day at sea, when Mr. Hart's glasses appeared, I recognized my decision: fall to the deck and literally drown in worthlessness, or stand up to the wave, the rage, and the violence—and focus on strength. It was my choice, my power. It wasn't until several years later that I could name the feeling of rage, and be consciously aware of how I had held on to it. By releasing the rage that day, held deep inside, I was able to redirect my focus from victim to power-filled survivor.

Compassion, too, played a role in my paradigm shift. Although much of this story started at age eleven, the true beginning may have occurred generations earlier. Three therapists have independently speculated that Mother suffered from mental illness, borderline personality disorder, starting in her childhood after her own repeated abuse. Decades before she was born, when Grandpa Lloyd was a child, Great-Grandpa slashed his son's tongue with a knife because Lloyd told a lie. I try to picture Grandpa's life as a boy. I remember his distorted speech as an adult. What might cause a parent to deform their child's tongue, to give their child a lifelong speech impediment, to silence their child? What might it feel like to be reminded of your shame whenever you spoke? What might cause a grandfather or neighbor to become a sex predator? Is there any room, not for excuses, but for greater understanding and possible compassion?

The winds of the past must give way to the present and future. Like the apocryphal butterfly whose wings fluttered and ultimately caused a storm on the other side of the world, perhaps a singular act of violence in a small house in Pennsylvania, or anywhere in the world, can have profound consequences for generations across time and space. Might this be true for singular acts of compassion?

Most of us carry stories from our past. While some stories lift us up, others can weigh us down and diminish or restrain our lives. The only control we have is inside ourselves in this moment. Might we find individual and collective ways to transcend these heavy stories, using them to strengthen and power us ahead? In the martial arts concept of nonresistance, one can redirect energy, movement, and forces against us to propel ourselves forward. This is achieved by being fully present and guiding, rather than resisting negative energy.

Today as my voice emerges, I stand with those facing challenges, listening and sharing our histories, our progress, and our hope. We hone and share creative acts to inspire transformation and growth. I crave new ways to express the paradigm shift I feel inside, and see in many others. I seek the language of moving beyond victim, beyond silence breaker, and beyond survivor. Courageous trauma survivors have had profound transformations, and become compassionate leaders and change makers. For me, the word "survivor" or even "thriver" does not convey enough. We are in desperate need for new words and a fuller vision of transcendence.

I long to be part of a larger community—a tribe of transcendence—where millions across the globe find and use their voices to illuminate the hidden effects of discrimination, misogyny, domestic violence, and sexual assault, and collectively champion human rights one voice at a time. In reclaiming our voices, our whole selves, we rise above the stories we carry to realize our dreams. For some this day has come; for others it's on the horizon.

While scientists say it is impossible to stop the images that flood our brain's amygdala, the survival part of the brain, therapists and mental health professionals know that we can learn immediate alternate responses to triggers. Over the last year I have worked with a renowned Harvard psychiatrist and several therapists and survivors to develop an alternate response and to publish a workbook, *Knowing Acts: Engage in Healing*. With the help of a multitude of generous souls we have donated several hundred books to rape and domestic violence response teams.

What souvenirs did I bring back from my journey and where are the travelers today? I have an expanded sense of the world's humanity. I have met many people from around the world who live vastly different lives than I, yet we connect like sisters and brothers. I hope to always carry the wisdom of the Guna, especially holding "Paradiso" within. For over 500 years they have created a society enhanced by gender equality and fluidity, cherishing the female spirit and the heart of third gender. Within their isolated island communities these traditions remain strong, however, as more of the Guna come in contact with Western culture and travel beyond the archipelago, they experience greater discrimination and resistance to traditional ways. Though the Guna have adapted to centuries of changes, anthropologists warn that rising sea levels due to climate change could force mass migration from their low islands and have a strong impact on their culture.

The Pacific Islanders have taught generosity, laughter, and to stand in both power and joy, like warriors with true strength and beauty. They wear markings on their bodies to remind them of who they are. They, too, honor and cherish the home nature provides. Like the Guna, while many of their cultural norms remain intact, climate change is a grave concern. Their experience is propelling them toward new dialogues and leadership roles at recent climate accords and beyond.

My understanding of Paul Gauguin, and the tropical illusions he painted, has shifted. As a child I viewed the artist as a discoverer of paradise; now his work has been critiqued with greater scrutiny and more discerning eyes. The art world has exposed sexist, racist, and misogynistic aspects of his life and work. Though his art still brings me a sense of wonder, I can no longer overlook his exploitation of thirteen- and fourteen-year-old girls. I don't personally advocate for censorship of his aesthetically beautiful, thought-provoking pieces. I do, however, applaud museums and art historians who are doing us a service by more fully illuminating artists behind their art. In her article, "Can I Enjoy the Art but Denounce the Artist?" Roxanne Gay concludes, "We can no longer worship at the altar of creative genius while ignoring the price all too often paid for that genius." Her statement is particularly relevant with our contemporary "Me Too" movement.

Many friends and teachers along my journey continue to demonstrate courage: my turtle sisters, Eileen, my compassionate teaching captain, my Everest-climbing therapist, and champions of human rights and social justice across the globe who inspire; their courage is contagious.

Regardless of her frailties and mental challenges, my mother in all her goodness showed me how beautiful and resilient we both are. Although she has passed, memories of her continue to foster greater understanding and forgiveness. Most of all—I wish her peace.

Brother Vern, who taught me how to wash his boat fifty years ago, is still out sailing and teasing me in endearing ways. He was the first in my life to demonstrate a love of sailing and always offers souvenirs of laughter. He also, thankfully, lets me know when my sails are losing wind.

Dennis is still full of life, a spunky, brave, risk taker. Some of our friends call him "Adventure Man." He constantly encourages me to rise above fear. We've just completed a second rally sailing on a friend's boat, from Antigua in the Caribbean to French Polynesia. His relentless gifts of restorative salves for my wounds have taught me compassion for others and myself. It is an incredible gift to be with someone I love who inspires me to grow into who I am meant to be. His two children are thriving. After years of living in California, they have returned to our home state of Maine, bringing with them sunshine, warmth, and a love of family.

Nico, my heart of hearts, is now thirty-one. He still champions the underrepresented. He has returned from Europe with an advanced degree in international development and works passionately to improve income inequality and fight for social change. He is now married to a very special woman who matches his interests in creating a better world. He has taught me the critical lessons of how to live dreams, stand up for beliefs, and be love. It was through him that I truly learned what love is.

I worked hard to give Nico a safe, happy home and to expose him to amazing aspects of the world, handing down wanderlust and compassion. My mothering skills throughout Nico's life however, were at times, lacking. Divorce is hard for any child. I suspect he also suffered from my own mental instabilities, and my timing for leaving on my grand adventure had an impact. Though I can find numerous faults with my past actions, I try to forgive myself and wonder if perhaps I did the best I could at the time. Regret is an energy I no longer want to hold. I hope I have at least severed the cumulative chain of generational violence. Above all, I love Nico deeply, am immensely proud of him, and exceedingly grateful he has graced my life.

As for me, I've come home. My five-year, 12,000-nautical-mile journey to Fatu Hiva provided the chance—and the choice—to shed the rage I had buried so deep that I had no idea it existed. I discarded tightly held, false beliefs of being unclean and "ruined for life." Cleansing tides washed away shame and uncertainty. The freshest of waterfalls poured over me and healed me. The child I once hated and the trauma within me have profoundly shifted to give me added strength.

Soon after I purged my rage, my perceptions changed. I felt larger, symbiotically connected to the cycle of life, a whole being, vastly greater than my original self. Later I found there is a word for this, coined by Australian philosopher Glenn Albrecht—eutierria—becoming one with the universe. While philosophy, science, and religion have a multitude of explanations for human transcendence, for me love filled my soul and my past, present, and future blended in harmony.

The wise Maya Angelou once said, *"A woman in harmony with her spirit is like a river flowing. She goes where she will without pretense and arrives at her destination prepared to be herself and only herself."*

Although I don't know where my next journey will lead me, I do know that I still have Nico's love held dear and my dad's wanderlust and compassion. Dennis' backpack is always ready to go, with me not far behind. The more I understand myself, the more I love exactly who I am and the path I am sailing. I breathe deep. I feel the wind on my face and experience the salty taste of joy. This moment fills me; it is as powerful as the wind that fills my sails. The salt and sea, love of family and friends, giving and receiving, the living of bold dreams—Paradiso, I laugh to myself and the sky—it is all that I need.

Roca Union, Isla Isabela, Galapagos (Photo/Dennis Jud)

Heidi with a playful sea lion, Isla Isabela, Galapagos (Photo/Dennis Jud)

Land Ho! Arriving at Nuku Hiva, French Polynesia (Photo/Dennis Jud)

Marquesan Warrior Teiki, Nuku Hiva (Photo/Dennis Jud)

Dolphins playing at *Centime*'s bow, Marquesas (Photo/Dennis Jud)

Centime anchored, Bay of Virgins, Fatu Hiva (Photo/Dennis Jud)

Heidi and Nico, Moorea, French Polynesia (Photo/Dennis Jud)

The elusive, healing waterfall, Fatu Hiva (Photo/David Balfour)

Another Book by Heidi Love

Knowing Acts—Engage in Healing
A Calming Practice Workbook for Emotional Balance

By Heidi Love, Art by Linden O'Ryan

"This inspiring book is a touchstone, a safe harbor to return to again and again as we navigate the courageous journey toward healing."

Anne Hallward, MD
Founder and Executive Director Safe Space Radio
Former Faculty, Harvard Medical School

If you or someone you love feels overwhelmed by grief, despair, anger, sadness, or feelings of panic, anxiety, numbness or loss, or would simply like to develop a calming practice, *Knowing Acts* can support mindfulness and healing.

Knowing Acts—Engage in Healing is a customizable workbook for a personal journey of healing. This colorful guide is brimming with over 100 pages of beautiful original artwork by Maine watercolorist Linden O'Ryan, and over 30 pleasant-to-do exercises with music, art, poetry, mindfulness, and more. It was developed by Heidi Love as she battled—and rose above—traumatic PTSD flashbacks at sea. It is infused with her own personal examples, anecdotes, and recommendations for brave books and free healing resources.

Singular acts of compassion can have profound consequences across generations. You never know whom you might inspire or where the inspiration might lead.

Available at HeidiLoveAuthor.com

Heartfelt Thanks

Rising above trauma and writing this book took more than a village and a five-year, 12,000-nautical-mile sail. For me it took a global sisterhood and a tribe of mentors, therapists, friends, and family. I will be forever indebted to those who not only laughed with me in the good times but sailed with me through rough seas.

To the Turtle Sisters: Judy Trepal, who was instrumental in designing this beautiful book, Bonita Crane, Layne Gregory, Irene Baltus, and honorary sisters and dear friends Eileen Morgen and Danielle LaPointe, and to my beloved Annie (you know who you are). Sailors: Mark Bigalke, Theo Quick, Michel Veilleux, Lauren Watkins, Jenny and Charlie McNamara, Randy and Dawn Ortiz, Noel Small, Bobbi McCorkindale and the Talulah Rubians, may you have fair winds, following seas, and always remember the Irish sailor's proverb, "There are good ships and wood ships, and ships that sail the sea, but the best ships are friendships and may they always be."

To our community of phenomenal mothers and their families: Joan, Dan, Alex, and Kathryn Sisto; Lisa, Bill, Evan, and Katie Strouss; Lynn Macfarlane and Stuart, Max, and Izzie Werman. I will always be grateful to you for making my family larger, more boisterous, and filled with joy and love.

To family members, brother Vernon Malin, who taught me how to wash his boat, navigate around our mother, and gave me a passion for sailing and the sea; to Sarah, Amy, and Adam Malin, and Ethan and Hannah Jud who bring sunshine to my life; and to Nico's dad for giving me my most precious gift—our son.

To the brilliant authors Meredith Hall, Anna Moi, Alex Marzano-Lesnevich, Tessa Fontaine, and Nancy Crochiere who nurtured my soul and made this book sail true; and to Cheryl Strayed whose inspiration and writing helped me face my fear.

To editors, the patient and thorough Lynda Dietz from Easy Reader Editing and dear Janet Clemons, and to the wondrous writers and authors Michael Darcher, Liesbet Collaert, and Stewart Engesser: without you this book would be misspelled, poorly written, and basically drab.

To insightful mentors: Susan Manfull, PhD, Anne Hallward, MD, my Everest-climbing therapist, my compassionate sailing instructor captain, Master Mola Maker Lisa, and Marquesan Warrior Teiki: you've changed my life.

To the creative, gracious people I've had the good fortune to work with, at the multi-platform agencies: Ethos and Vont, you make passions brighter and more achievable.

To inspiring musicians whose songs rang true in my heart across the scariest of passages: Procol Harem, Enigma, Anna Nalick, Bill Conti, and Pink who is most Fuckin' Perfect. And to my shining star, Sylvester Stallone, the one and only Rocky, all I can say is, "I did it!"

To my tenth-grade science teacher, Mrs. Drake, who helped me build my first saltwater aquarium and encouraged me to write to the Ecuadorian government, and to friends who watched out for me in Radnor and North Philadelphia.

To my courageous captain, Dennis. Sailors say when life on land is a five, life at sea is a zero or ten; you make my life the perfect ten. Thank you, my brave adventure man, for being my partner, my witness to my life, and importantly, my champion of bold and outrageous dreams.

To my heart of hearts, Nico. I could not be more proud, more indebted, or have ever wished for a more amazing son. You fill my life with joy and beauty. Thank you for teaching me what love is and encouraging me to live my dreams. I wholeheartedly hope you realize yours. You once told me, "in this world anything is possible" and now—I believe you! I love you "forever and for all the evers."

How Readers Can Help

Authors put years of time and tears into their books. *Laughing at the Sky* is my first memoir. If you found yourself moved or even just a little tickled, please consider posting a brief review at Amazon.com and Goodreads.com, or your favorite review site. Book review ratings greatly improve the chances of books reaching readers who might benefit. I also invite you to connect with me online at HeidiLoveAuthor.com. A thousand thanks!

A Note to Survivors and Their Champions

For leaders providing sexual assault recovery support, my heroes, Michelle Bowdler, Madeleine Black, Winnie M Li, Tarana Burke, and the late Maya Angelou, who have transcended what no one should have had to endure, I am grateful to witness you, rising above, lifting your voices to bring healing beauty and social change to the world. Tarana Burke once said, "An exchange of empathy provides an entry point for a lot of people to see what healing feels like."

For survivors of sexual violence, I hope this book extends the gift of support, courage, and our utmost empathy to you. You are part of an emerging tribe of transcendence. My dear friend Dr. Anne Hallward wrote this for you:

"The work of healing from trauma requires tremendous courage. It means finding safe ways to revisit what was unbearable, through the eyes and heart of compassion, until we can carry our own suffering with great tenderness. As we bear witness to our own stories with compassion, we can release the mistaken meanings we have made about what happened, and the ways we have blamed ourselves. When we can cultivate this compassion within, it becomes safer to share our story with others, and to bear witness to their stories. This capacity to be present and open-hearted in the face of suffering becomes a gift to so many."

Anne Hallward, MD
Founder and Executive Director Safe Space Radio
Former Faculty, Harvard Medical School

www.ingramcontent.com/pod-product-compliance
Lightning Source LLC
Chambersburg PA
CBHW052133070526
44585CB00017B/1812